DIAMOND

ALSO BY MARK HARRIS

DIAMOND

Baseball Writings of
MARK HARRIS

DONALD I. FINE, INC.
New York

Friends have said over the years that left-handed Henry Wiggen's wife Holly resembles in many aspects my wife Josephine. Josephine's and my son Henry plays baseball but right-handed exceedingly well. It is Henry's brother Anthony who is the southpaw. Their sister Hester keeps us thinking left-brained and right-brained. Add Michele, add George, all together we exist as truth and fiction in each other's minds.

—M.H.

ACKNOWLEDGEMENTS

"The Bonding" is reprinted with the permission of Macmillan Publishing Company from *Birth of a Fan* by Ron Fimrite, editor, 1993.

"Two actors," published as "Obedience to Self," in 1977, is reprinted by permission of Pittsburgh Magazine.

"Bring Back that Old Sandlot Novel," "Recalling the Joy of Watching Baseball on the Radio," "Rose's Fate Uproots Fan's Illusion," and "Maybe What Baseball Needs is a Henry David Thoreau," Copyright 1988, 1980, 1989 and 1969 by the New York *Times* Company. Reprinted by permission.

"An Affair of the Heart" is printed with permission of the San José Mercury *News*, Inc. as published in the October 15, 1989 edition.

"Ladies Day at the Game" first appeared in Mademoiselle.

"Jackie Robinson and my Sister" first appeared in Flashes of Negro Life.

"Each Game was a Crusade" and "The Iron Man" are reprinted with permission from TV Guide Magazine. Copyright © 1977 by News America Publications Inc.

"The Man Who Hits Too Many Home Runs," copyright 1957 Time, Inc. All rights reserved. Reprinted with permission of Life Magazine.

The following articles are reprinted courtesy of Sports Illustrated from the August 4, 1958, May 18, 1959, and September 28, 1959 issues. Copyright 1958, 1959, Time Inc.: "An Outfielder for Hiroshima," "You Can't Scout Desire," and "Love Affair in San Francisco."

"Baseball's One-Liners" is reprinted with permission from The Diamond, © 1993 by Fans Publishing, Inc., Scottsdale, Arizona.

"Tragedy as Pleasure: Giamatti and Rose" was originally published in Michigan Quarterly Review, Summer, 1990.

"Moralizers Make Sport When the Mighty Fall" appeared in Newsday.

"Of *Casey at the Bat*" copyrighted August 8, 1988, Chicago Tribune Company. All rights reserved. Used with permission.

Introduction to *The Baseball Chronicles* appeared in *The Baseball Chronicles,* edited by David Gallen, Carroll and Graf Publishers, 1991.

CONTENTS

PREFACE

◇ I STILL CAN'T believe it. There must be some mistake. I was not to have spent my life dawdling over baseball. Baseball was wasteful and pointless, leading a boy nowhere.

During my school days the only long poem I voluntarily committed to my memory was *Casey at the Bat,* for which I offer in this book a new reading of the very sort which now and again antagonized my teachers. They mistook my disrespect for the poem for disrespect for *them.* I questioned the whole basic premise of the poem from the point of view of sound strategy. Casey's striking out was a fraud. With first base open, the pitcher would have walked him.

I was said to be the bad boy of our school. It was the fault of baseball. At my little desk I nodded in a state of distraction, gazing out the window, sizing up the weather, thinking about green playing fields (ours was brown dirt), fantasizing victory, the humiliation of the enemy, headlines—

YOUNGEST BOY IN HISTORY PLAYS FOR THE GIANTS

The principal of our school was Martin H. Traphagen, for whom the school itself was afterward named. It was he, among others, who tried to persuade me how bad I was. I must have appeared unconvinced, irritating him, for at our frequent conferences he expressed his frustration by twisting my ears, poking me in my chest with his powerful finger. My teachers, unable to improve my behavior, sent me to his office bearing in hand a paper form known as "a lack of commendation slip"—that is to say, a paper on which the printed word "commendation" was rudely obliterated by the teacher with her blackest pen.

1

Mr. Traphagen warned me of fearful consequences. Unless I cured myself of my compulsions: disaster. In his outer office I sat many wasted hours beneath the electric clock until he was ready to receive me. Once each minute the clock gasped, its big hand advancing. I see those Roman numerals yet. The ladies of his outer office viewed me with disapproval. Whether he was in his inner office I did not know, and nobody told me. I sat in dread, waiting to hear what my fate was to be.

No doubt existed of the direction my punishment would take. It would be related to baseball. I would be suspended from the next game, forced to miss it, sit it out. Baseball was the devil who occupied my mind. Something about the whole idea of baseball had corrupted me and driven me to bad behavior. But baseball was also the "control" authority exerted over me. The warden exploits the prisoner's addiction. Only by depriving me of my game could our principal expect me to reconsider myself.

Mr. Traphagen, when at last he arrived from wherever he had been, praised my lovely mother and my industrious father who deserved so much better than this. Could I not see myself on the road to failure and disappointment? Didn't I understand that it was only *myself* I was hurting? I was wasting my brain, the wonderful endowment of my mother and father; I was throwing away my life, casting myself into the gutter. At this point or another Mr. Traphagen plucked my record from his file to illustrate for me, by comparing the predictions of my tests against the shabbiness of my performance, how capable I truly was *if only I cared enough to do it.*

Oh, but I *did* care enough to do it. We disagreed only on what was to be done.

Except on one occasion my offenses were merely petty. Only once was I vicious, and even then I hardly knew it, for I was thirteen years old and hadn't made much progress yet in moral apprehension. The day of my crime was Friday, May 21, 1937, and the moment was the first inning of an after-school game between our class and another. I was a base runner so desperate to fulfill my mission that I crashed into the opposing third baseman and broke his collarbone.

It had not occurred to me that my being safe at third base was of less consequence than another boy's collarbone. In the days which followed I began to realize that my zeal had been excessive, although nothing in my diary that night revealed remorse. "School. Beat 9–2C 4–3. Ejected in first inning after injuring Normie Cotter." Years later I saw the matter larger. In my novel, *The Southpaw,* when my hero Henry, pitching, hurts another fellow with his fast-flying baseball, he is truly contrite. No game was worth anybody's collarbone.

As for the word "ejected," I must already have learned it from the sports pages of the New York *Sun,* where I read of hotheaded big-league players *ejected* by umpires. The *Sun* was a social force. My father brought it home every evening.

The man who ejected me from the game was our gymnasium teacher, Dayton G. Blunt. Often I asked him his predictions for me. Could a small boy with thick eyeglasses become a notable big-league baseball player? One day he dismayed me by offering his idea that my chance for success at baseball was slim. "A boy in your situation," he said to me, "should take up golf." *Never* I thought, and I never did.

When, in June, 1937, my class graduated from our junior high school, my diploma was withheld from me. Never in the history of the school had such a shameful thing happened to anyone. I left that school on probation. If for one year I behaved well in high school I would receive my diploma *post facto.* I passed this test. On the day I returned to claim my diploma one of the women at work in the principal's office found it by sliding open a drawer overflowing with unclassified trash. I had expected something like a small ceremony, but she offered me none, wordlessly handing my diploma to me and turning back to her tasks.

I pasted my diploma into my scrapbook, for I was one who kept such a book, kept a record of myself. I have kept a daily diary from age eleven to last night, in just the most conscientious lifetime of preoccupation with myself, keeping a daily record of myself in the way people keep daily records of baseball players, their hits, their runs, their errors and much more.

In the long run the school system of Mount Vernon, N.Y., in spite of my having begun by being so troublesome, granted me a measure of recognition. The sins of my boyhood came to be seen as the basis of my virtue. I still can't believe it. There must be some mistake. Crime pays. For in 1988, fifty-one short years after my willful unfortunate collision with Norman Cotter, I was elected by respectable citizens to the Mount Vernon High School Hall of Fame. One of the achievements for which I was cited was my authorship of my novels of baseball, precisely that game said to have corrupted me. "He adapted *Bang the Drum Slowly,* one of his eleven novels, into the screenplay for the Paramount film. His early novels show a warmth of feeling for racial justice, the later ones a devotion to peace and harmony."

Many people have the idea that fiction arises from the author's exact knowledge of the events and locale of the story. Of my work this was not true at all. My baseball fiction arose mainly from my imagination. I had never been closer to the profession of baseball than the schoolyard. Once, with a friend in the dead of winter, when we were very young, I telephoned the residence of one Frank Frisch of New Rochelle, N.Y., two towns away from our own. Frisch, a big-league player nicknamed the Fordham Flash, astonished my friend and me by answering the phone himself. We asked him if he were really he, and he said he was, and that is as much of the conversation as I can remember. It was as close to professional baseball as I had ever come.

It was still as close as I had come when, in 1953, fifteen years later, I published *The Southpaw,* first of my baseball novels. However, with the publication of that book I became a designated expert. Editors in the magazine business supposed that I was just the man they needed. They assumed from my fiction that I had been *there,* that I had always known the baseball scene, not that I had invented all this, or even extrapolated the lives of baseball players from my own. Placing their faith in me, they assigned me to write about actual baseball people, concepts, ideas, thoughts, and to give out my opinion on one baseball matter or another.

In my new role I entered actual baseball clubhouses. I met genuine players, coaches, managers, sportswriters, executives, and discovered that editors' illusions were somehow true enough. I had already invented these people for my fiction.

Three of my earliest articles came from that part of me I had so agonized for myself. What was a boy to do with himself? How was he to live? This question in different ways and degrees preoccupies the baseball-playing boys united in this volume in a section all their own. The key to Ed Cereghino's existence was expressed by his mother, speaking of "the wee bean in his tail."

This seemed to me to be related to the word I had begun to hear so often from baseball managers and scouts: "desire." I had had my own problems with desire, wishing I were somebody my principal and my gymnasium teacher thought I could never become.

I had thought that baseball players had always wanted to be baseball players. However, when I began actually to meet real living players I discovered the error of my expectation. Baseball players, even after they were acknowledged, wanted to be all sorts of other things in pursuit of other interests and ambitions. I saw that ballplayers were often demonstrating golf clubs to one another, talking football and worrying about their future lives.

The joy of playing baseball meant little enough to that amazing fellow, Dick Stuart, who cared only for hitting home runs. Stuart's passion for money and fame ("The Man Who Hits Too Many Home Runs") amused me and gave me wonderful sentences to report. "Every home run gives me the deepest personal thrill, although I've hit droves. Last year at Lincoln I hit sixty-six, yet it was the deepest personal thrill every time I seen that ball flying nine miles out of the park." Said Stuart: "Money can buy nothing but happiness." He remains for me an American classic of frank and simplified desire at the far end of a spectrum of complexity separating him from Cereghino, whose truest desire was not to play baseball for the Yankees but to return to school.

Stuart's difficulty lay in his indifference to his development of those skills which would make of him the complete player. It was hard for me to understand why he did not simply buckle down and do as wiser, older baseball men advised him he must do.

That's what I'd have done now that my mind had enlarged twenty years beyond my junior-high-school crisis. I had become a tenured college teacher, and I still wished I were a baseball player. It seemed to me when I met the honest Stuart that for sheer maximum animal pleasure the life of a baseball player was the supreme existence. For several days I trailed around with Stuart and his teammates. How I envied them their muscular physical lives! They played ball at night and slept on the clean sheets of fine hotels late into the morning. How they poured sweat! Nothing I did called forth such sweat from me. These men were drenched, drained, soaked, having surrendered the fluids of their bodies to the cause of the great game. To play ball, to sweat, to shower, to receive the applause of one's mates, to go afterward for irrigation by beer, four, five, six tall glasses down like nothing, and steak and baseball talk—*that* seemed to me the height of useful occupation. All choice and responsibility were lifted from them. Their purposes were clear and unambiguous.

I recall my surprise at hearing from those baseball players how little they actually enjoyed themselves. They were not carefree, as I had foolishly imagined them. Their future lives were doubtful. I who had always envied baseball players heard from them now how in fact they envied me. I was a teacher in a secure job. They who had in so many cases skipped over education now wished for lives as free and safe as mine. My innocence of their lives moved them to doubt me. My innocence makes me ashamed, for I was like the wretched Paul, in Willa Cather's "Paul's Case," who romanticized the actresses of the stock company, "hard-working women, most of them supporting indolent husbands or brothers, and they laughed rather bitterly at having stirred the boy to such fervid and florid inventions."

Thirty years later, the downfall of Pete Rose affected me in ways I might not have anticipated. My heart went out to the bad boy of baseball. Memories of my own confrontations with my junior-high-school principal were fresh in my mind. I felt a greater affection for Rose than for the respectable principal, Commissioner Giamatti, who exiled him from baseball. Rose reminded me much of myself, carrying me back to the memory of myself as a boy, when I too had been overcome by senseless desire. Rose was self-consumed, as I had been, living at the limit of his desire, as I had lived at mine on that bad day when I broke Norman Cotter's collarbone.

In that awful long television morning of his being read out of baseball I could feel his pain, as I could not feel the pain of the school man Giamatti, commissioner of baseball—the principal—spokesman for the community of disapproving men, of whom I was now presumably one.

For several years, when I was a serious young man, I lost all interest in that frivolity called baseball. By 1946 I had ceased to be a fan of the so-called national pastime. How could we have called the game *national* which excluded so many people? No issue on earth or in space angered and bewildered me more than the issue of race relations.

Then quite suddenly something for which I had campaigned for a long time (or for what seemed to me a long time —I was only twenty-four) became a reality. The black baseball player Jackie Robinson was signed to a contract in the Brooklyn Dodgers organization. My interest in baseball revived. I wrote a letter to Robinson, congratulating him and wishing him good luck. My pleasure also took the form of my little satirical essay, "Jackie Robinson and My Sister." I carried it to the editor of a St. Louis magazine called Flashes of Negro Life, and he paid me ten dollars for my work.

My essay is neither so casual nor so good-humored as it

reads. The people who tied up the question by linking Jackie Robinson to my sister angered me beyond description. I stewed and fumed for days. My early interest in writing and my growing interest in social questions had now been joined by my revived interest in baseball. This essay was my first professional writing about baseball, and it seems to have amused anyone who has read it these fifty years.

It's a tired old thing to say that baseball is America, and I have made sure not to say it. In these writings I have on the whole been able to avoid analyzing the meaning of baseball, predicting its future, or telling its major-league proprietors how to run themselves. The next pitch is always a mystery— think of the odds of millions to one against the pitch that killed Ray Chapman, as told here in "Hit by pitched ball—By Mays (Chapman)," my article on the bleakest incident in the history of baseball.

Baseball makes no sense. Hitting a ball with a stick? You're nuts. To foreigners in America every pitch seems to produce the same unvarying result, but to baseball fans the variety of possibilities staggers the imagination. Everything is right and everything is wrong with baseball. It has gone mad with statistics, rumor, dispute, and money.

The growth and maturation of baseball has also led to its extension into literature and film as serious and literate subject matter. I have tried to tell about this in "Bring Back that Old Sandlot Novel" and also by including here the text of my screenplay of the motion picture *Bang the Drum Slowly,* which some people think may be the best film made with baseball at its center. I hope so. Maybe so, maybe not, but it was good to do, it was where life had led me from my unpromising beginning as the brutal playground boy, up from moral nowhere to apprehensions of that justice which is equality.

I tried very hard at the end of my article "You Can't Scout Desire" to formulate an idea of baseball as something other than the professional game played for pay. If one of these days the professional baseball players of America and the owners of their baseball clubs strike against each other and lock themselves out forever people will go on playing this game without them. Baseball as amateurs play it is seldom exciting to watch, but it is exciting to play, as anyone can tell you who has whacked the ball well or caught a fly ball on the run. One understands this game by playing it. It is good exercise for the body and the head and the spirit and the outlook, as I have tried to tell in my narrative of my own latter-day playing days, "The Bonding."

Play day by day, write day by day. Some of these articles of mine may be better written than others, the wiser work of experience. I like to think my writing grew better year by year, the later the article the greater its insight.

But I guarantee nothing. Once I met the pitcher Ken MacKenzie when he was a minor-league player for the Atlanta Crackers. I asked him if he thought he'd make his way into the big leagues. MacKenzie said he could not answer my question, he could only do his best from game to game and see where he ended. I followed his advice and did my best with each assignment as it came. If my work improved from time to time practically to the threshold of perfection, so much the better.

THE BONDING

◇ THE TELEPHONE RINGS. I know who it is. It is a chunky, powerful boy with a thick, bushy, red-haired mustache named Christy Ratherbiglongname I can seldom remember, and when I remember it I can't pronounce it. He wants me to come out and play. He is nineteen years old and I am sixty-nine.

One of the things that made me a baseball fan is its democracy. Lines of snobbish distinction go down. (On the other hand, I was fifty-five years old before I ever played with a black teammate.) On the telephone Christy calls me Professor. On the ball field he calls me by my first name. Only on the phone or at the ball field do our lives intersect. Baseball is our *lingua franca*.

"Where?" I ask.

"Lafcadio Park," he says. "It's a trophy game."

"When?" I ask.

"Saturday," he says.

"What time?" I ask.

"Get there maybe half-past seven, seven-thirty," he says, "give us time to warm up a little. Do you see what I'm saying?"

He needs me and I need him. He knows what I can do. I'd been recruited by Christy Ratherbiglongname at a Senior Citizens game at Chapparal Park, in Scottsdale. He'd been driving by and he just happened to stop and watch. So he said. My impression is that he'd stopped deliberately to see what he could see, and I was the man he saw. He'd be able to count on me. Nobody wanted me but him. I'd be grateful to be his eleventh man. I'd show up for every game. I could punch singles through the infield. I could play right field, first base, pitch, coach.

He was a supremely energetic young man. He slept four hours a night whether he needed it or not. My wife once said she was pleased he was not a military person—he'd attack other countries out of restlessness. "If you come and play with us," he said when he recruited me, "the church gives you a free T-shirt."

"I don't like playing at night," I said.

"We don't play at night," he said. This was absolutely false. The league I joined him in played half its winter games at night and *all* its summer games at night. But he knew that once I'd been bonded to the team I wouldn't mind his having lied. He had seen by my way of playing that I was longing to be bonded.

This sport I am talking about is an extremely popular variation of baseball called Slow Pitch. The pitcher pitches an underhand arc. Strikes are determined by whether the ball in its arc lands on the plate. If the pitch does not land on the plate the umpire calls it a ball. A third-strike foul is out.

The ball is larger than a Florida grapefruit, smaller than an Arizona grapefruit. It is not a hard ball but it is not a soft ball either. The most endangered player is the pitcher, who is often struck by line drives. The distance to the plate is fifty feet. Infielders are often struck by bad-bouncing ground balls, frequently in the crotch, which is painful for the victim and inspires other players to offer bad jokes as consolation. It is a hitting game. A player seldom strikes out.

The bases are sixty-five feet apart, much less, of course, than a hard-ball diamond. The distance down the foul lines is usually well under 300 feet. Players' batting averages are closer to .400 than .300. Although these are high-scoring games they move quickly. A nine-inning game seldom takes as long as ninety minutes.

Slow Pitch is an ideal game even for teams composed of skilled male players mingling with unskilled players. Hundreds of schools and communities sponsor "co-rec" Slow Pitch leagues in which women's participation is mandatory, and of course many women players play very well. Christy in behalf of the Salt River Pentecost Bombers led us into a male league. Thus we have no women players, although I have heard some of our players speak fondly of women.

1

I too was once the whip—

> *So was I once myself a swinger of birches.*
> *And so I dream of going back to be.*

—the Christy Ratherbiglongname of my team, pouring half my energy into the telephone, rounding up the guys, routing them out of bed, out of the house, rounding up our transportation, pleading with my players against their mothers' tying them up with dental appointments, music lessons, visits to their grandparents. Baseball was urgent. Its urgency addicted me. We needed to win every game. The urgency of baseball made me a fan. Every game was crucial. One might be casual about many other things in life, such as love, learning, literature, morals, ethics, politics, religion, and College Entrance Examinations, but baseball mattered. I hated those mothers.

My father took me to the first big-league baseball game of my life. I know that the place was the Polo Grounds, in New York, and the time must have been the summer of my sixth year. The immense expanse of the grass was awesome. The feats of the players were marvelous. For example, batters hit balls which seemed to fly so high and far they would never descend. Yet soon enough they descended into the hands of players waiting far out on the grass. Such a relationship in distance astonished me. I was breathless to observe that a ball should be struck by a man with a stick at one point of the vast universe, and be caught in a glove by a man far away at another.

I was entranced by one of the Giants outfielders. What a peculiar name he had! Ott. I see it yet in my memory of that day's scorecard, and often on the Hall of Fame outfield fence at Candlestick Park in San Francisco. Such a name began to suggest to me the diversity of the world: nobody on our block in Mount Vernon, N.Y., was named Ott. Rosenbaum and Schwartzman, yes. Ott, no.

Thus baseball expanded my provincial world. Ott's teammate Carl Hubbell was called the Meal Ticket. I had no idea what a meal ticket was. My mother put our meals on the table. The sportswriters offered thousands of figures of speech to amuse a boy who loved the way words could be slung all over the place in a billion combinations. Hubbell "hailed from" Carthage, Missouri. Ott was called Master Melvin. Bill Terry was Memphis Bill.

Carthage? Missouri? Baseball introduced me to geography. The cities of the east were New York, Brooklyn, Boston, Philadelphia, Washington. The cities of the west were Cincinnati, St. Louis, Chicago, Pittsburgh, Detroit, and Cleveland. West of St. Louis lay the Rocky Mountains and China. My active sympathies for people who did not live near big-league cities were mingled with a certain contempt for their having got themselves in such a fix.

Baseball made a reading fan of me. I was introduced to the connection by my father's evening commuting companion, the New York *Sun*. On the front page of the *Sun* one night I saw a boisterous, effervescent player named Pepper Martin sliding home on his chest to score the winning run for the St. Louis Cardinals in a World Series game against the Philadelphia Athletics. For me, that was the night of the wedding of baseball and reading, two pleasures conjoined.

As my mind embraced the game, the game enlarged my mind. Baseball taught me things even adults approved. *The game is never over until the last man is out.* Teachers and family relations thought this was a good philosophy of life. They liked to hear me say such things.

For me, however, traits of good character, if I had them, had nothing especially in common with life, only with baseball. Certain things adults morally approved I found simply useful.

Consider arithmetic. Adults approved my sitting there doing arithmetic problems, but in fact those were not problems I was doing. They were batting averages. It never occurred to me that this skill I was acquiring for the purpose of following the game would serve me afterward for other purposes. These arts or skills were pleasures in themselves. It was all one unified endeavor, baseball and reading and geography and history and arithmetic and newspaper report. I became a fan of baseball because I had once glimpsed the green expanse of serenity, and because the game called upon me for all those other arts and skills which were play in themselves, no matter what teachers or other adults called them.

As a boy I adored Camp Secor in the summer, especially our baseball games. I remember a game we played on a ragged, stony field against a team of boys from another camp on the other side of the lake. Their field was pocked with cowflop. So was ours.

When the game was over we boys of Camp Secor piled into the truck that had brought us there. Our driver was Uncle Arnie Cohen, who was also our counselor, mentor, and nature teacher. Beside our truck Uncle Arnie was shaking hands goodbye with his counterpart Uncle from the other camp. The moment remains in my head half a century later. The other Uncle says to Uncle Arnie, "Who's that little brat of yours who . . . ?" That was me he meant. Uncle Arnie replied, "That kid eats and sleeps baseball." I was proud to be one to whom such a laudatory phrase applied.

Once when we returned from a game across the lake I tried to convey to the folks of our camp the impression that I had won the game all by myself. Uncle Arnie challenged my report. "Nobody wins a game all by himself. Nobody loses a game all by himself."

Uncle Arnie taught me the idea of team, celebrated bonding. I understood as time went by that nobody wins a game single-handed. That was the thing that made me a lover of baseball, the bonding with one's fellows, the possession of their confidence.

Somewhere, some years in the past, I am playing my position. I think I am playing shortstop. Two men are out. The batter hits a pop fly. It should be mine. Everybody sees clearly that it is mine. I am under it. I gather it in. But even before I gather it in I feel around me my teammates begin to jog toward the bench. They know that I am going to catch that ball. They have confidence in me. They know what I can do. They know my skills side by side with my limitations, and I know theirs. We are bonded. Baseball was bonding.

Uncle Arnie also said, "In the field. Want that ball. Want that batter to hit the ball to you. Don't pray the batter hits it someplace else to save you disgrace. Pray that he hits it to *you.*"

"Two hands for beginners." Of course it wasn't original with Uncle Arnie. I caught fly balls two-handed. I still do. Uncle Arnie and every school coach in the universe commanded boys to clap that bare hand over the ball in the pocket.

It's no longer the style. The modern one-handed style is casual, confident, and cool. No matter how critical the moment may be—the final out of a one-run game, let us say—the outfielder plays the fly ball one-handed. He is too proud for precaution, for safety, his peers would laugh at him if he required two hands to do the work of one. But I haven't been able to change with the style, and I'm not sure I care to. I appreciate the security of that old-fashioned second hand.

Baseball was my model for the good life. "When a poor American boy dreamed of escaping his grim life," David Halberstam has written in *Summer of '49,* "his fantasy probably involved becoming a professional baseball player."

My life was neither poor nor grim, but I had my necessities. One summer, when I was a boy at Camp Secor, I wrote my fantasy in lying letters to a friend back home whom I meant to excite with envy. I have written about these letters elsewhere, but an account of them is relevant here, too. Fantasy and fandom were bred together. For me, to invent the richest possible dream was to weave it of the stuff of baseball. I could imagine no life more desirable than the life of a baseball player, the luxury of travel, hotels, and chambermaids, worshipful girls, players' uniforms, natty umpires, and perhaps above all the strictly scheduled reliability of life, for baseball could be relied upon to be present and to be prompt like nothing else I knew: if Cincinnati was to be at the Polo Grounds at 3:10 P.M. on August 12, *they were there.*

I do not know what name my mind gave to those letters—*letters,* I suppose, although I knew that letters were true and mine were not. Mine were wholly lies, fiction, deceitful inventions created to excite my friend's envy. At their core were descriptions of an elaborate Inter-Camp Baseball League, in which boys in the most elegant uniforms traveled about like professionals.

Each camp (I wrote) was required to maintain a perfectly barbered diamond and sparkling dressing rooms. Oh yes. Each camp was required to supply new, white baseballs—none of your old tattered, ragged baseballs held together with black electric tape. Umpires were to be formally attired. The grandstands were spacious, girls pressed forward for our autographs—how boring to be giving out my autograph all day!

In spite of that hardship (I wrote) I enjoyed myself. Saying this, I permitted a tone of world-weariness to creep in. Some people might find this sort of thing exciting, but I'd much rather be home with *him* all summer on the good old baking streets and good old rocky choke-dusted sandlots of Mount Vernon. Sometimes in a letter I'd "correct" an "error" of an earlier letter. I provided settings for the act of composition: today I am writing to you on the train between Camp Indian Pines and Camp Lakadaka. Listen to the dumb thing that happened: on this trip our clubhouse man packed our *home* uniforms instead of our *travel* uniforms, ha ha, that's life, I guess. Oh nuts, in this hotel the electric fans work very poorly, the chambermaids are very slow. Rochester looks so much like Buffalo looks so much like Syracuse looks like Troy like Utica it sure is boring I sure look forward to getting home to school in September. (Glad we don't play *through* September like the big leagues.)

These letters were written on my cot at Rest Hour at Camp Secor. We almost never left camp between the first of July and the end of August, and when we did it was to hike two or three miles with canteens slung across our shoulders in order to justify our mothers' having bought the canteens. My letters were mailed by the most careful calculation, bearing in mind our eight-day swing through Schenectady, complicated by the tedious necessity of coming back through Albany to make up a washed-out game. My dates were painstakingly computed. Thirty-one days hath July. No Sunday baseball at certain church camps. Follow the weather reports and allow for rain. Follow maps for useful details: in Ogdensburg (I wrote) I picked up some Canadian money, in Lockport some of the kids went to see Niagara Falls falling, but I stayed in the hotel resting my pulled muscle. I had never been to Ogdensburg, never been to Lockport, never pulled a muscle. Where I *was* was on my cot at Rest Hour at Camp Secor on my way to becoming a novelist.

2

My back aches. I want to go lie down somewhere. I want to call Christy and tell him I can't play ball with him any longer. Kid, it's over. Do you see what I'm saying?

Saturday has come at last. It is Saturday dawn and my alarm clock wakes my wife, and my wife wakes me. "Why do you set it if you're not going to get up?" she asks. "That's not fair."

"Of course I'm getting up," and to prove it I cover my head with my pillow.

"You were sure out," she says.

Yes, I had slept deeply. I'd had a little bedtime sedative to ease my back. "How's your back?" she asks, and I reply, it's okay, it's okay, but I don't really know how my back is. I won't know until my feet hit the floor. I don't really want to leave this bed, but I cannot disappoint Christy G., boy whip, who's expecting me, counting on me. Right at this moment I truly couldn't tell my wife or myself if I'm going to play ball today or if I'm going back to sleep.

But this is nothing new. This is how it was when I was a boy and my bruises from last week's game were raw and the scabs were still bloody wet and my mother said if I played ball unhealed like that I was inviting infection, infection would course through my body—"gangrene will set in"—the doctors would amputate my legs and that would be the end of baseball.

The day is cold. Even so, I swing myself out of bed. I am terribly stiff, I can hardly move. Even so, I know that I am going to play ball today. I am going to get loose. People advise: "Use it or lose it." I am going to play ball and might even play it well, might even win the game with a sharp ground ball sliced down the right side. That's my specialty. They play me to pull and I fool them.

Tonight I will not be able to believe the misery in which this day begins. But it has always been like that. Indeed, I quite retired from baseball on May 27, 1960: "I played center field for Language Arts, against Social Science. We lost, 7–1, my legs are unendurably stiff, & I have the feeling this may be my last game . . . Baseball is for boys." So said my diary one day when I was only thirty-seven and a half.

Baseball taught me to know I could rise to the occasion (once I got out of bed). Baseball acquainted me with my own resources, with the outer limits of my body. I rise, I dress. I pull over my head my Salt River Pentecost Church T-shirt, blazing blue bearing some sort of design on the back I have never really identified. I think it may be a box kite, though I don't know why it should.

Some of our T-shirts include the word Bombers. I don't know whether the word is an addition to the shirt or whether it had been there in the first place and was removed as an ethical afterthought. I have never been to the church for which I so faithfully play. I have never seen it. I do not know where it is. I do not know anyone who belongs to it except Christy Ratherbiglongname, who alludes to it often as a checkpoint on his daily rounds. But I have never heard any of our teammates mention it. (In 1941, when I was employed in New York by Paramount Pictures, I played on the Paramount baseball team. I slowly discovered in my sweet innocence that I was the only member of the team actually employed by Paramount.)

Once I told Christy my best religious baseball joke, but it offended him:

Two baseball players were lounging in their hotel room one night. One player was a pitcher and the other was a third baseman. They began to talk about heaven. They wondered if baseball is played in heaven. They agreed that whichever of them died first would notify the survivor whether baseball is played in heaven.

The years passed. The third baseman died. He remembered his promise to communicate from heaven. He spoke through the spiritual ether to his old-time friend and teammate, the pitcher. He said, "You know, I promised to find out if baseball was played in heaven and let you know first thing, and I've done it just like I promised."

"I knew you would," the pitcher said. "What's the scoop?"

"Mixed," the third baseman said from heaven. "There's good news and bad news. Which do you want first?"

"Start with the good news," the pitcher said.

"The good news is," the third baseman said, "that we play baseball all the time on a regular schedule in heaven."

"And the bad news—" the pitcher asked from earth.

"The bad news is you're scheduled to pitch tomorrow."

Christy did not laugh. The funny part eluded him, violated his picture of reality. "Going to heaven can't be bad news," Christy said.

I devour half a grapefruit and a slice of toast and half a cup of coffee. Play first, eat a second breakfast with the Bombers later. Small breakfast digesting, I lower myself to the living room floor. My wife leads me through a series of stretching exercises to prepare my back for the game.

I pack my equipment bag: glove, extra shoelaces, a small roll of adhesive tape, and my sturdy pair of Sportgoggle2.

When I leave the house I hurry. Apparently I am afraid of missing something. Butterflies flutter in my stomach. It was always true of me that I approached a baseball field, whether as player or as spectator, with a feeling of rising excitement, eager to be there early, fearful of something happening without me. Maybe I'm afraid of being left out, kicked off the team. "Late! You're off the team!" the tyrant manager shouts at me.

Full daylight now, dawn has dissolved, the temperature is forty degrees on a December morning in Tempe, Arizona, on the way to seventy, and the time is seven-twenty. I'll be at Lafcadio Park at seven-thirty, Christy will direct our warm-up, and at eight o'clock we'll take on those Ball Crushers.

We'll beat them too, I think. We have played them twice and they aren't much. These games are just fun, of course, but the fun is greater when we win than when we lose. When we lose we are filled with the necessity to apologize, to confess our errors as a way of emphasizing that they weren't the whole story, that it was the *team* that lost: our undoing was a collective enterprise. When we go for a second breakfast everything tastes better if we have won.

My car radio tells me the temperatures around the country. The wind chill factor is forty-four degrees below zero in Minneapolis. I arrive at Lafcadio Park. I have hurried to get here. Christy will be there before me, ready to start our practice. He is persuaded that practice is the secret of our success, and I am inclined to agree with him. When we practice we start each of our games with a thirty-minute advantage. Our slothful opponents are never warmed up until the third or fourth inning, and by that time we have sunk them. They have lain in bed too long.

Nobody is here but me. I am standing swearing to myself in the cold at 7:40 in the morning at Lafcadio Park. Not alone the Ball Crushers but the Salt River Pentecost Church Bombers lie home in bed. To hell with this childish game. I am through with it forever. I quit. I will never get out of bed again. I will rest my aching back.

Since I'm here anyhow I'll run my back a little. I set my equipment bag on the player bench and jog across the grass. A humorist has planted a flag on a stick in a small mound of dogshit behind second base. The American national game is cowflop and dogshit, then and now, from Camp Secor in the Hudson Valley to the Arizona desert. This is the first time this morning I have smiled. I move stiffly. I feel awkward. I jog toward the left-field fence. I decide to jog another fifty paces and turn and break into a run. I imagine that just as I make my turn I will hear the roar of Christy's truck and the clamor of our team leaping to play.

I am warming. I am getting ready to play. I turn. Now I am running well and reasonably gracefully. I no longer feel awkward. My back is loose. The home-stretching did good. I am grateful to my wife for her exercise leadership. The impossible has happened, as in bed I knew it would: my body has returned to me one more time. I will not hear from my back again until tomorrow.

But neither Christy's truck nor anything nor anyone else has arrived. When I reach the player bench I am breathing hard, and for a moment the mass failure of Christy and my teammates strikes me as an event of no consequence. Indeed, they did me the greatest favor. If I had not got up to meet them here I would not have run, and if I had not run I would not feel as great as I do this minute. I pick up my equipment bag and drive home. By the time I arrive home I am damn mad.

My wife says, "There just must have been some misunderstanding." "There was no misunderstanding. It's the price I pay for playing with kids. They don't think. They don't keep track of things. They don't write their appointments down. They don't remember anything." "They're not all kids," my wife says. "I thought you had one other old guy." "We got one guy about forty," I say. "I call forty a kid."

I telephone Christy. I reach his machine, which blesses me and instructs me to leave my name and number and the time of my call. I say, "Christy, this is Mark, I just want you to know how damn mad I am, I just got back from Lafcadio Park, I was there at half-past seven and I waited until eight and nobody came, so to hell with it after this, I'm just going to play with the Seniors in Scottsdale, to hell with you and the Bombers."

I return to bed. I sleep for one hour. I rise. I read pages in two manuscripts in progress, one of mine and one of a student.

My wife and I walk in the neighborhood. On the golf course the gray-haired snowbirds from North Dakota, South Dakota, Montana, and Minnesota fire away. Golf must be a great game. You do not need eighteen people to play. "I'm going to take up golf," I say. "I doubt it," says my wife. We return home.

A message is on our machine. "Hi, professor, this is Christy, got your message. The game is still at eight, we need you, be there at seven-thirty we can warm up. Do you see what I'm saying? It's a funny thing you went there this morning, trophy games are always night."

The night is as cold as this morning was, without even this morning's prospect of warming. I wear a jacket during batting practice. I slash a couple of pitches to the left side. I made good contact. I like the sound. Right away I know that I am hitting well tonight. My hands sting in the cold. A teammate says I should buy myself batting gloves. In my generation batting gloves were unheard of, unthinkable. God did not intend us to wear gloves while batting—nor to bat with aluminum bats. I slash two or three more ground balls to the left side. I feel that they were hard-hit. I do not think the Ball Crusher third baseman would have had an easy time handling them.

I jog to right field. If I play tonight that's where I'll play. I need to catch one fly ball for confidence. That will do it. However, none of my fellow Bombers hits anything in the air to me. We have only one left-handed batter, and he is a light hitter like me. He and I are the only players who have never hit a home run for the Bombers. (I have not hit a home run for *anybody* for nineteen years—I hit my last home run playing at the California Institute of the Arts in 1972.) He strokes two or three balls to right field but with only the force of singles. Playing them off the grass in no way assists my confidence—almost anybody can pick up a rolling ball.

As our practice ends my alert boy Christy considerately fungoes a couple of fly balls my way. The first ball Christy hits to me I catch almost without moving a step. For the second ball I backpedal a dozen steps to the fence, and as the ball smacks the pocket of my glove my confidence rises to its comfort level. Christy has done just what I need. He knows my requirement for confidence. He is grateful to any player who shows up. I am one of his faithful. I am ready to play.

Eleven Bombers are here tonight, and I see that I will not start. "You'll get in," Christy says. "Stay warm and coach third." We join him for prayer. Some time ago when I told

Christy I did not believe in God he said, "He won't mind." We form a circle around him, we extend our arms and clasp hands, we bow our heads, and Christy prays. His red-haired bushy mustache quivers. "Dear God, we sincerely love You and pray You will help us do the right things when we play this game right now. We know that You will keep us from doing anything we don't want to be sorry for doing, and in Your mercy help us show good sportsmanship to the adversary."

Our adversary is formed from a pool of discount-store employees and United Parcel Service drivers and handlers. We are a much better team than these Ball Crushers, and we are warm and they are cold. They have barely made their way into trophy play. I expect a lot of traffic to be coming my way at third base. I love it. I love waving my teammates home. I am their guide and protector. I also love halting them, keeping them safe. As they charge at me from second base I cry, "Look at me, look at me, look at me," and if they do as I say I will keep them from harm. Some Bombers base runners sometimes defy me, ignore my signals, charge past me, passionate to score, and although I am first and last a devoted team person I feel at such times a secret satisfaction at their getting their asses thrown out at the plate.

We score abundantly without delay. In the coaching box I am waving home so many of my mates that I heat up as if I were playing. We score ten runs in three innings. We are secure. We will never blow a ten-run lead. The Ball Crushers score once. We lead by 10–1. We lead by 11–4. We lead by 12–6.

After five innings our dependable shortstop must go home —not to home plate but home to his house. Our right fielder comes in to play shortstop, and I go to right field where I am instantly employed. The first Ball Crusher to come to bat hits a line drive to me. He is a right-handed batter. He had looked my way when he came to bat, and I knew he had it in mind to try the old man out. The ball begins to float, catching me unprepared. For a moment I am alarmed that I have misjudged it. I envision it sailing over my head. But I need only to rise on my toes and reach for it, and catch it in the pocket of my glove with a satisfying sound.

For some reason we Bombers cannot sustain the success with which we began, while the Ball Crushers begin to hit safely repeatedly. This is one of baseball's perpetual recurring mysteries: why does one player, one team, inexplicably lose its command, or another inexplicably exceed all expectations? The score is 12–8, then again 13–11, and soon thereafter 13–all.

Nothing comes my way in the air. At bat I ground very hard to third base, but the Ball Crusher third baseman throws me out. When I come to bat again a Ball Crusher calls out, "Watch the line." The third baseman moves toward the line, and I think I can hit it past him to his left, but once again I ground to him. They've got my number. They've got me "defensed."

This is not to be believed. We are really a much better team than they are. They go ahead of us, 16–15.

In the top of the ninth inning when my mates are on the bases and everything depends on me, and all the Ball Crushers are playing me to the left, I punch the ball down the first-base side between the wide-playing baseman and the line. Nothing is lovelier to me than the sight of the ball I have hit skipping over the dirt to the outfield grass.

I had done it again. It was my specialty. More than once in a late inning I've whacked the ball right through that wide-open space between the first baseman and his base. The Ball Crushers were playing me to "pull"—that is to say, to hit the ball in my natural direction, down the left-field side. They shifted to the left for me. The second baseman played almost on the bag. The first baseman played wide. The famous old logician said, "Hit it where they ain't," and so I did, and ran exalted to first base.

I am in paradise, I am praised by my mates. They say, "Hey, good job man." Christy says, "You did a smart thing, I knew you'd do it." They all knew I would do it. They knew that my moment had come. It was the secret we shared together.

In right field, in the bottom half of the ninth inning, beneath the bright lights and the depths of the blackness beyond, in the cool night growing colder, in my exhilaration, my spirit glows with triumph. Through me the voice of Uncle Arnie speaks out of the past, "I want that ball. Hit it to me. Batter, hit that ball to me, I pray you hit it to me." Whereupon, with two Ball Crushers on base and two men out the batter does in fact hit it to me. It is a soft fly ball, spinning in the lights. I am under it. But even before I gather it in I feel around me my teammates unburdened of their tension. They know that I am going to catch that ball. They have confidence in me. They know what I can do.

I think I'll make a one-handed catch of it. I'll join the modern world, stick one hand up and allow that ball to settle in, which it does, and then pops out again and falls to the grass, while our adversary dashes across the plate with the winning run.

Christy, almost as if he were not about to cry, rallied his men to his truck. He could not bring himself to look at me. Eliminated in the first round of trophy play! This was unspeakable. At last he looked at me and said, "You got your car, you don't need a ride. I'll give you a call." I always had my car. I never rode in his truck.

I was about to fall into depression. My worst moment would occur on the following morning, when I awoke to the dreadful memory of that ball's having popped out of my glove. It was a moment of my baseball life I will always want back. In the end I might deliver one of those oblique deathbed statements for which mildly eccentric men become famous: "I should have caught it two-handed."

But this is no fatal wound. It is a memory, not a traumatic incident. I am sustained by the truths I have learned from baseball. All the game's commonplace wisdom serves me. "You can be a hero one day and a goat the next." I was a hero in the top of the ninth and a goat in the bottom of the same inning.

"That's baseball."

"You can't win 'em all."

"People forget, tomorrow's a new ball game." I don't know about that. I don't think Christy has forgotten. He said he'd call. Where's his call? I'm waiting.

Everybody learns in her/his own way about losing. For me, baseball taught me losing and winning, taught me never to let anything get me too far down or too far up. You not only can't win 'em all—you can't win much more than half, hard as you try, long as you live.

Baseball was my path to self-knowledge. Baseball made me a fan by telling me truths about myself. It taught me to know what I can do and what I can't. I will make good plays and bad plays. Every so often the easiest pop fly is going to pop out of your glove. I don't care who you are. It's the iron statistics. It's fate. If baseball taught me—I heard it first from Uncle Arnie—that I don't win games single-handedly, then neither do I lose them, either. *It takes a whole team to lose a ball game.* Hey, look, I didn't blow that ten-run lead all by myself, did I?

BOOK INTO FILM

CONCERNING THE SCREENPLAY, BANG THE DRUM SLOWLY

◇ FROM THE BEGINNING there was always a document *like* this screenplay, and before there were documents there was life itself. I played and dreamed baseball as a boy and into manhood.

Beyond playing and dreaming came the document *The Southpaw,* my first novel of baseball. That was 1953. In the next year our fellow-student at the University of Minnesota, Regan Brackett, in and out of the hospital, silently died, trying to keep his secret from the rest of us, as the dying man does in the document he inspired.

The new document was a novel trim and lean except at its overweight end. The editor Joe Fox at the publishing house of Alfred Knopf served me memorably by persuading me to cut the manuscript brutally hard at the climax, in order to prevent its falling into sentimentality. I lamented all that hard-won prose swept to the basket, but I profited by having learned to live with the sophisticated idea that less may be more. The process of cutting was to play a crucial part in the making of the next document, the screenplay, when at last I arrived at that point in 1972, sixteen years after the publication of the book.

Sixteen years devoured! For some reason not then clear to me the attempt to make a screenplay of my trim novel had proved to be extremely difficult. Yet it had looked so easy, like playing baseball itself, seen from the grandstand. Its story line was so marvelously *simple*! At least it seemed simple at first to the several screenwriters eager to try it. But as soon as they got to work the story line became complex.

Some years passed before I discovered sufficient confidence in myself to try to succeed where all those other adaptors had failed. At first, my own efforts also failed. I wrote several big fat screenplays each entitled *Bang the Drum Slowly,* from which films eight or nine hours long might have been made. Frequently my versions of the work departed from the book. Losing my way, I told myself I was exploring new ideas, enlarging my awareness, breaking new ground. Tired of my simple story line, I complicated it, transforming my characters to talkative philosophers, importing newly conceived characters.

In 1971, when I lived in California and thought I had cured myself of the habit of writing screen adaptations of the book, a Chicago attorney named Maurice Rosenfield telephoned to inquire whether he and his wife, Lois, might produce a moving picture of *Bang the Drum Slowly.* They had the money to do it. "They own all the banks," says Dutch, the manager, indicating Maurice, gray and distinguished, who in the film he made played the small part of the owner of the Mammoths baseball club. I too was to have played a small part—I was to have been a sports reporter in Scene 48—but by the time my turn came to play my scene Maurice had expelled me from the shooting location in Florida.

Maurice as attorney had done not only well but good. He had accomplished admirable work for civil rights; once he had performed that noblest of all legal work—he had saved a man from execution. His interests lay also in theater and film. He had never produced a motion picture and I had never succeeded in writing a screenplay. We pooled the wealth of our inexperience.

John Hancock, whom Maurice engaged as director, had had more experience of theater than of film, but in any case more of film than either Maurice or I. He brought to the enterprise a truly alert imagination for which I was to be grateful, and the obscure, hard-working young actor Robert De Niro.

Michael Moriarty joined us to play the part of Henry Wiggen, star pitcher, putative author of the book which tells the tale, and therefore called Author, except by his tin-eared roommate, Bruce Pearson, who calls him Arthur.

Bill Badalato, associate producer, introduced limitless intelligent energy to a company of talented people assigned to jobs I had never known existed. Richard Shore became our director of photography, Richard Marks our film editor, and we were extraordinarily lucky, I was told, to have them.

We still required a screenplay. I now felt that I could write it. I sat from time to time in California or Chicago with Maurice and John, the novel on the table before us, considering the general question which scenes of the book, in what order, lent themselves to conversion to film within the limits of our resources. After our meetings I went home and wrote into the form of a script my impressions of what we had agreed upon.

"Since I am not as movie-centered as they are," Jessamyn West wrote of the making of the movie of her novel *The Friendly Persuasion,* "my meetings with Mr. Wyler haven't seemed as important to me as they have to [others]. My feeling is script-centered rather than Wyler-centered. Can the script be bettered? If so, how?" I too was script-centered. I was neither Maurice-centered nor John-centered. I wanted the script to make good *reading,* to be a good literary work I'd be proud of when at some time in the far future (like right this minute) I should be able to prepare it for strangers to read without loss of my writer's pride.

I eventually saw, however, that the flat screenplay on mere paper was only the barest beginning of the rich film we finally see. Reading the screenplay, you have got to dream the whole world in. Nothing on paper can be as lively as Tootsie's catching up Henry with her eavesdropping, nothing as haunting as the theme music. Reading, not seeing, not hearing, you've got to create whole baseball crowds, whole stadia in your head with no help from anyone. But then, that was how we did it in the old days, when Babe Ruth lived, the "national pastime" was lily white, and blind radio did it all, as I try to tell in my essay, "Recalling the Joy of Watching Baseball on the Radio."

I who had been writing nine-hour screen adaptations of my

novel was beginning now for the first time to see how one might make a large film from the appearance of a small screenplay. My idea had been that a script was language, people speaking. John Hancock, however, declared at many moments that we could serve a scene better with a gesture or an action than with words. I was beginning to learn to place my faith in "the magic of cinema"—John's ironic frequent phrase—by which he meant the power of film to achieve in a few seconds the effect of many lines of writing. Cut, cut, cut, sacrifice treasures to the wastebasket, as I had given up pages of the novel itself to the house of Knopf.

At the opening of this film you will hear sounds and see images before you hear words. You will listen a while to the first sound before you will even be able to guess what it is or see the people who are making it. The sound may be unfamiliar to you. It is the sound of somebody running in spiked baseball shoes down the cement runway from the clubhouse to the field. You may recognize the runners now, as you would not have recognized them in 1973, when the film appeared, as the actors De Niro and Moriarty playing the roles of Bruce and Henry. The broad contrast of working methods and personal style between the two men was striking and instructive to me. I have tried to tell something about them in the essay "Two Actors" in this book.

They jog on the cinder path circling the breathtaking green field. We see by their uniforms that they are teammates, and when we catch glimpses of Henry's protective sidewise glances at Bruce we may begin to guess at their deeper relationship. Henry seems to be Bruce's guardian or protector. We have not heard them speak a word.

In Scene 3 Henry wears a white fur-lined storm coat he purchased in Minneapolis. In Scene 14 his wife Holly carries it home with her. That is the last we see of that handsome coat. From the novel we know where and why Henry bought the coat, what transpired between Henry and Aleck Olson in Minneapolis, between Henry and the airplane stewardess en route from New York to Chicago, and on the phone to Goose's wife and Joe's wife in Chicago.

I had made movie scenes of those book scenes. John cut them from the film. In doing so, he enhanced the thrust of the film, achieving a momentum the film never surrenders. But later scenes, dependent for their humor on our knowledge of places and occasions now absent, have lost their connections to their sources, and viewers are deprived of the wit and quickness of Henry's inventiveness in parrying Dutch's fierce strategies.

I'm not sure anybody in the world misses those things as keenly as I. Yet, on the theory that readers might relish pages of the novel which reconnect several scenes to their sources, I publish in the present book the first chapter of the novel as an independent prose selection for the interest we may have in knowing what happened before the film began. The chapter gives us in addition a good taste of Henry's prose in its fullness weighed against the efficient sparse language of the screenplay.

In January, 1972, with photography planned for March, I met with John at the company suite on the nineteenth floor of the Warwick Hotel in New York. I had brought with me the script of 179 pages I thought we had agreed upon in Chicago. I had come to New York to work only on "minor revisions"— my diary says so, so it must be true.

However, as I gained confidence in John, and as I began to get the hang of his method of solving plot problems as often with sights and sounds as with language, I began to see how amazingly we were able to reduce the weight of my script. One hundred and seventy-nine pages were many too many. Consider, for example, Scene 58. On the telephone Bruce assures Katie that Henry is attending to the matter of the contract. She does not believe him. What does she say? I wrote many replies for her to deliver in her lovely Southern rhythm. But no words of Katie's could have spoken with the cruel force of the unspoken sound for which John Hancock optioned —the dial tone of her hanging up.

On March 26, requiring brief winter filming before the snow was gone, Hancock, Moriarty, De Niro, and a crew of film workers shot Henry and Bruce's drive from Minnesota to

Georgia (Scene 3), simulated by the magic of cinema in Maine and New Jersey.

On the same day Maurice phoned me from Chicago. "He seems uneasy about John's changes in the script," my diary says. He complained in the following way: unauthorized changes had been made by an unproved young director and an uncredentialed screenwriter in the script they had agreed upon in the producer's very house in Chicago. Maurice as the producer should have been consulted. Things seemed to be missing. It all seemed so awfully much *shorter* than it had been. Yes, Maurice in March was where I had been in January.

I told him of my increased confidence in John's way with the script. I made a somewhat ardent defense of "John's changes," which I thought of as *my* changes, too. Briefly Maurice was at ease. Three days later on the phone we "had a good talk. He is optimistic about everything. He says that John & others have seen rushes of the Maine shooting & are delighted." But that was our last cordial conversation.

We went to New York for three weeks of rehearsal before "the shoot," where I felt an increase of tension produced by my frustration and Maurice's mistrust. I was writing new scenes. I felt that I was only now beginning to learn how to make certain scenes effective. But Maurice may have felt—indeed, he quite said so—that the hour was late for me to be learning new tricks. At an expense of thousands upon thousands of nonrefundable dollars Maurice and Lois had committed themselves to scores of people for a shoot that was to begin in a few days. We had better stop experimenting with the script.

—I'm making discoveries every day, I said.

—Very nice, but this was no time for discoveries, said he.

—I'm beginning to understand my characters more fully, I said, I see them bursting from my book into a life better understood, more richly revealed, more fully developed.

—No, said Maurice, I want to make the book I bought. I haven't got time right now to film your new developments.

When I became, as Maurice felt, too argumentative, he

commanded me, as our contract permitted him to do, to go home, far away from Florida, clear to California. He said to me, "You're a fine writer but a rotten human being." I agreed with only half his sentence. His wife and coproducer, Lois, according to my diary on the day I was fired, accused me of being "cruel" to Maurice, of attempting to hurt him because I thought of him as "a dirty old businessman."

Of those possible subconscious motives I could not be certain. No doubt my tongue had got away from me. In writing I could state my argument more clearly. For four days, between the day he fired me and the day I finally left Florida, I sat in my hotel room stating myself in letters to Maurice I deposited in his mailbox in the lobby below.

In the twenty years since the release of the film I have lost track of the number of times I have seen *Bang the Drum Slowly*. I'm guessing that I have seen it seventy-five times, most often at academic conference occasions, where a screening of the film precedes a question-and-answer session. It is the only motion picture I can lip-read. My interest in the film grows greater.

One afternoon during the rehearsal in New York I felt especially sane and well rewarded. We were in Scene 34—Dutch's lecture on the unity of the ball club, the unity of mankind— when one of the ballplayer/actors burst forth with astonishment, crossing the room to me to say, "Hey, you know, this is supposed to be a *serious film*."

I saw it first at its preview at the Film Society of the Writers Guild of America West in 1973 in Los Angeles, attended mostly by—of course—writers and their spouses and friends.

At the beginning of the film, when my name blossomed on the screen, the audience applauded. At the Writers Guild people definitely applaud the writer no matter how bad the work. I do not enjoy being applauded and I mistrust people who do. The test would be whether my fellow writers would applaud at the end. I mean *really* applaud.

At the end, my fellow writers applauded with true enthusiasm because they thought it was a good film. I thought so, too. I thought at that hour and with increasing conviction watching it seventy-five times more that it is really and truly almost the only baseball film ever made. It is true to the sport. It avoids sentimentality almost entirely. Baseball films have been fake and phony and unauthentic, sentimental, lacking in realism, just the most awful drivel, just absolutely disgraceful. I had wanted this film to be meaningful. I did not want to spend the rest of my life answering the question, "Why did you let them do that to *Bang the Drum Slowly?*"

The screenplay before the reader is not the script written in advance but only a portion of it. It is the record of the shooting which was actually done and survived all the cutting— that fraction left of the mass we once had, published now for the first time.

This film preceded De Niro's fame. He complained ruefully to me that his name was misspelled even on the records of the Rosenfield company itself. When the shooting was over he went on to a career often dominated by films of violence and gore and guns. In our film guns play no part in the outcome. One shot is fired from a pistol, by the character Goose, the only member of the UCLA Drama Department, he told me, ever to play on the varsity baseball team. Goose fires Piney Woods's pistol into the ceiling of a hotel bedroom, to douse the light, all in fun to celebrate an occasion (in Scene 52) nobody will name. They are celebrating Bruce, whom they cannot address directly on the tender subject of his death. "Celebrating what?" asks the uninformed rookie Piney Woods. "Celebrating—*celebration,*" replies the learned Red Traphagen, graduate of Harvard, the only pipe smoker on the ball club.

As that celebration scene begins Henry comes down the hotel corridor dangling his room key in his hand. He is puzzled to hear a big party in progress in his room. He turns the key in the lock. That much of the scene was made on the fourteenth floor of the Fort Harrison Hotel in Clearwater, Florida. The action of the noisy party which follows was filmed in New York six weeks later. Six weeks to cross that threshold! To a novice of filmmaking such inside knowledge is a wonderful bonus.

In Scene 4, Gem, the Pearsons' black housekeeper, speaks four words of welcome to Bruce, home from Minnesota. "You all better now?" They embrace, kiss. When I saw that scene for the first time at the Film Society at the Writers Guild in Los Angeles I may have thought to myself, This is it. This is where the whole thing is going to break down. This was the sentimental thing I had been afraid of.

My opinion was that Bruce would not have kissed and embraced the black maid. That was not the Bruce of the novel. In our old fat script my stage direction says that Bruce replies to Gem's inquiry "without turning around for a colored person."

Maurice envisioned Bruce as the baseball player an audience *expects* to see, a celebrity in sports clothes, slick, stylish, fastidious. Maurice wanted Bruce to be *nice*—a nice guy, a real nice guy with whom an audience would identify, with whom it would see a likeness to its ideal self.

In fact, Bruce Pearson is established in the two novels in which he appears as antiblack, anti-Semitic, the obedient warrior who killed many people willy-nilly in the war. He was not your everyday liberal. I was distressed now by the ingratiating change in his character. Bruce kissing and embracing the black servant, Bruce cleaned up for company, Bruce the well-liked man—I was shocked.

Bruce Pearson in his original fictional setting was a veteran of World War II. In our film the war is updated to Vietnam, trains are updated to airplanes, and dollar figures are inflated. Bruce is seen now as a veteran of the Vietnam war America was powerless to condemn until *our* middle-class boys began to die in it. Boys who pissed in the sink were not ours.

I had wanted us to embrace Bruce not for the particulars of his code but because he is human, not because he comes to us redeemed but because he comes to us in his own terms as a suffering person for whom our sensation of kinship must arise in spite of *our* prejudices against his.

I make much of this because it was at the heart of my quarrel with aspects of the film in the making. The trouble with baseball films is always their sentimentality, their social unrealism, their pandering to the expectations of the moviegoer. The idea of a humane life, it seems to me, is to care not only for *our kind* but for other people's kind, too. Those were the terms upon which I thought we needed to love Bruce, not because he was easy to love but even because he was not; not because he fell familiarly into our sympathetic arms but because he did not; so that we would have the experience of loving someone not ourselves, not our own son but somebody else's.

Far into the period of our filmmaking Maurice was troubled by certain violations of his expectations. He felt the need to reply at least to his own objection with a scene mentioning Bruce's poor fashion taste, demonstrating at least that the filmmakers were aware of it. The result is Scene 24, embracing funny monologues by two players lecturing Bruce upon the necessity of studying men's fashion magazines and learning to scrub his yellow teeth. This scene popped up as a surprise before my very eyes. I did not write it. Somebody wrote it when I was in exile.

"It's his one day off," says Bradley Lord the company lackey in Scene 13. He is telling us that Dutch is going to be angry if we awaken him, and somebody in this room is going to pay for the consequences. I marvel to recall how John, Maurice and I struggled over that simple-sounding line. What was our problem?

We must have been trying to establish something we thought was crucial. We must have wanted to avoid confusing our viewer. Twenty years and seventy-five screenings later I am still jarred by the word "one"—"It's his one day off"— which feels terribly awkward and must have been the key to whatever it was we were trying to establish or avoid. I have stopped the film on my VCR to see if I *can* remember why three grown men struggled over that sentence, but for the life of me I cannot.

In Scene 36 the curtain blows softly at the window, giving the illusion of summer. For an hour John Hancock had fussed with somebody invisible outside the window, to make a concealed electric fan deliver the breeze just right. The moment was tense. It seemed to me that day, as it may also have seemed to Maurice, who was paying for the time of two dozen people standing around waiting, that John was making more of this fan-hitting-the-curtain than it would finally be worth. But now, when I see those curtains gently blow, the summer breeze bathes my face.

What is this game called Tegwar? People often ask me how I thought it up. I didn't think it up, though I invented the name. I heard about it from Oscar Serlin, a man of theater and movies, who described it to me as a game he had seen the Marx Brothers play in hotel lobbies at the expense, in more ways than one, of tourists and traveling salesmen awed by those famous fellows, proud to play a game of cards with them.

Bruce wanted to know how to play that game. It was one of those smart big-league tricks to which he'd never been privy. He had been left out of most things. Bruce's chance at last to join his teammates in their private trick on the public fool registers the heightened life Henry was able to help him to enjoy during his final months.

In this connection, De Niro in Scene 21 is especially interesting to me for his total comprehension of Bruce's rejection. His face shines with delight when he believes that Goose and Horse are taking a friendly interest in him. But then with a phrase his antagonists turn his hope to humiliation. The disappointment on his face measures his deep chagrin that he had been fool enough even to hope.

Oscar Serlin, who had seen the faces of the Marx Brothers plain, and given me the makings of Tegwar, also gave me Tootsie the telephone operator. One day he called me from a Los Angeles hotel with news of a project. He was cautious. We must not speak too freely on the phone. Switchboard operators were eager to pass precious news to their cohorts, as Tootsie passes secrets to Henry in exchange for ball park tickets "not behind no pillars nor posts." Screenwriter Selma Diamond's Tootsie served both the necessity of exposition and the pleasure of unfailing amusement.

Each time I see this film I feel that someone is soon going to organize a reunion of the cast and company. I think this feeling comes from the fact that I *do* so often get together with everyone, and watch it through one more time.

Selma Diamond is dead. Phil Foster is dead who plays Joe Jaros the Tegwar-playing coach. Bruce's father Patrick McVey is dead. Vincent Gardenia is dead; he plays Dutch, whose little speech I always relish for its power to make the whole theater laugh: "What teach English? People speak English already." Other men and women of the company have no doubt drifted to the other side without informing me, like Regan Brackett, whose shy death inspired my book.

Dozens of actors and actresses played bit parts and "extras." With only a couple of hundred extras John Hancock packed thousands of fans into the stadium. One enthusiastic cheering young woman attracts my notice with her leaping breasts. I watch for her every time, to make sure she has not left the park. It is as if the actors know what they are doing. They had come to the shoot for a day, two days, to make scenes out of sequence from a script they had not read, seldom knowing what they were saying or why, grateful for a moment's employment. I wondered if they would ever see the film. "Be on the lookout for it," they all said as they departed.

Where can I reach them to invite them to our reunion? Is this all that's left of them—these feet and yards of film? Dell Bethel, credited as our "baseball advisor," has been out of touch with me these many years. He taught De Niro how to make the plays, run the bases. He flashed De Niro complex signs from third base. Earnest unsmiling Mr. Rogers, the detective, was last seen departing forever for Minnesota to develop further information. Big Benjamin Scotland, who struck out 312 batters for the Mammoths in 1901, threw one last pitch for us in Scene 20. *Burn it in, Ben, burn it in.* Gem the servant. Bruce's mother walking strong in the cemetery. Miss Industrial Progress savoring her free meal while Katie tries to sell her to Henry. The umpire dusting the plate during Bruce's final seconds of baseball. In the hotel lobby (Scene 46) when Henry asks home-run king Sid Goldman "Where is everybody?" Sid replies with truth enough, "Nobody knows."

Birds sing while Bruce fishes in the river. Dogs bark in the night when he burns his life's papers in the backyard. Who captured the birdsong for us? Who made the dogs bark? One day I passed an open door marked SOUND. A man and a woman were repetitively transcribing singing birds and barking dogs from one piece of sound film to another, producing as many singing birds and barking dogs as the director might wish. Would they come to the theater to hear their birds and dogs? "Be on the lookout for it," the woman said.

TWO ACTORS

◇ I HAD A LITTLE glimpse not long ago into the characters of two film actors. One was Obedience and the other was Self, and I began to think that those might be the broad options of the worker in the arts.

The actors were at that time unknown to everyone but a few colleagues, a few friends, and a producing company which had engaged them at a lucky moment when their talents were much more highly developed than their wages. One of the actors was Robert De Niro, who has become that awkward thing called a "star," and the other was Michael Moriarty, who has thus far been noticed less.

We were filming a baseball story. The day's work was done. I was standing at dinner time at the window of my hotel room, looking down several floors into the outdoor swimming pool. Nobody swam at that hour but De Niro, and he swam alone, cutting through the water in a businesslike manner—in, across, up, out.

His was a small body. Most people will be surprised to learn that De Niro is a little fellow, not so much a sturdy hero as a growing boy. In life little, on the screen big, his passionate obedience enables him to become someone he is not. He loses himself. He gives himself away to become that "star" he means to be. His art is illusion.

I suppose his swift little swim refreshed him, relaxed him, by which I mean to say he had not swum for fun but for use. He had not come to frolic but to work. From the pool he went to his room and stayed there, studying the script for tomorrow, I am sure. I would not see him again before morning.

For his role De Niro learned to bat a baseball, catch it,

throw it and run the bases. Since he had never played baseball this was dangerous work and he went about it with a dangerous directness. He did not teach himself to play baseball in some general gradual manner, as you and I would have done, by teaming up with other slow fellows and looping baseballs back and forth to get the old feel of it. No, De Niro strapped on the catcher's gear and squatted behind the batter and came into instant relationship with baseballs thrown at him from the time-honored distance of sixty-feet-six-inches at a speed of a hundred miles an hour. He learned to catch thrown balls. He couldn't have caught a pop foul—but then he wouldn't have wanted to: the script didn't call for that. He learned only as much baseball as he needed for his role. I doubt that he ever cared to touch a baseball again.

In the same way, I understand, he has since learned to play the saxophone. He needs what he needs when he needs it. I saw him one day on the set plunge his fingers down his throat to bring tears to his eyes by gagging himself, and this he did not once but forty times to accommodate every "take," every trial shot. Try gagging yourself forty times of a summer day.

Where was Michael Moriarty when De Niro was swimming alone at the dinner hour? Moriarty was taking dinner with friends of the cast and company, sitting with them afterward in the hotel tavern until a late hour. Moriarty lived in the world in ways De Niro didn't. During the evening, when rushes were shown, Moriarty was there to see himself on film, and I think he enjoyed the critical talk which followed, the praise, the theorizing, the second-guessing, and the inevitable tendency of people in a nervous profession to settle upon people to blame things on.

Moriarty was never aloof from discussion on any topic. Beside the pool at swim-time, glass in hand at happy hour, tensely across a table in the tavern at night he was inquiring, accessible and open. If De Niro was small, dark, solitary, Mediterranean, Moriarty was tall, handsome, and fair. He drew a crowd to his table, he was at the center of hubbub, and because he was reachable, touchable, he was popular. People thought well of his friendliness. People in a nervous profession like to be mixed with.

From De Niro's point of view, a room full of tense people watching rushes was the gateway to hell. He cared nothing for all that jabbering, all that speculation. Such a scene was pointless, like chasing pop fouls. Superfluous. Whether De Niro had sufficient confidence to ignore the rushes or too little to risk exposure to torrents of talk I could not decide. For whatever reason, he remained in his room studying. If not studying, alone. If not alone, fabulously discreet.

De Niro's career advanced. The baseball catcher became the taxi driver became the Godfather became the last tycoon became the saxophonist. His talent is obedience. From the producer's point of view, it is a money-saving obedience. De Niro is no "troublemaker." He seems to believe in the system. He seems to play the game. When he receives *his* Academy Award he does not send an Indian woman to make a speech on rights and abuses. Someone has quoted someone in print as saying that De Niro as actor is "pliant," and someone else has called him a "robot."

But art is labor, talent, luck, origins, and De Niro has combined them into a self-denying discipline. Perhaps he learned from his painter-father that an artist pours all the energy of ego into the service of his daily work. Ignore the vulgar producer. Respect the director. Defer gratification. At least *appear* pliant. In that strategy De Niro has been masterful.

Moriarty may yet become so. After the baseball film Moriarty played for several months with distinction on Broadway, and opposite Katharine Hepburn in *The Glass Menagerie* on television. But in a letter to me three years after our brief acquaintance he felt compelled to express his skepticism by enclosing the word "success" in quotation marks—"these past 'successful' years," he wrote.

He mistrusted acclaim, the sudden rush of admiration from people who seemed to confuse Michael Moriarty in the flesh with Michael Moriarty's image on the screen. He cared to be loved not for his reputation but for himself. The world he had hoped to enter as a "star" now presented itself to him as vulgar in ways he could not ignore. This was not the game he meant to play. The end of so much talking, so much mingling, was a realization of Self which estranged him from Obedience.

He seemed to drop from sight. For a while he was a waiter in a restaurant. He was unable to play roles representing people he was not, at least until he discovered who he was. Time passed. Two years after his letter I saw a headline in the press, MORIARTY RECOVERING FROM FAME, BITTERNESS. I hoped so. Obedience was coming into balance with Self, and that was good for him and all of us.

BANG THE DRUM SLOWLY

The Screenplay

Scene 1. We hear the sound of spikes on cement. Henry and Bruce, in baseball uniform, with towels about their necks, emerge from the interior of the vast baseball stadium, and jog down the tunneled alleyway, onto the field. They jog together around the field.

At one point, as they run, Henry turns his head to glance solicitously at Bruce, as if Bruce were under his care—as if Henry knows himself to be Bruce's guardian.

Scene 2. On the steps of the Mayo Clinic in Rochester, Minnesota. Henry and Bruce are departing. Bruce shakes hands with the physician.

Scene 3. Henry and Bruce are driving across the wintry countryside in Bruce's weathered car. There is a good deal of snow on the ground, diminishing as they travel. Day turns to night and then again to day. They are traveling from Minnesota to Georgia. They cross a big bridge. Henry wears an expensive white fur-collared storm coat he purchased in Minneapolis.

Bruce is driving. He chews tobacco.

HENRY (*voice over*): Actually you get over it fairly quick. You might not think so but it's true. You're driving along with a man been told he's dying and yet everything keeps going on. I mean, it was hard enough rooming with him when he

48

was well. He chewed this disgusting tobacco. He pissed in the sink. And as a catcher he was a million dollars worth of promise worth two cents on delivery. Most people didn't know he was with the club. And dumb. He was almost too dumb to play a joke on. And now he been played the biggest joke of all.

Scene 4. The driveway of the modest Pearson rural home in Bainbridge, Georgia. Bruce drives up the driveway, honking loud. Mrs. Pearson is the first to see him. She summons her husband, who comes running, carrying a beekeeping mask.

MRS. PEARSON: Bruce. (*Summoning her husband.*) Bill, oh, Bill. I'm so glad to have you—

MR. PEARSON: Hey, Bruce, Bruce, how are you, son, so good to see you. How you been?

BRUCE: Oh, I'm fine, I been fine. Daddy, momma, I want you to meet Henry. You can call him Arthur.

MR. PEARSON: Oh, tell you, it's an honor to have you here, Henry Wiggen. I can't believe it.

HENRY: I can't believe I'm here.

MRS. PEARSON: Wonders never cease.

Gem, the black housemaid, appears. She and Bruce kiss and embrace.

GEM: You all better now?

MR. PEARSON: We was worried.

BRUCE: Yeah, I was in good hands.

MRS. PEARSON: I bet it was cold up there.

BRUCE: Not too damn cold, momma.

MR. PEARSON: What was wrong?

BRUCE: Nothin'.

Scene 5. On the shady bank of the Flint River. Birds are singing. Bruce and Henry are fishing.

BRUCE: Arthur? Tell me why I swam up and down in this mud a million times and I never drowned. Why I never got killed in the war in Vietnam, and why I never got plastered by a truck, or I come clean through all that and now I get this disease? Arthur?

HENRY: Don't ask me questions I can't answer.

BRUCE: Boy, I been handed a shit deal, boy. I'm doomed. Arthur, you remember that game you and Joe Jaros played— Tegwar? How do you play it?

HENRY: Tegwar? You don't know how to play Tegwar? Spell it. T-E-G-W-A-R. It stands for The Exciting Game Without Any Rules.

BRUCE: T-E-G-W-A-R. No rules? No rules at all?

Scene 6. Bruce, Henry, and Mr. Pearson are playing cards on a table in the backyard. Henry is dealing fast, confusing Mr. Pearson: confusion is the point of The Exciting Game Without Any Rules.

MR. PEARSON: I'm not too sure I'm understanding this game.

BRUCE: You might never.

HENRY: Throw down in the middle, sir.

MR. PEARSON: Why, nobody else threw down in the middle.

HENRY: It's your fish-fly card.

MR. PEARSON: How can you tell?

HENRY: The rules.

MR. PEARSON: What rules? I haven't noticed any rules. They seem to keep changing.

BRUCE: Five and six are eleven, that's what.

HENRY: Attaboy, Bruce.

MR. PEARSON: The rules concerning what?

HENRY: The rules of arithmetic.

MR. PEARSON: I wouldn't play this game for money I can tell you.

HENRY: Don't be discouraged.

BRUCE: Don't be discouraged.

HENRY: See it was no double birdie.

MR. PEARSON: Double birdie?

BRUCE: Whereas it might have been a spread eagle.

HENRY: Probably you been playing Southeastern Tegwar all your life but in the majors the boys all play western Canadian style which for my money is much faster. That means you're free for a butchered hog most any time whereas—

Mr. Pearson: Whereas what?

Bruce: Whereas it keeps you from dropping dead on the board.

Mr. Pearson glances suspiciously from Bruce to Henry. He has seen that something is amiss. He sees that his son is animated and joyful, different from his usual silent isolated self; that some important change has come over him.

Scene 7. Henry's wife, Holly, arrives by car at the Pearson house. She has joined Henry and Bruce here to continue south with them to training camp.

Henry: Hello, old lady.

Holly: Hi, Henry. Bruce.

Bruce: Seeing you here is a real pleasure.

Holly: Thank you.

Mr. Pearson: My son's talked a whole lot about you.

Mrs. Pearson: Wonders never cease.

Holly (*to Bruce*): How are you?

Bruce: Oh, I'm fine, never better.

Scene 8. Night. Holly and Henry are together on the balcony of the house, overlooking the backyard. Dogs bark.

Henry: Here's some medical papers just in case—the doctors give me in Minnesota. God, it was cold up there.

Holly: What did you think of your contract?

HENRY: I didn't read it.

HOLLY: Hell you didn't read it.

HENRY: I was taught in school where slavery went out when Lincoln was shot.

HOLLY (*a new subject*): Henry, who knows about him?

HENRY: You know, I know, Mayo Clinic knows, maybe his father.

HOLLY: And Bruce knows.

Scene 9. In the yard below the balcony Bruce has made a small fire of his paper possessions, mainly newspaper clippings recording his successes as an athlete. We catch sight of one headline, GEORGIA CELEBRATES BRUCE PEARSON DAY.

Scene 10. At the spring-training baseball field, Aqua Clara, Florida. We have moved suddenly from the silence of the night to the roaring noise of Piney Woods driving into camp on his motorcycle. He is a rash, innocent young fellow who does not know whether he'd rather be a baseball player or a cowboy. His ever-present guitar is strung across his chest.
    News photographers are taking pictures of the players.
    Reporters are interviewing the manager, Dutch.
    Henry and Holly are standing apart. Since Henry has not signed his contract he is not in uniform.
    Batting practice: Horse Byrd is hitting balls thrown to him by a machine.
    Diego and George. George speaks no English. Diego is his Spanish-language interpreter.

HENRY (*voice over*): The talk of the Aqua Clara camp that spring was a kid name of Piney Woods, a wild and crazy catcher out of a place called Good Hope, Georgia. The sportswriters all called him Dutch's good hope from Good Hope. In the catching department Dutch needed hope.

Photographer (*to a group of catchers*): Stand close. (*To Goose Williams.*) Put your arm around Pearson—

Goose: I'd rather not.

Dutch (*speaking of Piney Woods*): I'm very high on him, very high, got all the tools, he hits them a mile, he runs like a deer, his backside's one mile wide by actual measure where his power is.

Reporter: Who will stay?

Dutch: How do I know in February who I'll love in April when the flowers bloom.

Piney: No no, flowers bloom in May, it's April showers.

Dutch: Smartest prospect in years.

Holly: Henry, how many catchers on a team?

Henry: Never that many.

Diego: George says, sign your contract, Author.

Ugly (*giving Henry an insurance-premium check*): Morning Author, Holly. I believe this brings my insurance up to date.

Henry: Keep it coming, it's your future.

Ugly: Well, I have to save something for the present, however, such as these little girls running around here with their eye on handsome ballplayers. How much you holding out for?

HENRY: One hundred and twenty-seven thousand five hundred.

UGLY (*laughs*): Well, even if I believed you you'll never get it. Look, as a veteran of many a holdout let me give you a picece of sound advice. Don't hang in the park because your eye gleams, your hand itches, and you wish you were playing ball. This shines through, Author, and it'll cost you money.

Scene 11. Henry, Holly, and Bruce are reclining on the hotel-room bed, watching TV. The phone rings.

HENRY: It's the boss.

HOLLY: Don't be too comical, just answer it.

HENRY: Let it ring awhile. (*He answers it.*) Fishing pier. Tapeworms for sale.

On the other end is Joe Jaros, Mammoths coach, phoning from the lobby of the hotel.

JOE: Hey, Author, how about coming down and playing a game or two of Tegwar?

HENRY (*to Holly*): It's not the boss, it's Joe Jaros.

JOE: Author, come on down, this place is swimming with fish.

HENRY: All right, we'll be right down.

JOE: Who's we?

HENRY: Me and Bruce.

Joe: Bruce Pearson?

Henry: Yeah, him and me played quite a bit of Tegwar over the winter.

Joe: No.

Henry: Forget it for today, Joe.

Holly: Henry, you go, Bruce and I'll stay here.

Henry: I'll be right down, Joe.

> *Scene 12. In the cheery sociable lobby of the hotel. Henry and Joe appear to be engaged at cards. A smiling, eager tourist stands between them, watching their game. He wears a porkpie hat and a yellow shirt and a big campaign button announcing that he is Feared In The Deep. He wishes he could join the card game with such an illustrious fellow as Henry.*
>
> *We hear paging announcements. Soon we will hear Henry being paged.*

Feared in the Deep: Would you mind if I watch?

Joe: Quarter of eleven.

Feared in the Deep: No, I said would you mind if I watch. You're Henry Wiggen. Would you mind if I sit in. You know, I read your book, too.

Joe: I didn't read your book, Author, but I will, I will, I plan to. So far I've just been concerned with the parts that concern me.

Feared in the Deep: Hey, who did you used to be?

JOE: I'm Joe Jaros. I'm a coach. I used to be a baby. (*Excited by his cards.*) Here's a fitten two, a fitten queen—Red Rooster—Banjo! That's the first natural banjo since the day that Joe DiMaggio—in St. Petersburg—

HENRY: Fifteen plus fifteen is thirty-one.

FEARED IN THE DEEP: Hey, what's the name of this game?

JOE: Fifteen plus fifteen is thirty-*two*.

HENRY: Oh, that's right. That's a double honey bee.

FEARED IN THE DEEP: I'm not sure if I'm too clear on some of these new rules.

JOE: What new rules? There hasn't been any new rules since the Black Sox scandal 1919. Big league Tegwar is big league Tegwar known to every big-time ballplayer from Boston to California.

HENRY: And this is the last time we play without Pearson, too.

JOE: Author, your mind is crumbling, he's too damn dumb.

HENRY: Promise me, Joe.

JOE: I promise you, I promise you, I promise you on a stack of cards. Anyhow the way that banjo's been hitting Pearson's sure to drift down and out.

HENRY (*alarmed in Bruce's behalf*): They're sending him down?

JOE: I didn't say nothing.

HENRY: Well, Dutch said then. They're releasing Pearson?

JOE: Well, don't it look quite obvious?

HENRY: They can't do that.

The paging announcements keep imploring Henry to pick up the house phone.

JOE: Forget it, Author. Stick around.

HENRY: It's the boss. I got to go, Joe.

JOE: Damn it, Author, stick around.

Scene 13. The management suite. Present are Mr. Moors, his daughter Patricia, and stout Bradley Lord, the management flunkey. Henry enters talking. On the table is his contract, across which, in heavy pencil, he has written, "I was taught in school where slavery went out when Lincoln was shot."

HENRY: Fair! You call that fair! I was taught in school where slavery went out when Lincoln was shot.

MR. MOORS: Yeah, so you wrote across your contract.

HENRY: Not across *my* contract. Maybe the contract of some turnstile turner.

BRADLEY: Young ballplayers often end up old turnstile turners.

PATRICIA: All right, let's all calm down.

HENRY (*to Patricia*): You're looking very healthy this morning.

PATRICIA: Henry, you keep talking about $125,000. I can't do business that way.

BRADLEY: We'll just have to get along without him.

PATRICIA: Some of those pitchers out there yesterday afternoon looked very promising.

HENRY: So I hear. Any one of them might win four or five games if God drops everything else.

PATRICIA: I have in my mind an absolute maximum figure of—

BRADLEY: Sixty thousand dollars.

MR. MOORS: If you have a good year this year we'll make it back to you next year.

HENRY: I will go on year after year being paid for the year before. Now that shorts me a year in the long run.

BRADLEY: We've heard this one before.

HENRY: Every time Bradley Lord opens his mouth I'm raising my absolute minimum figure.

BRADLEY: All right, Henry.

PATRICIA: Bradley . . . Bradley. I have in my mind an absolute maximum figure of $60,000—

BRADLEY: But—she has in her heart ten thousand more.

PATRICIA: That's $70,000. I think you'd jump at that arrangement.

BRADLEY: Leap at that arrangement.

HENRY: I'll take it.

PATRICIA: Good. Well, then it's settled.

HENRY: There's something I want instead of money.

MR. MOORS: Nothing's instead of money.

PATRICIA: Money can buy nothing but happiness.

HENRY: There's one clause yet to go in my contract.

PATRICIA: All right, shoot.

HENRY: There must be a clause saying that I and Bruce Pearson must stay with the club together or else go together. Whatever happens to one must happen to the other. Traded, sold, whatever. We got to be tied in a package on any deal under the sun.

BRADLEY: I never heard of such a thing.

PATRICIA: No, absolutely out of the question. Reason one, Dutch will never hear of such a thing—

BRADLEY: Look here, Henry, if you want to have to get started this way you're—

PATRICIA: Let's not talk before we speak. We won't bother to write it down. I give you my solemn word.

HENRY: No verbal words. It must be wrote in.

PATRICIA: Bradley, call Dutch.

BRADLEY: It's his one day off.

PATRICIA: Call him.

Dutch enters from sleep, adjusting his nightclothes.

DUTCH: They should put zippers on pajamas.

PATRICIA: Tell him your clause.

DUTCH: Oh, so it's you with a special clause, Author. I bet it's a dilly. Bradley, run get me a wet rag. Everybody thinks they're special. Sterling must be shot for hay fever with medicine made out of the piss of a horse. Carucci must have contact lenses. Gonzales must have a buddy along to translate in Spanish, and Goldman must go home for Passover. What do you want now, Author? Chinese New Year's?

HENRY: I want a clause tying me in a package with Pearson.

PATRICIA: I bet he owes you money.

Dutch squeezes the wet rag Bradley has brought for him.

DUTCH: Jesus, Bradley, you ain't got much strength in your hands. What do you mean tied in a package?

HENRY: If he's sold I must be sold, or if he's traded I must be traded same place. Wherever he goes I go.

DUTCH (*thinking it through*): This is telling me who I'm keeping or not, which nobody ever told me before and nobody will ever tell me again as long as I'm upright. If it's money talk money and good luck. They own all the banks. (*He means Mr. Moors and Patricia.*) Talking money is one thing, but talking business is another. I'd as soon trade the whole club for a tin of beans as leave *anyone* tell me who stays and who gets cut loose.

HENRY: I'm sorry to hear that, because without that clause there'll be no contract.

DUTCH: Well, then there'll be no contract? Then I must suffer along the best I can.

Mr. Moors: Some of those young pitchers looked good out there yesterday.

Dutch: Yeah, good for what?

Bradley (*ridiculing Henry*): Will you go sell insurance? You don't know a soul on earth to sell insurance to outside of ballplayers. Will you sell insurance to other insurance agents? And where will you find people with money with the language you speak? Henry, I hardly ever even saw you wear a necktie.

Dutch: Bradley, shut up will you? Go get me a Coke. What's up between you two, Author? Are you a couple of fairies or something? That can't be. It's been a long time since I run across fairies in baseball. Jesus, this is too much for me.

Henry: You'll understand it some time.

Dutch: When?

Henry: Oh I don't know, maybe soon, maybe not—

Dutch: Oh, I'll certainly be hanging from my thumb waiting to hear. Christ Almighty, I've seen you on days when you hated Pearson, when you ate him out as bad as I myself ever ate him out. I saw you once get up from the table and walk away.

Patricia: That could be love as well as hate.

Henry: It ain't love.

Patricia: I don't mean fairy love.

Dutch: I remember one time you come storming into my office—you caught him pissing in the sink in Pittsburgh.

HENRY: Cleveland.

BRADLEY: Urinating.

DUTCH: Must this clause go on forever? I have four catchers. I have a catcher that's old on the sauce, and a black catcher that cannot hit, and a motorcycle catcher wild and crazy, and Pearson just plum dumb. I'd give both my right eyes for Sam Mott off Cincinnati, but Cincinnati wants Author, and I can't give Author, or if I give you I must have Scudder off Boston which the son of a bitches won't give me except for all my right-hand power. I could spare my right-hand hitting if I could trade with Pittsburgh, but Pittsburgh wants Author, and I've already give you to Cincinnati on paper for Sam Mott. So, I must play my old catcher on days when he gets himself sorted out, play my black catcher on days when my hitting is hitting, and play my motorcycle catcher on days he ever comes to his senses, which so far he's give me no sign of really having any. I'll ship him down to Queen City and see if they can talk him off his motorcycle. (*Fiercely, as if the motorcycle is really the problem.*) We must never have another motorcycle in camp. I been trying for days to get some sleep. You know, when I stop and think about it I'm liable to wind up using my plum dumb catcher more and more.

HENRY: Some day you'll understand.

DUTCH: No, no, forget about it, that's too much to ask. All right, I will agree to the clause. I've never done such a thing before and I wouldn't do it now except there's a look in your eye that tells me I've got to.

Scene 14. Henry, Bruce, and Holly on the street in front of the Fort Harrison Hotel. Holly is leaving for home in New York. They are loading her car. Among her luggage is Henry's white Minnesota storm coat. Henry slams the car trunk shut. Holly kisses Bruce goodbye.

BRUCE: Have a good trip.

HOLLY: I will, thank you.

UGLY (*strolling by*): You drive careful now.

HOLLY (*to Henry*): I'll call you collect tonight, okay?

Scene 15. Hotel room. Bruce is playing loud music on his radio. Henry is examining the medical papers.

BRUCE: I hope that if it happens it won't happen at a bad hour.

HENRY: It might or might not probably never happen. I have no faith in those cockeyed doctors up there.

BRUCE (*spitting out of the window*): Curve ball.

HENRY: Too bad a fellow can't pitch spit.

BRUCE: Yeah, I'd have the breaking stuff all right. See the dip on that. Arthur, if you was on one club and I was on another what kind of book would you keep on me.

HENRY (*deeply considering Bruce's character*): If I was to keep a book on you I'd say to myself, "No need to keep a book on Pearson 'cause Pearson keeps no book on me." Because if I strike you out on something, like a change-up in here, you don't come back to the bench thinking "That son of a bitch Wiggen struck me out in here so I'll be on the lookout next time." No, you come back to the bench thinking "I think I'll eat a frank," or "Gee, I see a great pair of jugs up there in the stands," so by the time you come up against me again you forgot all about the time before, so I'll just throw you in the same place again. You've got to think, Bruce, think and remember.

BRUCE: I'm going to start keeping a book.

HENRY: Yeah, either in your head or better still on paper for a while. You already have terrific power, but power plus brains is the difference between nobody and somebody.

BRUCE: Yeah, well, I always been pretty much of a nobody, though, so I guess what I got to do is I got to develop brains.

HENRY: Plus confidence. Power and brains are nothing without confidence.

BRUCE: You always had confidence. I never had confidence, Arthur.

HENRY: No, but I always *looked* like I had it, didn't I? Days when I'm tired and my curve is hanging *bullshit* gets me through. You got to crowd in, look fierce—works wonders— and half the pitchers you're facing they're just country boys like you, or country boys from the city

BRUCE: Country boys from the city?

HENRY: They're no smarter than you.

BRUCE: Yeah, but I never been smart, that's the thing.

HENRY: Everybody's smart. You've been dumb on one count only—you let somebody tell you you were dumb. Didn't you buy an Arcturus insurance policy?

BRUCE: Yeah.

HENRY: Didn't that prove to be a smart move?

BRUCE: Well, now as far as that goes I can't argue against that.

HENRY: Is Dutch smart?

BRUCE: Oh yeah, he certainly is.

HENRY: Then if you're so dumb why ain't Dutch cut you loose?

BRUCE: Well, he might yet.

HENRY: Oh, no. Piney Woods goes down and you stay up.

BRUCE: Who says so?

HENRY: I heard it with my own ears.

BRUCE: Yeah.

HENRY: Yeah.

BRUCE: Shoot, now that's the best news I heard so far.

Scene 16. Rockefeller Center, New York. The ball club is home.

Scene 17. Henry and Katie in a bar. Katie has the most charming Southern accent anyone has ever heard.

KATIE: What's wrong with Bruce?

HENRY: Who says anything is?

KATIE: He says.

HENRY: He says what?

KATIE: He says marry him and cash in on a big surprise.

HENRY: He's nutty. You get that way from sitting on the bench too many years.

KATIE: What was he doing in Minnesota?

HENRY: He had pneumonia.

KATIE (*laughing scornfully*): What would you go all the way to Minnesota with pneumonia for?

HENRY: Well, whatever it is it isn't catching. Do you think I'd be his roomie if it was?

KATIE: Living with him is one thing, loving is another.

HENRY: Oh, Katie, honey, why don't you get yourself married and raise yourself some exemptions?

KATIE: Why don't you play baseball for free, Author? Why should a girl go amateur when she's got the stuff to be professional? I don't know why you can't tell me what's wrong with him.

HENRY: Katie, if I knew I'd tell you.

Scene 18. Katie and Bruce are dancing to slow music in a dark bar. They kiss. Elsewhere in the bar Henry sits watching them—keeping his eye on them, monitoring them.

Scene 19. Opening Day at Mammoths' Stadium. Several marching bands come and go this way and that. Many flags fly in the April breeze.

The male voice on the public address system announces "our national anthem." The Mammoths players are lined up in front of their dugout. Some of the players cover their hearts with their caps, but others are distracted by one thing or another.

Henry is last in the line of the players. He is joined by Piney, in cowboy clothes, his guitar slung across his body.

PINEY: Why are they sending me down?

HENRY: You'll be back up, Piney.

PINEY: I should be back up now.

HENRY: They'll teach you to stay off motorcycles.

PINEY: I love motorcycles. (*He spies Goose.*) Look at that old washout.

HENRY: Don't lose your ticket. Take care of your banjo.

PINEY: Guitar.

HENRY: Say hello for me to everybody down in Queen City.

PINEY: Maybe somebody'll drop dead up here, open up a slot for me.

HENRY: Well, anything's possible.

PINEY: Life is unfair, I'll tell you that.

Scene 20. The Mammoths fan out to their positions. Standing at his place in his field-level box seat, Big Benjamin Scotland winds to throw.

PUBLIC ADDRESS ANNOUNCER: Ladies and gentlemen, your attention please. Today we honor a recently elected immortal, Big Benjamin Scotland. Big Ben, pitching for your New York Mammoths, struck out three hundred and twelve batters in the year nineteen hundred and one.

Big Benjamin Scotland throws the ball to Jonah, the Mammoths catcher.

JONAH: Burn it in, Ben, burn it in.

Scene 21. The game is on. Bruce, Goose, and Horse sit on the dugout bench.

GOOSE: Say, Pearson, I always wondered, exactly how tall are you?

HORSE: He always did wonder.

BRUCE: I'm exactly five feet eleven inches.

GOOSE: I never knew shit piled that high.

Scene 22. The game continues.

HENRY (*voice over*): We were a strong club. We had great pitching with both hands, and good relief if F.D.R. Caselli come through. We had the best outfield in baseball, bar none, and the best double-play combination. In fact, I didn't think there was anyone that could beat us—except maybe ourselves. We started ragging each other.

Scene 23. The game is over. The players are coming up the alleyway which is the entrance to the clubhouse. A dispute seems to have occurred among the members of the team.

HORSE (*angrily*): I heard you discussing my personality in Spanish. Spanish is the same as Italian.

Scene 24. In the clubhouse, quiet moment. Bruce is being addressed, but he does not respond.

UGLY: I don't know about you, Bruce. You know that goddam tobacco you chew. You ever hear of Old Yeller? That's what they're going to call your teeth.

ANOTHER PLAYER: That hairdo you wear. You ever seen that commercial with Joe Namath or something about the greasy kid stuff? You got to get hip like them guys, man, that's part of the whole image of being a baseball player. He has to look *good*. Why don't you like—you know—read some kind of fashion magazine, something like Esquire. Me and the other guys read the Esquire and Playboy and things like that. That's why we dress well. But you—you read the farmer magazines.

Scene 25. On the baseball field. Henry is pitching.

Scene 26. The players are again coming up the alleyway after the game. A fight erupts between Horse and one of the black players. They are separated.

Scene 27. Beside Henry's locker in the clubhouse. The sign on the door says KEEP YOUR COOL. *Dutch with a bat in his hand has some questions for Henry.*

DUTCH: Author, Joe tells me you been playing cards with Pearson over the winter.

HENRY: Yeah, why not?

DUTCH: When?

HENRY: Just before camp begun.

DUTCH: Where?

HENRY: Down at Bruce's.

DUTCH (*as if he's onto something*): Oh. What were you doing down there?

HENRY: You mean besides playing cards?

DUTCH: Quit stalling. Why did you go there?

Henry: He always wanted me to see what his folks were like and all his old stamping grounds and various beautiful whereabouts.

Dutch: Was the missus with you?

Henry: Sure.

Dutch: You drove down there by car?

Henry: Yes indeedy.

Dutch: Very welly. Now we got you and your wife located by car in Georgia. Let's back up the car to where you spoke to Goose on the telephone in Chicago. You drove to Georgia from New York by *via* Chicago, did you?

Henry: I never did speak to Goose in Chicago.

Dutch: You never did? In other words you told me Goose is a liar?

Henry: No, no, I suppose what he means is I spoke to his Mrs.

Dutch: You know very goddam well what he probably means. Don't procrastinate, Author. You're stalling the wrong man. When was this?

Henry: Probably around in February.

Dutch: What were you doing in Chicago?

Henry: Besides speaking with Goose's Mrs.? I was only changing planes.

Dutch: For where?

Henry: Minneapolis.

DUTCH: For what?

HENRY: Insurance matters.

DUTCH: Name me somebody you planned on seeing on insurance matters in Minneapolis.

HENRY: Aleck Olson.

DUTCH (*calls*): Joe, where's Alex Olson from on Boston that swings like an ice chopper?

JOE: Olson?

DUTCH: Yeah.

JOE: Minneapolis.

DUTCH (*back to Henry*): Did you sell him any insurance?

HENRY: It's only a matter of time.

DUTCH: This is all lies.

HENRY: I got Olson in the palm of my hand.

DUTCH: I got a feeling that all your little statements are true, but what they add up to is one big lie. Am I right?

HENRY: About what?

DUTCH: About the feeling I got?

HENRY: I don't know what kind of feeling you got. If you say you got this feeling I guess you do.

DUTCH: You should be wrapped in a sack and threw in the river, all except your pitching arm.

Scene 28. In the interior of the stadium between the club-houses. Henry meets furtively with Aleck Olson of the Red Sox.

HENRY: Dutch called you.

ALECK: Yeah, what's it all about?

HENRY: What he say?

ALECK: Oh, was you in Minneapolis. I said—bought a coat, that's all that I know. Oh, he asked about insurance—did I buy insurance off you. Is *he* selling insurance?

HENRY: What else?

ALECK: He asked me then what—I said you got on a bus to see Pearson. That's all I knew. What's up, Author? You got a girl or something?

HENRY: Did you tell him where I went to see Pearson?

ALECK: I figured if you got on a bus to Rochester you're going to Rochester.

HENRY: Ain't there any places between Minneapolis and Rochester?

ALECK: Cannon Falls?

HENRY: It just so happens we met in Cannon Falls.

ALECK: You can meet anywhere you want to meet except what would you be doing in Cannon Falls?

HENRY: Fishing.

ALECK: In nine feet of ice?

Henry: Hunting?

Aleck: Yeah, but you'd be most likely to go up north of the city—I mean that's where most people go. You guys got girls in Cannon Falls? Author, concerning insurance I want to—

Henry: No, no, no, no, up north is exactly where I'd never go —that's where everybody goes, packed in like sardines. Thanks, Aleck.

Aleck: For what? I just wanted to talk to you about insurance. I mean, combining insurance with annuity, you know—

Henry: Next time, I got to warm up.

Aleck: Yeah, but I—

Scene 29. Playing ball. Somebody hits a comebacker to Henry, who throws out the batter at first base.

Henry (*voice over*): We started out near the top, neck and neck with Baltimore and Cincinnati, but all spring we kept floating, never dropping far back but never gaining either, staying alive with pitching one day and power the next, never putting the two together. It wasn't pulling like a club. I was worried, but Dutch—he was going out of his mind. It's not surprising he was hounding me, trying every which way to figure out what was happening to the club.

Scene 30. Dutch is in the clubhouse whirlpool bath. He has summoned Henry to meet with him. Dutch smokes a cigarette: during this scene he will smoke more than one. When he is through with a cigarette he orders Henry to "flip up the bowl" so that he can throw the cigarette into the toilet.

Sign on the wall says, NO WOMEN ALLOWED BEYOND THIS POINT.

HENRY: Ain't you afraid you're going to burn a hole in your chest?

DUTCH: I'm sitting here with this Chicago book. I keep trying to figure the son of a bitches out. But then you know what I wind up thinking about? Wiggen and Pearson. Goddam it, Author, you told me you went back home from Minneapolis.

HENRY: So it's this again. No, Dutch, I don't believe I told you that.

DUTCH: You led me to believe it, which is the same thing. Did you see Olson?

HENRY: Sure I seen Olson.

DUTCH: About what?

HENRY: Insurance matters. By the way, he mentioned you called him. Dutch, I wish you wouldn't push this thing too far.

DUTCH: Why not?

HENRY: It's a personal matter.

DUTCH: Flip up the bowl. How so?

HENRY: Well, you're probably going to think I'm some kind of heel and all that, but there's this airline stewardess.

DUTCH: Her name being what?

HENRY: Mary.

DUTCH: Mary what? Smith, Jones, Brown?

HENRY (*improvising "piss" from the toilet*): Mary Pistolo-glione.

DUTCH: Go on, I'm trying very hard to believe this. So you piddle along between Chicago and Minneapolis and then you get on a bus in Minneapolis and you go where?

HENRY: Didn't Olson tell you?

DUTCH: You tell me.

HENRY: Cannon Falls, Minnesota.

DUTCH: For what?

HENRY: To hunt.

DUTCH: You never hunt.

HENRY: I'm taking it up.

DUTCH: What kind of a gun do you shoot?

HENRY: No kind, I only went there because Pearson asked me to.

DUTCH: What did you catch?

HENRY: Nothing. We changed our minds, we went back.

DUTCH: Back where?

HENRY: Back home—him to Georgia and me to New York.

DUTCH: You've probably drilled him up to the eyes by now, but I'm going to hear how this sounds from him anyway. (*He calls.*) Bradley. Send Pearson in. (*Back to Henry.*) I don't believe this cockeyed bull story about Mary Pisstacallioni for one minute, but you're making a very big mistake. Anybody with a wife like yours should count his blessings.

Bruce enters.

DUTCH: What plane took you up to Minnesota, Pearson?

BRUCE: No plane, sir, I had my car.

DUTCH: Is Cannon Falls a nice town?

BRUCE: Oh, yes.

DUTCH: Well, tell me, what's it like.

BRUCE: Well, it's a pretty nice little town with a main drag, a few stores, but very cold.

DUTCH: Oh.

BRUCE: Yeah, we couldn't fish, the ice was nine foot thick, we went hunting.

DUTCH: What did you shoot?

BRUCE: Nothing. Well, we started hunting but then we changed my mind so—I didn't feel like killing anything any more.

DUTCH: Knocks the hell out of hunting.

BRUCE: Yes, I guess it does.

DUTCH: Then where did you go from Minnesota?

BRUCE: Back home.

DUTCH: Alone?

BRUCE: Yes.

DUTCH: You're sure?

BRUCE: Yes, yes, weren't we, Arthur?

DUTCH: You two went back from Minnesota by car?

BRUCE: Yeah.

DUTCH: Flip up the bowl again. Very well, Author, I think we might be heading toward something at last, for two days ago I asked you who drove your car down to Bainbridge and you said you and your wife did, and now I hear something else again. Did you go down there and back home for your wife, or did her and Mary Pisstacallioni maybe drive down there with Aleck Olson or otherwise what the hell is going on here because you know as sure as your name is that I'm going to get to the bottom of this.

HENRY: Well, Dutch, the joke's on you.

DUTCH: I'm laughing my ass off.

HENRY: Because if you'll back the whole thing up you'll re-member I called you during this time on the telephone and give you a little patter. Right? And I told you I was up home when all the time where we were we were right downtown St. Louis. We would have went out and seen you but we weren't dressed. And we didn't want to see the Mrs. like this, so we made a gag out of the whole thing. Well, you can understand me not wanting to give away a gag like that I might want to use again some other time.

DUTCH: Get out. Get out.

Scene 31. The baseball field. A game is in progress. Henry is pitching. Now Bruce is hitting. Henry is in the dugout. Bruce, at bat, receives complicated signals from the third-base coach. Bruce hits, rounds first base—a single.

A PLAYER: Attaboy, Pearson.

HENRY: Not bad, huh, Dutch?

Scene 32. Hotel bedroom. Henry and Bruce are preparing to leave for the ballpark. Bruce wears a shirt with a smiling face on the front. He is humming the song "Katie." The word "beneficiary" does not come easily for him: he pronounces it "benefishoorary."

BRUCE: Arthur, how do I change my beneficiary?

HENRY: Who do you want to change it to?

BRUCE: To Katie. She's going to marry me at last.

HENRY: When? When you change your beneficiary?

BRUCE: Arthur, you got no right telling me who I can and who I can not change my benefiary to.

HENRY: Why didn't she marry you last year or the year before?

BRUCE: Well, she never loved me before.

HENRY: Before what?

BRUCE: Before now.

HENRY: How is now different?

BRUCE: Author, will you change it for me or will you not change it for me?

HENRY: I'll write away to Arcturus.

BRUCE: When?

HENRY: Tuesday.

BRUCE: Why not now?

HENRY: Because it's time to go to the ballpark.

BRUCE: Oh, I've seen you dash off many a letter standing against the wall or when you're in a cab.

HENRY: This is a matter of one hundred thirty-seven thousand five hundred dollars. A large figure like that has got to be handled sitting down with plenty of time to wet your pencil.

BRUCE: Well, okay, but don't forget and do it Tuesday.

Scene 33. Beside the hotel switchboard. Tootsie at the switchboard is tending her business and other people's business, too. Bruce is dozing on a couch in the lobby nearby.

TOOTSIE: Hey, Author, come here I want to talk to you.

HENRY: How are you, Tootsie?

TOOTSIE: Pretty good. I want to ask you something. Why don't you Mammoths get it together, for Heaven's sake? What's with this squabbling? You know, considering the personnel of the organization you'd be on top of it if you guys hung together. What do you guys do on the road anyway? I think that's what's wrong. (*Answering her phone.*) Oh, I'm sorry, this hotel does not provide such a service. I'm *sorry*. (*To Henry again.*) I wish somebody'd tell Dutch to bolster up the catching. You know I'm going to tell him myself if I see him.

Joe approaches Henry.

JOE: Author, come here, for God sake this place is full of fish.

HENRY: Yeah, I'll get Bruce.

JOE: Let him sleep, it's Tegwar.

HENRY: Let him sit in for me.

JOE (*extremely angry*): He can't do it. Don't you understand that?

HENRY: He wants to join us.

JOE: Let him sleep.

HENRY: You promised me.

JOE: Promised me, promised me, sound like a song. (*He sings.*) "O promise me that we will never part." What are you two anyhow, Romeo and Juliet? One can't play cards without the other?

HENRY: Forget it for today, Joe.

JOE: Romeo and Juliet, I don't know which is which.

BRUCE (*waking up*): Oh Joe, how's the show?

JOE: I will make you sorry for this, Author, I really will. You're going to *pay* for this, Author.

BRUCE: What's the matter with him?

HENRY: Nothin'. What are you reading?

BRUCE: I know you're not going to believe this, but I'm reading how some girl was seduced by Dracula.

Scene 34. In the clubhouse. All the players are assembled. Dutch mounts the scales—his lecture platform. While he lectures he is somewhat distracted by Diego, who is translating his remarks into Spanish for George. More than once Dutch tries to restrain Diego, but Diego cannot resist continuing.

DUTCH: Boys! Today we start shaking the son of a bitches off for good. You know, to me they're like a fly buzzing around your head while you sit and watch it for a while without raising your hand until you say, "You buzzing fly, buzz me one more time and I will snatch you out of the air and you will buzz me no more." Diego, forget it. This isn't so much for George anyhow as certain other people who can't control their feelings toward their teammates. Rule one. No dissension. Baltimore, enough is enough. I should have pulled away from you by now, and now I think I will simply pull myself together and squash out your miserable life. Fly, you are done for. Whack! But only one thing is wrong. I look down in my hand and I see no fly. And I ask myself "How could I have missed it?" when I already seen the whole league around east and west and I know that I am the winner if I work together. Diego, forget it.

DIEGO (*consulting his dictionary*): Forget? What is forget? Ah, forget is not to remember. But mister, it is too quick not to remember, she just now boom happen, no?

DUTCH: Forget it means—screw it. Why did I lose when I should have won? Because the fly flew through my hand. And the reason that the fly flew through my hand is because the fingers did not work together. The first finger says to the second finger "I don't like you because you won't play cards with me," and the second finger says to the third finger "You should hear what finger number one has been saying about you," and the third finger says to the fourth finger, "I don't agree with the color of your skin," and the fourth finger says to the fifth finger, "Let's you and me cut finger number three dead and tell our goddam wives do the same and bring up our children likewise." (*He is screaming.*) Boys! Boys! This is suicide. Work together! Play together! This way when the World Series time comes around you'll be there, you won't be home watching it on electrical television. (*He sings the Gillette Razor Blade song.*) "*Look* sharp dee dee dee dee dee, *feel* sharp dee dee dee dee dee—"

Scene 35. In the Mammoths bullpen. In the distance we hear the canned ballpark band playing hollow, tinny, distant, time-killing joyless carnival music. The music supports the mood of the mournful, pivotal scene which follows.

Henry and Goose relax on the bullpen bench. Joe enters the bullpen.

HENRY (*voice over*): I was liable to wake up some morning not even speaking to myself. The ragging was even getting to me.

JOE: Hey, Romeo, where's Juliet?

HENRY: Romeo was a great lover, Joe. You jealous? Because if you're jealous I believe you can buy these little pills give you back your pep in bed you lost when you were young like me.

JOE: Mind your tongue, boy. Be careful how you rag your elders.

HENRY: Don't pull your rank on me. Give is give and take is take.

GOOSE (*to Henry*): How's your wife?

HENRY: Nice of you to ask.

GOOSE: I ain't took my wife to a ballgame in eleven years.

HENRY: Take her when we hit Chicago.

GOOSE: First laid eyes on my wife in a ballpark. Probably looked like you back there. Shaved my face every day. Had high hopes of making the big cash.

HENRY: It's never too late for an Arcturus annuity.

GOOSE: It's much too late. I'm too old.

HENRY: No-o-o-o, with World Series money I can fix you up with a plan as a starter.

GOOSE: You know, I been meaning to ask you. A man my age hates to ask a punk like you for tips on things.

HENRY: What do you own?

GOOSE: What do I own? I own two catcher's mitts and a baseball autographed by each and every member of the New York Mammoths. Put it all together and you can get a fin in any hock shop in Chicago. What I own is debts.

HENRY: That's simple. We'll declare bankruptcy.

GOOSE: That's something for a fellow to look forward to. How?

HENRY: I'll show you but you've got to do me one favor.

GOOSE: What's that?

HENRY: You got to lay off Pearson.

GOOSE: I just joke around. It's something to keep up my spirits, that's all.

HENRY: He's dying.

GOOSE: Soon? Any day now?

HENRY: It could happen any time.

GOOSE: Does Dutch know?

HENRY: No, and you mustn't tell him either. Only me and you know.

GOOSE: Only you and me will ever know.

Henry and Goose shake hands.

Scene 36. Henry's and Bruce's hotel room. It is the middle of the night. Once again the summer breeze blows the curtain at the window. Henry is asleep. Bruce is wakeful, restless, feeling ill. A large photograph of Katie stands on Bruce's bedside table.

BRUCE (*calling weakly*): Arthur. Arthur. Arthur. Arthur. Something's happening. Something's happening.

Scene 37. The hotel corridor. Henry runs down the hall in his pajamas. He knocks on a door. Horse answers the door. Goose is right behind him.

HENRY: Where's Goose? I need help.

HORSE: What for?

HENRY (*to Goose*): You know.

GOOSE: What do I do? You can talk. Horse knows.

HORSE: He told me.

HENRY: You weren't supposed to mention it.

GOOSE: Only my roomie.

HENRY: You got to go get this doctor—Dr. Charleston P. Chambers.

Scene 38. Back in Henry's and Bruce's room

BRUCE: I'm really sorry to have woke you. I was hoping it wouldn't happen at a bad hour.

HENRY: Make it back to me another time.

BRUCE: No, there's not going to be another time. Dutch'll probably bring Piney Woods back up now. And he's going to be real happy. Is the doctor going to come?

HENRY: Oh yeah, Goose went after him.

BRUCE (*laughing in confusion*): Goose? Why Goose?

HENRY: He's right down the hall. Goose has got a heart of gold.

BRUCE: Yeah, I guess it never really showed. Probably you told him or something.

Henry and Bruce laugh together.

HENRY: I—I never told a soul—

BRUCE: Probably everybody be nice to you if they knew you were dying.

HENRY: Everybody knows everybody's dying, that's why people are as good as they are.

BRUCE: I'm scared. Hold on to me.

Henry and Bruce embrace. The doctor arrives. He is accompanied by Goose and Horse. The doctor is very businesslike. He studies the medical papers Henry has carried with him from Minnesota.

DOCTOR: Who's the sick baseball player? (*To Henry.*) Are you a baseball player, too?

HENRY: Yes, sir, Henry Wiggen, sir.

DOCTOR: I heard that name. Not that I follow the game. I've detested it from early childhood. It's a dying game, I'm told. (*He examines Bruce.*) I think it's something else.

HENRY: You mean something else besides what they said in Minnesota?

DOCTOR: I couldn't say about that. I only mean that—I don't think there's any danger right at this minute.

BRUCE: Oh boy, it sure felt like it.

HENRY: Now you can do me one favor. Please send a bill care of my wife in Perkinsville, New York, and also not leak anything to the papers.

DOCTOR: I'm not in the habit of leaking my house calls to the papers.

Scene 39. In Dutch's office. The walls are decorated with New York Mammoths symbols and souvenirs, team photographs, star photographs, and photographs of Dutch looking fierce. Also present in the office is one Mr. Rogers.

DUTCH: Author, meet Mr. Rogers. Mr. Rogers is a detective. Sit down. Mr. Rogers been down to Bainbridge and is now on his way up to Minnesota filling in some facts for me. However, you can save us some time by filling in the rest of the story Mr. Rogers has begun.

HENRY: I'll surely try my darnedest.

DUTCH: Tell him what you discovered.

MR. ROGERS: In Bainbridge, George, the subject's domicile, I developed the following information. I interviewed a Mr. Jay Clark and a mailman, and a colored woman named Gem—

DUTCH: Never mind the facts. Give me details.

MR. ROGERS: The details are that the subject, Pearson, told various people that he wasn't feeling so good and went to the hospital in Atlanta. The hospital in Atlanta recommended the hospital in Minnesota—

HENRY: If you'd actually spoken to anybody worth the while you'll learn that Pearson has this old-time habit of running back to Atlanta maybe once or twice a month. No doubt you developed that much. No need telling you where he *went* in Atlanta. Everybody knows that.

MR. ROGERS: Naturally.

HENRY: And you know what you sometimes pick up in such places. Which he did. And which he rather not have them treat in Atlanta so close to home for fear of it getting back and embarrassing his mother. So-o-o-o, off he goes to Minnesota with his fishing gear, forgetting that the ice is nine feet thick that time of year, checks in with the Mayo Brothers, gets himself shot with a couple of miracle drugs, flirts with the nurses, checks out, meets me in Cannon Falls, we hunted—

DUTCH: What? What? Goddam it.

Something has alarmed Dutch. He runs out into the hall calling for help.

DUTCH (*calling*): Where's Pearson? Bradley, get me Dr. Loftus.

MR. ROGERS (*to Henry*): What's the sudden interruption?

HENRY: I don't know. You're the detective.

DUTCH (*reenters office*): I see the girl he runs around with. She'll give it to the whole club. She'll run right around my infield.

Doc Loftus and Bruce arrive at Dutch's office.

DUTCH: Take down your pants. Are you over the clap yet?

BRUCE: Oh yes, sir, long ago.

DUTCH: How do we know? Check him over, Doc. All I need is the clap running through my ball club now.

BRUCE: Hey, Arthur, what's going on around here? Sometimes I don't know what's going on sometimes.

DOC LOFTUS: He looks just fine to me. Never better.

Mr. Rogers: Shall I develop this information farther in Rochester, Minnesota?

Bruce (*to Henry*): Rochester, Minnesota?

Henry: Where you got shot for the clap.

Bruce: Oh, yeah.

Dutch (*to Mr. Rogers*): Stay with it. Some things have yet to be explained.

Scene 40. A Mammoths game is in progress. Bruce bats.

Henry (*voice over*): In July we dropped a couple more games off the pace. It was strange. The team was going lousy—and yet I led both leagues in wins. And for the first time in his life Bruce played regular. He didn't bust down fences left and right, but he hit steady, two-sixty-five, two-seventy, not that great, but for Bruce—fantastic.

Scene 41. Henry and Katie are dining in a restaurant.

Katie: Wouldn't you say that if the Arcturus Company discovers that you been writing phony letters to prevent Bruce from changing his beneficiary—

Henry: Oh, that's not a phony letter. It's a real letter.

Katie: Who wrote it?

Henry: The company wrote it.

Katie: Or if you didn't write it your wife wrote it, that's my guess, and several baseball players tell me I'm probably right. Maybe I'll go check this with the company themselves. They'll take away your license.

HENRY: Throw me in jail.

KATIE: Ruin you as an insurance agent.

HENRY: Well, if you say anything to the Arcturus Company I'll stroll down to a certain police station on Sixty-Six Street and swear out a complaint against a certain—answering service.

KATIE: I'm not really anxious to complain to the Arcturus Company. I don't see any reason why you and I can't arrange a settlement just between us.

HENRY: A deal?

KATIE: A compromise.

HENRY: I can't compromise with his money.

KATIE: That's none of your business. You're supposed to do what he wants.

HENRY: I'm deciding what he wants.

KATIE: That's illegal.

HENRY: I know.

Scene 42. A baseball game is in progress. Henry is pitching and Bruce is catching. Mr. Pearson is in the dugout. The theme song plays. We hear it now for the first time on an unseen guitar.

HENRY (*voice over*): First week in August his father hit town.

Henry is being shelled. A line drive comes back at him. He must fall to the ground to get out of the way of it. Another opposition player hits a double. From the stands someone shouts, "Get a job, Wiggen, get a job." Henry is shelled some more. Dutch strolls to the mound to take Henry out of the game.

DUTCH: All right, Author, it's just one of those days.

Scene 43. Henry is alone. He walks up the alleyway to the clubhouse. Mr. Pearson is waiting for him before the clubhouse door.

MR. PEARSON: Henry.

HENRY: Hello, Mr. Pearson.

STADIUM GUARD: Please move on, don't detain the ballplayers.

HENRY: That's okay.

MR. PEARSON: I am intruding on you, I know.

HENRY: No you're not.

MR. PEARSON: You been intruded on enough.

HENRY: It's a ball game, sir, you win 'em and you lose 'em.

MR. PEARSON: I mean regarding my son.

HENRY: Sir?

MR. PEARSON: You know about—the condition of my son.

HENRY: Yes sir.

MR. PEARSON: So do I.

HENRY: Yes sir, I suspected you did.

MR. PEARSON: How—how can he be so sick and play so well?

HENRY: I really don't even know, sir. If I knew I'd say.

MR. PEARSON: —and not playing so well but better than ever, and that's a fact.

HENRY: That's a fact, sir, there's no mistake about that.

MR. PEARSON: So I been wondering if they didn't make some kind of a mistake out there at that hospital in Minnesota because it's hard to believe that it can be true.

HENRY: I don't think I'd count on it, sir. They got an awful famous reputation up there.

MR. PEARSON: I know it's been a terrible strain on you.

HENRY: It's a lot worse on him, sir. And on you.

MR. PEARSON: So I been thinking—I don't generally swear—

HENRY: You go ahead and you swear, Mr. Pearson.

MR. PEARSON: Plain old mother talk ain't nowheres near strong enough to describe such a terrible mixup as life, Author. I'm swearing. My son's been handed one shit deal.

HENRY: Yes sir.

Scene 44. Henry enters the clubhouse. Only Bradley Lord is there. Henry's meeting with Mr. Pearson has brought down upon him the weight of Bruce's experience; he is also frustrated by his poor pitching performance. In the clubhouse he begins to throw things around. He beats a table with a stool. He punishes the clubhouse in every way that comes to hand. He hurls a baseball at the water cooler, smashing the five-gallon glass bottle.

Bradley dodges this way and that in a surprisingly agile manner for a fellow so stout, trying to stay out of range of Henry's wrath. Bradley is ignorant and unsympathetic.

BRADLEY (*on the run*): What are you doing that for? Calm down. They bombed you out early—why didn't you use your energy in the game instead of—everybody's going to be very —save your energy for the game, what are you doing it in here for? Don't wreck that stuff. Everybody—

Scene 45. Henry is alone in his hotel room, sitting on his bed, writing in a notebook. Joe enters.

JOE: You writing a new book, Author?

HENRY: No, Joe, I'm being interrupted by somebody busting in my room.

JOE: About you and Pearson?

HENRY: What makes you think so?

JOE: I didn't understand the situation.

HENRY: What situation?

JOE: The situation you're probably writing a book about.

HENRY: Probably what situation?

JOE: The way I feel about it is this. I believe that Pearson is a better Tegwar player than I ever realized. He should play with us all the time. I swear to God, Author, I'm shaking yet, my knees are trembling, my heart is sick. He told me on the airplane.

HENRY: Who told you what?

JOE: Goose told me.

HENRY: What?

JOE: I been calling Pearson Romeo and Juliet, which is which
—see—

HENRY: Now who'll you tell?

JOE: Nobody, Author, absolutely nobody. I told the wife and
that's the end of it.

HENRY: Why told the wife?

JOE: Author, I tell the wife everything.

*Scene 46. In the hotel lobby. Sid, the mighty home-run
hitter, now in a batting slump, sits on a sofa, testing his
eyes by placing a hand over one, then the other, and
squinting into the distance.*

*Doc Loftus walks past in a purposeful way, as if he has
been called to an important meeting in the hotel—which
he has.*

HENRY: What's up? Where is everybody?

SID: Nobody knows.

HENRY: I'll bet Tootsie knows.

TOOTSIE: Knows what, Author? I know something is up. The
long distance been flying far and fast. I could use two
grandstands any weekend or night.

HENRY: Tickets are going to be scarcer and scarcer from here
on in. Why did I see Doc Loftus just pass through?

Tootsie: Oh, Doc Loftus in the hotel. (*She pages him.*) Doc Loftus, telephone please.

Henry: Who wants him?

Tootsie: Dutch wants him.

Henry: Who's sick?

Tootsie: I don't know—somebody in Minnesota. I'm not clear. Look, I only catch a little bit now and then. And besides, who understands this medical talk they're talking? But I *believe* he has a leak in his blood somewhere. Room service? Just a moment, please. Nothing serious, but I don't know who. I never heard of it. But for two more grandstands on the following day I can tell you something else.

Henry: Yeah, I hate to hear it.

Tootsie: *You* are in the doghouse. Why you? You've been playing your heart out. It's some of those other so-called baseball players been dragging their foot. That's why we haven't won it yet.

Henry: Why me?

Tootsie: Because of your contract—Pearson—Mr. Rogers the detective broke it open. You see, very easy, Joe Jaros and Goose Williams spent the winter in Minnesota with Pearson. You know, I didn't even know they were that friendly. Well, it takes all kinds. (*Into the phone.*) The time is eight-oh-six. Third base side, Author, lower deck, not too far back, and not behind no pillars nor posts.

Scene 47. The executive suite. Present are Dutch, Dutch's wife, Doc Loftus, Bradley Lord, Mr. Rogers the detective, Mr. Moors, Patricia Moors, Joe, and Joe's wife. Henry enters.

DUTCH: I told you. I told you I'd get to the bottom of this.

HENRY: Good morning to all.

DUTCH'S WIFE: I wonder why I'm not crying.

JOE'S WIFE: Keep your hanky handy, dear.

DUTCH: Don't you think we discussed it enough as far as how horrible it is? Tonight is another ballgame as usual.

PATRICIA: Maybe we can get help from the commissioner.

MR. MOORS: We can't get help there and keep it in this room at the same time.

DUTCH: Well then let the facts out.

DUTCH'S WIFE: It wouldn't be human.

DUTCH: Is it human to lose? We're calling in Piney Woods from Queen City for extra catching.

BRADLEY: Ready on your call to *Professor* Traphagen.

DUTCH: Do we really need him? He was the greatest catcher I ever saw. Author, you were his boy. You talk him into coming back to help us. He won't play. He'll instruct the catching. He'll steady us. Help us make it to the end. How much can I offer him?

PATRICIA: The sky's the limit. And I'm sure the boys will vote him a full Series share if we win.

DUTCH (*on the phone*): Red—oh, trouble, Red. Lots of trouble. Author wants to talk to you. Yeah, it's Author who got us in trouble in the first place.

HENRY (*on the phone*): Red, we got a crisis here and we need your help. You get a full Series share if we win it.

DUTCH (*seizes the phone again*): Red, how do you like the sound of a thousand dollars a week? Can't find a substitute to do what? Teach English! What teach English? People speak English already. Red, Red, it's urgent, I swear you won't have to play, just instruct the catching. Right. Hop on the nearest plane. Love and kisses, Red. (*He hangs up.*) I hate him. Have you thought up anything yet, Doc?

DOC LOFTUS: I'm thinking.

DUTCH: You're a slow thinker. This thing—what is it called?

DOC LOFTUS: The disease is named for Hodgkin. He's the man who identified it.

DUTCH: Find him. Is he alive himself? Maybe he thought up a cure by now that those jugheads up in Minnesota didn't hear about yet. What the hell kind of a place is that anyway to build a goddam hospital? In the wilds of nowhere? Doesn't a man freeze his ass off by the time they get him down in bed? (*To Henry.*) You. You were there. You sneaked out there in the middle of winter and all the rest was horse-feathers, you and Mary P for Palooka and hunting through the ice and miracle drugs for the clap and tricks on the telephone.

Scene 48. Piney Woods enters the clubhouse, followed almost immediately by Red Traphagen. Piney, with guitar, dressed like a cowboy, is greeted by the players with good-natured mockery. Red, on the other hand, is received with the respect reserved for an honored veteran of the game.

A PLAYER (*to Piney, mimicking a cowboy on horseback*): Did you come out from Queen City on horseback?

SECOND PLAYER: Hey, it's Red Traphagen.

RED: What's up, Author?

HENRY: Damned if I know. You know I'd tell you if I knew.

THIRD PLAYER (*to Red*): It stinks in here.

RED: Human perspiration smells, it doesn't stink. Wouldn't have it any other way—huh, Author? (*He is alone with Henry.*) How are you? Jeez, you've been having a great year.

HENRY: The best year of my life. I bet you get no reception like this in San Francisco.

RED: Nah, they pray I don't show up for class.

REPORTER: What's up, Red? Why are you here? (*To Dutch.*) Is he going to play?

DUTCH: He's here to coach the catching and Piney's here to back up the catching in case anything happens.

REPORTER: Why now?

DUTCH: Mental lapse, that's why. (*To Piney.*) Where's your gun?

PINEY: Right here, partner.

DUTCH: Hand it over. I'm in no mood to see anybody get killed by a bullet wound. I hear you have bullets with it too.

PINEY: Yes sir, they're in the gun.

DUTCH: Why in the hell didn't you tell me?

PINEY: I didn't think it'd go off. I'm always very careful.

DUTCH: That's what everybody says. That's why the hospital is full of babies. Jonah.

JONAH: Yeah.

DUTCH: You shot guns in the war.

JONAH: No sir, I played baseball.

DUTCH: Some hell of a war. Canada.

CANADA: Yes sir.

DUTCH: You shot guns in Vietnam.

CANADA: Right.

DUTCH: Here. Take and empty this gun.

RED: Why am I here, Author?

DUTCH: Boys, I want to welcome Red back from the Coast to bolster us and steady up the instruction. (*The players cheer.*) I want to welcome Piney Woods back from the wild wild West to ride along with us all the way now is what I'm hoping. (*Cheers again.*) You've all been doing very good jobs. Maybe now and then some baseball player or other type of person gets the idea that I'm not human. Well, for example, even Pearson here thought that I sometimes wasn't human.

Dutch has presented himself as having chosen to speak of Bruce as if Bruce were an accidental choice lending himself to illustration: "Well, for example, even Pearson here . . ." Dutch stands beside Bruce at his locker and speaks with great guilty emotion.

BRUCE: No sir.

DUTCH: I probably ate you out now and then, but never without a reason.

BRUCE: No sir, you only ate me out for doing dumb things.

DUTCH: No no no no, I ate you out for the good of the club and for your own pocketbook. Never for anything personal, because I know that you know that personally I never had anything but the greatest respect for you as a human being.

BRUCE: Yes sir, that was how I always felt.

DUTCH: When I die—(*He realizes what he has said. Nevertheless, he repeats himself. He leaves Bruce. He steps on the scales.*) When I die the papers will write in their headlines "The son of a bitches of the world have lost their leader," but many a boy will shed a tear or two that rode along with me into the big money, and that's why maybe now and then I ate Pearson out or some other type of person.

JOE: Time, Dutch.

DUTCH: Yeah. I'll say it's time. Let's go, boys.

The clubhouse clears. Henry, Bruce, and Red remain.

BRUCE (*to Red*): Tell me what you see because I know I got faults. I always did.

RED: Throw the ball back to the pitcher better. Make it easy on him.

BRUCE: All right, I will, I really will, I'll do that.

HENRY: I told you that a thousand times. When he tells you you believe him.

BRUCE: Yeah, but he's a catcher. You ain't no catcher.

RED: We're of the tribe of catchers. Oh yeah, when you hit don't chew. There's a system to your chewing. You give yourself away.

HENRY: When he tenses up he stops chewing.

RED: That's it. Oh, one other little thing. Use a lighter bat. I always thought you used too heavy a bat. Big, strong boy like you, just meet the ball, don't murder it.

BRUCE: Okay.

Scene 49. In a restaurant. The piano plays. Henry, Katie, and Miss Industrial Progress are dining—Miss Industrial Progress very enthusiastically: she never interrupts her eating. Miss Industrial Progress has long, golden hair. She speaks in a Southern accent, like Katie's. Perhaps Katie has brought her to New York from her own hometown.

KATIE: Is she familiar to you?

HENRY: You bet, I seen her on TV.

KATIE: Plus she was voted Miss Industrial Progress not so very long ago.

HENRY: I believe I recall the event.

Katie: Tell Mr. Wiggen your present business address.

Miss Industrial Progress: Sixty-Six Street.

Katie: Where you got a golden lifetime pass to just as soon as I lay my hands on that change of beneficiary form to You Know Whose policy. Miss Industrial Progress is a baseball fan from way back, aren't you, honey?

Miss Industrial Progress: I sure am.

Katie: You can't play ball forever. You got a short life. Why not live it up a little bit? Why worry so much about—You Know Who and his family and his little old policy? Why? *Why?*

Henry: I don't know why you don't live it up all the time when dying is just around the corner, but you don't. You'd think you would but you don't. I don't know why.

Scene 50. The piano fades to thunder. The rain pours down on the ball field. A dozen or more uniformed men— the groundskeeping crew—are pulling an immense tarpaulin across the infield.

In the Mammoths clubhouse the uniformed players begin to wait out this game delay. They play cards. In Bruce's locker we see the large photograph of Katie we have seen at his bedside.

Piney strums his guitar and sings the song sometimes known as "The Streets of Laredo," sometimes as "The Cowboy's Lament." We have heard the melody of this song through the film.

Not until now, however, have we heard the words. Bruce at his locker sits with eyes cast down, as if he were not involved. His teammates, however, take in the words in their full meaning; all but Piney, who has not yet taken possession of the secret.

PINEY (*sings*):

> As I walked down in Laredo one day
> I spied a young cowboy all wrapped in white linen,
> Wrapped in white linen as cold as the clay.

PINEY (*speaks*): Then the cowboy speaks.

HORSE: Try a different song.

GOOSE: Yeah, I don't like that song.

PINEY: No, the cowboy speaks.

HORSE: I don't want to hear the cowboy speak.

PINEY (*sings*):

> I seen by his outfit that he was a cowboy
> As I walked near him these words he did sigh,
> "Come sit down beside me and hear my sad story,
> Shot in the breast and I know I must die."

GOOSE: Do you know another number, Piney?

HORSE: Song stinks.

A PLAYER: It's a cornball song.

SECOND PLAYER: Hey, I think it's letting up.

PINEY: Come on, sing.

THIRD PLAYER: Yeah, it sounds good.

PINEY: Cowboy tells his sad story. (*He sings.*)

> It was once in the saddle I used to go dashing,
> Once in the saddle I used to go gay,

First down to Rosie's and then to the card house,
Shot in the breast and I'm dying today.

Get sixteen gamblers to carry my coffin,
Get six pretty maidens to sing me a song,
Take me to the valley and lay the sod o'er me,
I'm just a young cowboy and I know I done wrong.

Piney pauses to address his fellow players.

PINEY: Come on, boys, why don't you join in like they do?

Piney resumes his song.

Oh bang the drum slowly and play the fife lowly
Play the dead march as they carry me along.
Put bunches of roses all over my coffin,
Roses to deaden the clods as they fall.

Scene 51. The deserted ball field. The tarpaulin covers only the home-plate area.

Scene 52. Henry strides down the hotel corridor, swinging a room key in his hand. We hear the sounds of a boisterous party in the room he is about to enter. Men are singing and laughing. Henry is puzzled. What is going on in his room?
Henry enters the room. He is welcomed by cries of "Author" and "Hats off."

BRUCE: Come on in, Arthur, come on in and join the celebration.

HENRY: I guess I will. I live here. Celebrating what?

BRUCE: Celebrating.

RED: Celebrating—*celebration.*

BRUCE: Hats off.

PLAYER: Hey, Piney, he said hats off so take your hat off.

PINEY (*who now knows the secret*): Whatever Bruce says I'll do, for in my opinion there's no greater catcher in baseball today.

The players cheer and applaud. Joe Jaros enters the room to make a slightly depressing announcement.

JOE: Baltimore won.

BRUCE: Well, that's okay, because they ain't going to beat us.

All sing.

HENRY (*voice over*): I thought I might be dreaming. I figured I'd wake up and they'd be ragging each other and slinging horseshit as usual. But it was real, and Bruce amongst them. It was a club.

Goose wrestles the gun out of Piney's holster and shoots the light out, silencing the room.

BRUCE: Arthur—

HENRY: Are you all right?

BRUCE: Yeah. Oh, are they a great bunch of boys! They always was.

Scene 53. Henry, Bruce, Joe, and a victim are playing Tegwar in the lobby of the hotel.

JOE: I'm betting right now—I want five dollars more.

THE VICTIM: What are you betting on?

JOE: I'll tell you after you put in the five.

BRUCE: And I'm going to raise you two.

Here follows a confusion of voices Henry, Bruce, and Joe do nothing to clarify. They are having great fun—"What are you holding? . . . I want to see your money . . . and two better than that . . . I want to see his money . . . I can't play unless you put in your money . . . put in another two dollars . . . there it is . . . a jack and a three"—

JOE: Can you beat a Coney Island Katie?

THE VICTIM (*protesting*): What about this double-A deuce?

JOE (*gathering in all the money*): I wish you a lot of luck with it.

Scene 54. Playing baseball. Labor Day. A montage of baseball flies by at a quick pace, accelerated by fast music. The Mammoths are batting. The Mammoths are making great plays in the infield. The Mammoths in the dugout are applauding themselves. The Mammoths are running down fly balls in the outfield. Bruce, catching, throws out a runner at second base. Bruce tags out a runner sliding into home. Dutch is arguing with an umpire.

HENRY (*voice over*): It was a club like it should have been all year but never was. We begun to pull ahead.

Scene 55. In a television studio.

VOICE OF THE ANNOUNCER: Please welcome for a return engagement on this program the Singing Mammoths and their newest member, Bruce Pearson.

Six Mammoths—Henry, Bruce, and others—sing and dance to a lively, corny old jig which now and again repeats the meaningful refrain, "When all is said and done I'm not the one you really took me for . . ."

Scene 56. The music of the Singing Mammoths carries to the ball field. Bruce is at bat. Henry is watching from the dugout. Bruce lines out a hit, he rounds first base, he runs toward second, his cap falls off, the music of the Singing Mammoths speeds him along, he races toward third base, the ball is coming on a bounce behind him; but he beats the throw to the base. In the dugout Henry applauds.

Scene 57. In the clubhouse. The players are in a celebratory mood. Although they have not yet clinched the pennant they prematurely indulge the tradition of pouring beverages on each other's heads.

Scene 58. Henry and Bruce's hotel room. Bruce is stricken.

HENRY: I'll call the doctor. Okay?

BRUCE: No.

HENRY: Is it the real thing?

BRUCE: Well, yes and no. I just feel a little dipsy. Maybe if you open the window. (*He dials the phone.*) Hi, Katie. I'm okay. Well, I feel a little dizzy. No, I don't think he did. Oh, he's getting to it. No, he's getting *to* it. Yes. Katie? But I didn't— Katie?

We are startled by the rudeness of the dial tone: Katie has hung up. Bruce pretends to be talking to her, but he does not deceive Henry, who averts his eyes.

BRUCE (*continuing*): Katie? Well, okay, yeah, and I love you too.

Scene 59. Before the ballgame. Bruce walks down the alleyway to the field. Henry assists him. Bruce walks weakly, unsteadily, leaning on the rail.

HENRY: I'll get Perry to warm me.

BRUCE: No, no, I'm okay. Am I throwing the ball back better?

HENRY: Oh, yeah. It's helping me a lot, too.

Scene 60. The game is in progress.

HENRY (*voice over*): Everything had been going our way. And when the Pirates came to town we had ourselves a big cushion. We were unstoppable. It was only a matter of time.

Bruce is catching. We hear a volley of hard cracks of the bat, as if we were as close to the action as he. Bruce returns the ball weakly to the pitcher. He is struggling.
The umpire behind the plate observes that Bruce is behaving in a peculiar way. He effectively halts the action of the game by dusting off the plate.

UMPIRE (*to Bruce*): You all right? You don't look all right.

HENRY: He's all right, we'll take care of him.

Bruce is at the bat. The third-base coach sends him complex signals. He swings weakly. Then he swings well for a single. He rounds first base.
In the dugout Doc Loftus is alert.

HENRY: He's not too clear in his head, Dutch.

Dutch: Look for your sign off the bench.

Henry: Tell Horse to cover pop flies around the plate.

> *We follow a passage of visual action.*
> *Bruce catches many pitches coming at him with force and frequency. Henry covers first base on a ground ball to the baseman. Henry pitches. The Mammoths complete a double play. The crowd is extremely excited, chanting as if the climax of the race is within reach.*
> *An opposing batter hits a high pop fly near the plate. Bruce is looking for the ball. He cannot find it. Horse comes in from first base and catches the ball.*
> *The game is over. Bruce in a bewildered way is still searching the sky for the ball. The Mammoths shake one another's hands and start off for the dugout. Henry and Joe retrieve Bruce's cap and mask from the ground and turn and follow him from the field.*

> *Scene 61. Henry, Joe, and Red are in the waiting room of the hospital.*

Nurse: You can go in now.

Joe: It's sad. It makes you want to cry.

Red: It's sad. It makes you want to laugh.

> *Scene 62. In a patient's room of the hospital. Bruce is sitting on his bed. He wears a hospital gown.*

Bruce: Hi, Joe.

Joe: How you doing? (*He has brought Bruce's clothes.*) I hope I brought the right combination.

Bruce: Anybody bring my chews?

JOE: Yeah, sure.

Henry winds a belt around a few of the personal items Bruce brought to the hospital with him from his last ballgame: his uniform; a pair of spikes; a baseball cap. Red helps Bruce to untie the back of the hospital gown. He helps Bruce on with his shirt.

Scene 63. At the open-air check-in desk at the Eastern Airlines gate of a small airport. Henry has come with Bruce to see him off.
   A sign reads: TICKETED PASSENGERS ONLY BEYOND THIS POINT.
   Bruce, carrying his suitcase, struggles beyond the gate toward the airplane. He turns back to Henry.

BRUCE: Thanks for everything, Arthur. Thanks a lot. And I'll be back in the spring. I'm going to be in shape. You'll see.

HENRY: I'll see you then, Bruce. See you in Aqua Clara.

BRUCE: Hey, Arthur, don't forget to send me the scorecard from the Series. Okay?

HENRY: You bet I will.

BRUCE: Okay. I'll see you.

Henry watches through the wire fence as Bruce walks with effort from the ticket gate through the fine daylight to the waiting airplane.

Scene 64. At the cemetery. Henry, Mr. Pearson, and Mrs. Pearson are walking among the gravestones. Henry walks somewhat apart from Mr. and Mrs. Pearson.

HENRY (*voice over*): We breezed through the playoffs and wrapped up the Series on a Sunday. My win. I took the scorecard home and threw it on the shelf and left it lay there. It would have been simple to shove it in the mail. How long would it have took me? Couldn't I afford the stamps? On my Arcturus calendar for December tenth it says "DeSoto visited Georgia 1540." This hands me a laugh. Bruce Pearson also visited Georgia. I was his pallbearer, me and some local boys. There were flowers from the club, but no *person* from the club. They could have sent somebody. He wasn't a bad fellow and probably better than some, and not a bad ballplayer neither when they gave him a chance, when they laid off him long enough. From here on in I rag nobody.

THE END

BANG THE DRUM SLOWLY

From the Novel

◇ ME AND HOLLY were laying around in bed around 10 A.M. on a Wednesday morning when the call come. I was slow answering it, thinking first of a comical thing to say, though I suppose it long since stopped handing anybody a laugh except me. I don't know. I laugh at a lot of things nobody ever laughs at except her. "Do not be funny," she said. "Just answer it." But I seen her kind of listening out of the corner of her eye.

"Triborough Bridge," I said.

"I have a collect call for Mr. Henry Wiggen from Rochester, Minnesota," said the operator.

"I do not know a soul there," said I, "and I do not accept collect calls under any circumstances." I used to accept a lot of collect calls until I got wise to myself.

Then behind the operator I heard this voice saying, "Come on, Arthur."

Well, there is only one person in this world that calls me "Arthur," and the first thing I thought when I heard it was I got this picture of him in jail in Rochester, Minnesota. Do not ask me why jail, but that was the picture I got, and I said to Holly, "Bruce is in jail in Minnesota," and she sat up in bed, and I said to the operator, "Tell him this better be important."

"Arthur, Arthur," said he, "you must speak to me," and I said I would.

And then it was like speaking to him always is, where all he can say is this one thing his mind might be on, like he might get up in the morning saying, "I must write a postcard

113

home," and says it while dressing, and says it at breakfast, and says it maybe 3 or 4 times all morning, or he says, "Arthur, I must have $20," and says it again all the way to the park and all the time dressing and drilling, and then might say it in the middle of the ball game when you are trying to keep your mind on what you are doing until you finally give him his 20 and he stops saying it and becomes silent, and he said, "You have got to come and see me."

"What did you do?" I said. I still thought he was in jail.

"You have got to come and see me," he said. "I am in the hospital."

"With what?" I said.

"You have got to come and see me," he said.

"I cannot afford it," I said. "I am up to my ass in tax arrears." This was the statement of a true rat, and you can imagine how it must of sounded to him. But I knew nothing of the circumstances at the time. If he had of hung up on me then and there he would of had a right to do so. Yet who could he of called besides me? There was a silence, and I personally cannot stand silence on long distance, especially if I am not sure how deductible it will be, and I said, "Say something! Do not just stand there!"

"You have got to come and see me," he said.

"All he says is I have got to go and see him," I said.

"What did he do?" she said.

"He is in the hospital," I said.

"Then you have got to go," she said.

"I will come," I said.

All we threw was one change of clothes in a bag because we naturally had no idea, plus my Arcturus kit, figuring if I done some business along the way we could call the whole trip deductible. "He would not be in Rochester, Minnesota, if it was not serious," she said. "I do not like the look of it."

"He has got North Pole coverage," I said. When I am trying to sell a total policy I say, "This policy covers everything except sunstroke at the North Pole." It is good for a laugh. However, I never wrote such a total policy except the one I sold to Bruce, $50,000, the first I ever sold, and the fastest, selling it to him in 5 minutes flat in the hotel in Boston one night, not even trying to sell it to him but only just tuning my line you might say, the seal not yet even broke on my kit and my license scarcely dry because only that afternoon I polished off this course I took. I took the course bit by bit all that summer, every time we hit Boston. I said, "Leave me point out just a few advantages of protection of this type," and he said, "Arthur, show me where I sign." I did not write another policy for a month. I have sold about 70, all to ballplayers except one to Mr. Jacob Epstein, my former English teacher at Perkinsville High. The reason they call it "Arcturus" is because Arcturus is the nearest star, or else the brightest. I forget which. Maybe both. They told me in the course but I forget.

"Surely his coverage is not all you can think of," she said.

"No," said I, "naturally not," though it was. First you think about money. I used to pee away money like wine until I got wise to myself.

We made a fast stop at the bank, and then she drove me to the depot. "Take care of 600 Dollars," I said, which was what we kept calling him before she was born. She was 3 months pregnant at the time. She said she would, and I kissed her and said I would be back in a couple days. I was not back for 6 months.

I flew through a snowstorm from Albany to Chicago, the stewardess going up and down the isle smiling with her big white teeth and singing, "Tra-la, this is nothing but a snowstorm." She said we were over it, but it looked to me like we were *in* it. It got very dark inside the plane, and I started getting these flash pictures of the whole goddam machine coming to a dead stop 30,000 feet over Indiana or somewhere, and the stewardess said to me, "Are you *the* Henry Wiggen?"

I said I was. It made me feel pretty good, for it been some time since anybody asked me that in just that way, not selling me anything, only asking. In the summer of 52 I was the toast of New York, but 2 years later I couldn't of got a traffic ticket squashed. She said, "I bought a copy of your book at the American airport in Cairo, Egypt." She had very big white teeth and quite a lovely smile and all, and right away my X-ray eye started seeing through her uniform and down to the girl herself. You know how you do. One minute you are picturing yourself dead in Indiana and the next minute a girl glides in view and gives you a smile and a little thing like a snowstorm at 30,000 feet don't seem to make much of an impression any more.

The upshot of it was we wound up over coffee in the airport in Chicago. She told me what a lonely and gloomy city Chicago was on a snowy night. "I will probably just lay on my bed curled up with a magazine," she said, and now I begun getting pictures of her curled up like a girl does.

"No doubt you have got a roomie for company," said I.

"Oh yes," said she, "but she is on a flight to Mexico City," and she yawned, and I started telling myself it was insane to go on in a snowstorm, besides which what could I do when I got there and how much more sense it would make to get there in the morning fresh as a daisy, and on and on. But then I said to myself, "Henry, what a louse you are with a wife 3 months pregnant that you kissed goodby not 7 hours ago!" "I have got to make a couple phone calls," I said.

I called Goose Williams. I could not of sold Goose anything, and I knew it, but if I didn't at least try I wouldn't of had the nerve to list the trip deductible. He used to hate me. His wife said he went out for a loaf of bread Sunday and was never seen since. "I do not know which is worse," she said, "having Harold home or having him away."

"I wish to speak to him concerning insurance matters," I said.

"Harold already cashed in all his insurance," she said.

"He should not of done that," said I.

"Harold should not of done a lot of things," she said, "and a lot more things he should of done he never quite tended to. Tell me, Henry," she said, "is Harold at the end of the trail?"

I could not get used to her calling him "Harold." "Goose?"

said I. "At the end of the trail? That is the most ridiculous thing I ever heard of."

"Tell me the truth," she said. "He is at the end of the trail. He has not got as much as one full season left in him. He has got only his wife and his debts and his children, and all of them a pain and a burden to him," and I held the telephone away from my ear and looked out through the glass at the stewardess. She was twisted around on the stool, studying the seams of her stockings. "He will be 35 come August," she said. The stewardess twisted her body first one way and then the other, and I said to myself, "It is true that you have got a wife back home, but it is also true that you only live once, and furthermore she practically as much as invited you up." "I wish you was Harold," she said, "and Harold was you. How old are you, Henry?"

I do not even think I answered. She begun crying a little, and I eased the phone back on the hook and slid the door open and started out. But right away I got these further pictures of Holly back home worrying about me and probably following me on the clock and no doubt picturing me rushing in one plane and out the other, and I quick closed the door again and called Joe Jaros and spoke to his wife. It was Joe's wife later left the cat out of the barn. Usually I do not hang with the coaches much, but me and Joe become fairly friendly on account of Tegwar, The Exciting Game Without Any Rules, T-E-G-W-A-R, which nobody on the club can play but me and Joe because nobody can keep a straight face long enough. I will be hilarious on the inside but with a straight face on the outside, and I was smiling while his phone was ringing while poor Goose's wife was probably still crying in a dead phone at her end which shows you the kind of a thoughtless personality I have. Joe was out baby-sitting his grandchildren. His wife give me his number, but I did not even take it down. "My Lord," she said, "Joe has got insurance with 3 or 4 different outfits."

"You do not have insurance," said I, "unless you have got Arcturus."

She laughed. She asked me how long I planned to be in

town, and I said I did not know. There were the pictures of Holly and the pictures of the stewardess curled on the bed plus more pictures now of Joe Jaros baby-sitting his grand-children, all cozy and warm with a snowstorm outside, not tramping the streets like Goose nor with girls in a number of towns, not drinking up all his credit in the saloons until all of a sudden one day the girls and the credit begin to give out at once. I seen it happen. I seen too many old-time ballplayers hanging around clubhouses telling you what a great game you just pitched (though you might of just got the hell shelled out of you) and could you by any chance loan them 5 to tide them over, which I used to loan them, too, before I was in so damn deep I was playing winter ball and hitting the banquet circuit and *still* getting in deeper with every passing day until Holly took a hold of things. I said, "Henry, look at Joe. He did not flub his life away chasing after every pair of big white teeth he run across," and I slid open the door again and cir-cled around and went out a side door saying "Positively No Admission" and listing a number of fines and penalties and prison terms you could get for passing through that one door, and out in the snowstorm and back up in the air.

The only time I was ever in Minneapolis before was in June of 53 for an exhibition in St. Paul, the night Red Traphagen split his finger and walked in to the bench with the nail hang-ing off and said to Dutch, "That is sufficient," and stepped out of his gear and never even went back east with us but went to San Francisco and taught in the college there.

I fell asleep in the hotel wondering what I might of missed not following through with the airplane stewardess in Chi-cago, kicking myself for not having took a stab at it, yet knowing that I would of kicked myself all the harder if I done the opposite, laying there thinking how life was one big prob-lem after the other and feeling sorry for myself and I suppose actually thinking I had any problems, not knowing what a real problem was.

I hardly knew a soul in town. I called Rosy Ryan in the

morning, general manager I think they call him of the Millers, once a right-hand pitcher for the Giants, the first National League pitcher to ever hit a home run in the World Series, which he done in 1924, but he was out. I personally never hit a home run in 4 years up. The TV said, "Today's high, 15 below zero." I figured I heard wrong.

I called up Aleck Olson, the Boston outfielder, and he come rushing down, and we had coffee and gassed and talked about annuities, which he was very interested in and bought one off me later in the summer. I did not wish to sell him one on the spot but told him check around and compare Arcturus with the others, because I knew he would find nothing better, besides which they never do check around anyway, and he went with me to The Dayton Company and I bought a storm coat with a fur collar and earmuffs and gloves, $70, all deductible, business. I would not of needed them if I was not in Minneapolis and would not of been in Minneapolis except on business. Holly says the same. Me and him started floating around town like a couple old buddies, which handed me a laugh. All summer a fellow is just another ballplayer on somebody else's ball club until if you run across him in the winter it's a horse of another color, and he laughed, too, not knowing why, like Bruce does, laughs when you laugh without knowing why, which I bawled him out 500 times for but never made a dent.

Well, you know me, if I get to a place hungry the first thing I do is eat. When I got down to Rochester, Minnesota, I stumbled across this kosher restaurant, being very fond of kosher food, and when I was done I went to the hospital. He was not in the room. Yet I could tell it was his by the smell of this shaving lotion that he uses about a quart and a half of every time he shaves. And for who? For a prostitute on 66 Street name of Katie that he thinks he is in love with and goes around telling everybody he is about to marry. A nurse popped her head in the room and said, "Are you Mr. Wiggen at last?" and I said I was, and she left, and soon I heard the sound of his shoes racing along the hall and finally sliding the

last 6 or 8 feet like we used to slide in the hallway in Perkinsville High, and in he come, all dressed, all fit as a fiddle,
looking as tip-top as I ever seen him, and I said, "This is sick?
This is why I dropped everything back home and risked my
life in a snowstorm and went to the expense of a new ward-
robe in Minneapolis?"

"Hello, Arthur," he said.

"And do not call me 'Arthur.' If you would trade in these
gallon jugs of shaving lotion on a bar of soap and wash out
your ears you would hear something."

"Do not be mad," he said. "They do not wish me to leave
without a friend."

"Then stay," said I.

"I was even here over Christmas," he said.

"For what?" I said, and right about then 3 doctors walked
in, and the head one spoke, saying, "Sit down, Mr. Wiggen,"
and they all begun to smile, first smiling at Bruce and then at
me and then at each other, and one of them offered me a
cigarette, though I do not smoke and did not take it. "How
will things be going with the Mammoths?" said the doctor.
But he did not really care. You could tell. He started flipping
through papers on a clipboard, and then he turned the whole
thing over and did not look at them, and he said, "Unless we
have made a terrible mistake somewhere Mr. Pearson is suffering from Hodgkin's Disease." He then begun telling me
what it was. It was bad.

"Exactly how bad?" I said.

"It is fatal," he said.

I could not think what "fatal" meant. It is like a word like
"cancel" or "postpone" that for a couple seconds I can never
think what they mean but must ride with them, or like being
told an X-ray is "negative" which always sounds bad to me
until I remember that it is not bad but good. "What is that?" I
said.

"It means I am doomeded," said Bruce.

"You goddam fool," I said.

Then I closed my eyes, and time passed, and when I opened
them he was standing in front of me with one of those little

tiny hospital cups, and I drunk it down all in one gulp, and he took the cup and run back across the room and filled it again from a pitcher. He kept running across the room like that about 4 times, too stupid to bring the pitcher over. But I couldn't say anything. I couldn't talk, and I seen the doctors there like 3 bumps on a log. "3 phonies," I said. "3 monkeys that I doubt could cure a case of warts. You are the boys that send me 50 letters a day looking for contributions for your rotten hospitals. What do you do with the contributions I send?"

"We done many great things," said the first doctor. "We are only human and cannot do everything."

"I will never send another penny," said I.

"This is not a pleasant occasion for us," said the doctor, "no more than it is for you."

"It is some world," I said. "I say turn the son of a bitches loose and leave them blow it up," and I got up from the chair but sat down again, very weak in my knees.

"Anyhow, Arthur," said Bruce, "I am covered by North Pole coverage. It is all paid right down to the end."

"I doubt that you have even got what they say," I said.

"We are naturally hoping we are wrong," said the doctor.

"You never looked better in your life," I said. "What do you weigh?"

"185," he said.

"That is your weight," I said. "Why do they not put you on a scale? I suppose that would be foolish, however, since I doubt that these knucklehead individuals could read a scale."

"Be calm, Arthur," said he. "You must be calm and listen to what they say, for they know best," and I sat back and listened without believing them. It was all too impossible to believe.

LITERARY

BRING BACK THAT OLD
SANDLOT NOVEL

◇ THE FAN OF the game who is also a reader of books takes up his position before the television. On a nearby table lies a new novel. The jacket of the novel shows a man in what appears to be a baseball uniform sliding into a white cushion that appears to be a base on a baseball field. You assume that the book is about baseball. But you might be wrong.

Earnest people devoted to the salvation of novelists have long been moved to insist that baseball novels are not at all about baseball, that they are really about the grander themes of life, death, God, theology, art, morals, or that they are, at the very least, mythical representations of legendary America. A serious writer, they say, forsakes lowly baseball for symbolic heights.

When, as a boy, I read novels about men who were pitching and batting and sliding into bases, I was reading, as far as I knew, pure novels purely about baseball. And later, as time passed, and I crossed from reading to writing, I drew upon whatever funds I possessed of joy and experience, playing out memories of my sandlot pleasures. Nothing in life had yet been as real to me as baseball, and so it assumed the same reality for me in my novels as heaven and damnation for somebody else.

Or had I been fooled? Had we all been fooled? It's not difficult to see with hindsight that the baseball novels we loved best equally were books about success. William Heyliger, Ralph Henry Barbour, and John R. Tunis arrived on the

125

shelves of our magical public library in the wake of a vigorous tradition of the novel of success, to which they were subtly related. The basic plan of books by Horatio Alger (*Brave and Bold, Do and Dare, Paul the Peddler, Phil the Fiddler,* among a hundred others) was the dream of personal wealth and prestige. That was also, to a significant extent, the basic plan of the novel about baseball.

Alger's *Mark Manning's Mission* and Lester Chadwick's *Baseball Joe in the Central League* are rich with plots and subplots pollinated with characters weaving through incredible coincidences. Their heroes, Mark and Joe, are deserving young men instantly identifiable as proper heroes. The boys of Alger and Chadwick are spectacularly honest, clean-cut, fearless, heroic, and have a marvelous sense of humor.

When I had read one Horatio Alger story, I had read them all. I had also read *Baseball Joe in the Central League,* published in 1914. Baseball Joe arrives home from Yale one day "swinging a heavy valise as though he enjoyed the weight of it. . . . 'Hello, Mother,' he called gaily." He loves his mother, as Mark Manning does. He calls her Momsey, and his sister Sis. Joe has quit school to play baseball—something any red-blooded book-reading boy would have done if it had not been out of the question.

Soon Joe is off to the South to baseball training camp. He wins a place on the team. The pennant race goes down to the last game. Joe is to pitch, but he is late to the ballpark because a jealous teammate tampered with his watch. Luckily, Joe is able to reach the park in the fifth inning and help his team come from behind and win. And "when the last batter had gone down to defeat in the first half of the ninth Joe drew off his glove and, oblivious to the plaudits of the crowd and his own mates, hurried to the dressing room."

Everything had worked out. I closed my book and dedicated my life, as other bookish boys also did, to years of labor in pursuit of distinction worthy of plaudits to which we could be oblivious.

Michael Oriard, in the scholarly journal of sport, *Arete,* has observed of juvenile sports fiction that "one of the things that makes the overwhelming majority of juveniles so deadeningly dull and similar is the lack of any distance between the hero and the ideal." True of *Baseball Joe* in 1914, it was still true in 1948 of Tunis's *Highpockets,* a somewhat contrived tale of the reform of an arrogant loner. "Look here, Highpockets, why don't you quit thinking about your batting average and play for the team? Why don't you be a nice guy like the other boys on the club?" Highpockets mends his ways. At last he becomes "a part of the team, not just a longball hitter out there slugging for himself." And the fans are "quick to recognize the right guy, the team player."

Thus, as late as 1948 the world had not yet known the pleasure of a book about baseball that anyone could have thought of as art or as literature. There was one important exception: Ring Lardner's *You Know Me Al,* published in 1916 and applauded by a number of people who took literature seriously. Among these were H. L. Mencken, who relished the accuracy of the vernacular of the baseball rookie, Jack Keefe, and Virginia Woolf, who saw the book as an authentic description of American life. Classless America, Woolf said, was bound or unified by games, as England was bound by the class system.

Lardner himself, however, never viewed *You Know Me Al* as literature, nor himself as a literary man. As most of the world viewed him, so he viewed himself. He wrote for a living as a journalist, for enormous fees to support expensive habits. A writer who wrote about baseball was a sportswriter, not a literary person.

Eleven years after its publication he wrote a one-page preface to a reprinting of the book, reflecting the grounds of his diffidence:

"The writer has been asked frequently, or perhaps not very often after all . . . Who is the original of Jack Keefe? . . . The original of Jack Keefe is not a ball player at all, but Jane Addams of Hull House, a former Follies girl . . . The writer wishes to acknowledge his indebtedness to Mayo brothers, Ringling brothers, Smith brothers, Rath brothers, the Dolly sisters, and former President Buchanan for their aid in instructing him in the technical terms of baseball, such as 'bat,' 'ball,' 'pitcher,' 'foul,' 'sleeping car,' and 'sore arm.' "

You Know Me Al belonged to no tradition of baseball writing; it emerged from the tradition of the American vernacular. The best-known novel in that vein is undoubtedly *Huckleberry Finn,* and one of the best-known in our own time is *The Catcher in the Rye,* whose narrator, Holden Caulfield, tells us that his favorite writer (apart from his brother D.B.) is Ring Lardner.

The tradition it clearly rejects is that of the Horatio Alger story. Lardner's Jack Keefe does not make good in any sense of which Alger would approve. He has not troubled himself to speak well, to become literate. He spells by ear. When he threatens to jump to the Federal League, he reveals that he has never developed corporate loyalties. His marital difficulties are mean and violent—no Momsey, no Sis. He thinks about money on every page. He drinks, he carouses, he tells jokes about underwear. Even so, we like him, or at least I certainly liked him when, as a boy, I read him in the 1930s in Mount Vernon, N.Y., in *The Saturday Evening Post* on the cold stone steps of our apartment house.

And yet, I must confess now that when my own baseball novel *The Southpaw* appeared in 1953, I committed an act of repression arising from real or imagined necessity. I denied the influence of those boys' books of Horatio Alger and of Lardner.

My novel, along with Bernard Malamud's book *The Natural,* was "the first serious adult baseball fiction," according to Peter Bjarkman, the historian of sports literature, who dwells also on the oddity of the fact that these books had not appeared until "more than a full century after baseball had been crowned the American national game."

But *The Southpaw* is clearly descended from Alger and deeply influenced by Lardner, hard as I denied it. My boy, Henry Wiggen, *does* succeed, *does* grow rich, *does* protect and preserve his moral virtue. For, of course, my novel had a great deal in common with that success tradition from which

I emerged as boy reader and which I perpetuated as young-man writer.

I denied the influence upon me of the Baseball Joe books—right there on the jacket of the first edition of *The Southpaw,* in the words of the publisher's publicist: "Obviously Henry has nothing in common with Frank Merriwell or Baseball Joe, just as *The Southpaw* has nothing in common with the sentimental, saccharine, and completely improbable sagas which keep bobbing up under the general category of 'base-ball books.' "

In 1952, just a few months before *The Southpaw* was published, Malamud appeared with a novel called *The Natural.* One thing Malamud and I deeply shared was our self-consciousness about what we were doing. We insisted that we were creating *literature* just as earnestly as Ring Lardner, almost forty years earlier, had insisted that he was *not.* None of us had yet been liberated to think of baseball as legitimate literary material. We had not yet achieved sufficient self-assurance to recognize that our own experiences of sand-lot memory, the mighty prose of the sports pages and the powerful voices of sport on radio were as genuine realities as any we might ever know.

No doubt this confusion, in one form or another, characterizes writers of all generations. Had that not been the American problem to begin with: who will read an American book? At the time of the publication of *The Southpaw,* I was a graduate student at the University of Minnesota, and I certainly did not want my professors, upon whom my success depended, to think of me as frivolous. Therefore, I scrambled to claim a literary standing for my work. Lardner, no; Baseball Joe, no. If anybody wanted to know the source of my inspiration, it was *Huckleberry Finn,* so widely respected in the English department.

Malamud, too, struggling upward in academic life, enforced a connection between his novel of baseball and his literary texts. "During my first year at Oregon State," he has written, "I wrote *The Natural,* begun before leaving New York City. Baseball had interested me, especially its comic aspects, but I wasn't able to write about the game until I transformed game into myth, via Jessie Weston's Percival legend with an assist by T. S. Eliot's *The Waste Land,* plus the lives of several ball-players I had read, in particular Babe Ruth's and Bobby Feller's. The myth enriched the baseball lore as feats of magic transformed the game."

As the years passed, and baseball formally merged with the literary matter of America, scholars trumped Malamud's rude beginnings. "Many a glassy-eyed scholar," an observer wrote in *Arete,* "has ravaged *The Golden Bough* searching for one more applicable motif to attach to [*The Natural*]. It has been . . . compared to every mythical personage from Apollonius of Rhodes to Shoeless Joe Jackson."

All this intellectual self-consciousness was placed into compact focus by the critic Ben Siegel in a scholarly article following the appearance of Philip Roth's extravaganza of baseball, *The Great American Novel.* Baseball lover that he was, and usually audacious, Roth the novelist nevertheless hesitated many years before taking up the game. He felt the need, he told Mr. Siegel, to overcome his own "snobbishness" before he could persuade himself that baseball contained enough "seriousness or profundity" to merit a place as his subject.

Mr. Roth's confidence in his literary impulses had been a long time arriving, but when it did, he came out of the closet, confessing his absorption in baseball, even as he had confessed to his adolescent sexual obsessions in 1969 with *Portnoy's Complaint.* Masturbation wasn't naughty enough for Philip—now baseball.

Not only Mr. Roth but hundreds of scholars, novelists, story writers, and poets have been liberated at last to commit their art to scenes of baseball without denial or apology and without pretending that baseball novels are really about something else, except in the way that all literature is metaphor.

Mr. Bjarkman counts eighty novels of baseball since Mr. Roth trotted into the game in 1973. In this enlarging body of fiction the tradition of Horatio Alger has quite disappeared.

Instead, there is a diversity of topics and themes far beyond the imagination of Baseball Joe. The issues are as psychological as athletic—racial and romantic dilemmas, drugs, fathering, neuroses, fears, phobias, and homosexuality.

The baseball fiction of recent years, challenging an older ethic, has finally established a natural distance between the hero and the ideal. Bad guys win and nice guys lose. In literature the national game is played now in the image of reality, money, sex, egomania, told in the fully expressive range of the English language denied and suppressed by the creator of Baseball Joe and the heirs to the Alger tradition.

The legitimized field of play adjoins the clubhouse, the front office, the hotel, the airport, town, and city, like other scenes of common life and labor, like factories and sailing ships. (When Mr. Siegel asked Mr. Roth why he had chosen to write about baseball, Mr. Roth replied, "Because whaling has already been used.") The baseball field has evolved—it has become a baseball field. The man on the book jacket is wearing a baseball uniform. The real player slides into a real base in real life. The novel of baseball can no longer be imagined as a mere representation of something else.

PREFACE TO *THE SOUTHPAW*

◇ L<small>ORD HELP US</small> all, especially me, it is eleven years now since I was writing *The Southpaw,* living with my wife and new-born girl in a wooden two-room cottage outside Denver (the "Queen City" of the book), composing my novel in a lean-to late at night, first feeding the baby and sacking her out. Our backyard was bigger than the house. The landlord said we might use the cellar for storage, but it was a cellar you couldn't stand up in. It didn't matter. We had nothing to put there. We had no surplus in those days. I was a student at the University of Denver, saying it the right way by day for my teachers there, and wrong for myself in my private book at night. Henry Wiggen don't speak the King's English, nor the Queen's neither.

My friends, who were nervous beginners and ridden with caution, were often most traditional. Baseball was for boys, they said, not for literature, but I wrote my book anyhow, out of the faith that if I was moved and amused by what I was writing somebody else was bound to be, betting on my humanity that way.

Even hard cash I gambled. In the summer of 1951, in the middle of my manuscript and less than penniless, I signed a contract as a counselor at a summer camp run by the Jewish Community Center—$210 with the promise of more if the head-count rose. Torn between the glory and the money, I finally begged out of the contract, so it was a meager living for a while, but never an ultimate regret.

In the years since the publication of *The Southpaw* the question I am most commonly asked is, "How did you ever know so much about baseball?" Alas, I confess it was amateur love. The only professional players I met were a few Denver Bears one night. Since then, mainly on magazine assignment, I have met some of the "real" people of the game, though confronting them, and spying on their secret meetings, or even listening for the meaning hidden beyond the word, has told me very little I hadn't already known or guessed. The man of fiction, Henry James tells us, takes an ell when he's handed an inch. I knew, not so much by going and looking as by sitting and analogizing, and by reading between the lines of the gross newspaper facts. One sportswriter (later turned drama reviewer, and finally dissolved by alcohol) apparently spent the decade of the fifties attempting to alert a more or less yawning public to the fact that my box score at the end of Chapter 24 doesn't "check out." It became an obsession with him, maddening him quite beyond reason. He bankrupted himself making abusive long-distance telephone calls to anyone who praised the book, plunging himself into his grave, still sounding in his final hour the argument that Truth is Fact.

Let us not be deceived. No game is so much its intricacies as its states of mind. I was raised on the playground at William Wilson Jr., Junior High School, in Mount Vernon, N.Y., playing baseball from morning to sundown as the law allowed. I knew, if not the subtler matter of the box score, the wonderous physical feel of the movements of the game—a ball well-fielded, cleanly played, perfectly thrown; best of all, solidly hit; and beyond that the splendid sensation of the dependence enforced by team-play, each boy upon the next, and all upon all, calling, beseeching, crying to one another, singing as my men sing to Henry upon the day of his ascension, "To me, Henry, to me . . . to me, to me," in the same chapter as the faulty box score.

The names of some of my playground companions— Schnell, McKenna, the Carucci brothers—are engraved herein. Their faces I shall probably never see again. The heroes of my boyhood were the New York Giants, especially the left-handed pitcher Carl Hubbell, and the mighty outfielder Mel Ott. My father carried me on his shoulders down the long ramps of the Polo Grounds, to the first game I saw. The principal of our school was Martin H. Traphagen, who twisted my ears to interest me in reading and writing, and for whom I named my fictional catcher some years before the school itself was renamed in the same way.

Then the body slows. Only the memory of sensation remains, a longing and a yearning. I would deal with the Devil for one more summer.

Henry Wiggen, who comes of age mid-season in *The Southpaw,* is nine years my junior. Now he is the age I was when I wrote him, his summer done but his life ahead. What will he do?

Probably he will become a manager of men, and succeed, for baseball taught him everything, as an art teaches. He took ells for inches by guess and by hunch. His pace is mature now. "It used to be that I went out there and fired them through. I always wanted to be pitching. But I learned to take my time and think about what I was doing and not just go ahead and fire like a lot of boys will do." At the mature pace he says it better now, less awkward, less profane, not now in the vulgar tongue, tighter now, with absolute economy and fierce compression. Not with less passion, but in fewer words. All the things he hated then he hates still—exploitation and false report. Walking with his father he saw "the worst rundown houses I ever seen. Pop said that people lived in the houses." Henry was astonished; aghast; he is still astonished.

The clubhouse is a place of mortal ache and higher woe, life is short, dismissal imminent, the rivalries brutal, and we are all anxiety. What Henry did best was to turn his hatred to style and story, and so shine good. He knew to keep from imitating hate. Above all, he wrote his own book in his own voice, suffering consequences along with rewards.

I learned from him, as he from me. In his honor I have named my newest baby Henry, whom late at night I feed, then sack him out. The bottles are disposable plastic. Time strides, and we all grow more efficient. The baby I fed in the two-room cottage is old enough to read this book and tell me of its several grammatical flaws. But Martin H. Traphagen is dead, the lady to whom the book is dedicated is dead, School-boy Rowe is dead; the DiMaggios (my Caruccis) have passed from baseball. Brooklyn was still in the League in 1951—and my League itself, which struck us then as merely spurious, sounds downright archaic now: it has only eight competing cities, none farther west than St. Louis. Bruce Pearson, Henry's roommate, died in a later fiction.

The Mammoths—those Giants of my boyhood—have followed me to San Francisco. I saw Carl Hubbell not long ago. He was wearing a blue business suit. We go to the same dentist. And Mel Ott is dead of violence, of whom it was said by Leo Durocher, "Nice guys finish last." Yet Henry Wiggen, defying the harvest, has been given life again and again over the years, and now once more. I am delighted to see him reissued, coming out again, renewing acquaintances, adding new friends, shaking hands all around.

MEMORIES

AN AFFAIR OF THE HEART

◇ WE HAD A friendly dentist in San Mateo named Ed Brown who had many patients, among them Carl Hubbell and Harry Danning, who had played for the New York Giants across the decade of the 1930s, into the 1940s. Both had appeared in the World Series—the subway series, New York City's version of a BART series—between the Giants and the New York Yankees, in 1936 and 1937. They had lost. Their whole *team* had lost. It was one of the agonies of my New York boyhood that my Giants were always smothered and humiliated by the Yankees.

After their playing days Hubbell and Danning came west to the Bay Area, each for reasons of his own, and settled into separate lives but the same dental chair.

Bright and early one morning, Dr. Ed Brown, looking over his lineup for the day, saw that Mr. Hubbell was to come to have his teeth observed at almost the very hour reserved for Mr. Danning. Thereupon Dr. Brown considered a plan. He thought what he would do—this kind dentist—was to allow the two men to encounter each other in his waiting room.

Dr. Brown, author of this dramatic scene, stationed himself out of sight to observe the joyful reunion. Mr. Hubbell arrived for his appointment and sat himself in a chair in the waiting room with a magazine, and Mr. Danning arrived soon afterward and sat himself in another chair with yet another magazine. One had been pitcher and the other catcher, and although for long hours the catcher had worn a mask at his trade his actual face could not have been unknown to the pitcher, for they had traveled thousands of railroad miles together from one National League city to the next, ridden the same hotel lobbies together and patronized the same restaurants.

But Dr. Brown had not quite taken into account the weathering effects of time. The two men had not met in fifteen years. From moment to moment, although they glanced at each other, they revealed not the slightest, scantiest, smallest sign of recognition. They read their magazines and waited for the dentist, who at length burst from his hiding and cried, "Don't you guys *know* each other?" He reintroduced them and they embraced.

Hubbell's name is painted large on the fence at the Giants' Candlestick Park, for he is a Hall of Famer among other notable Giants—Bill Terry, Mel Ott, Willie Mays, Juan Marichal, and Willie McCovey. Not so Harry Danning, nor even Harry's brother Ike, whose lifetime batting average was .500. Yes, Ike Danning played in two big-league games for the St. Louis Browns in 1928, came to bat six times, hit safe thrice and retired. Why did he depart? Wouldn't you think that a man who batted .500 in 1928 would be called back for another look in 1929?

City series, subway series, Bay series follow me around. But my Giants have not won an inner-city series since 1922. In the month before I was born those good Giants defeated those bad Yankees in four games played on five days: Game Two was a 3–3 tie canceled on account of darkness after ten innings, though "the sun was high in the sky when the game was called," says the *Baseball Encyclopedia,* and the baseball commissioner "was so irate at the decision that he donated the (day's) receipts to charity."

Never again in all human history could the Giants defeat the Yankees in a World Series. In 1936, when they next tried, I assisted within my limits. In the spirit of a subway series I journeyed by subway long before dawn carrying my mother's sandwiches to a $1.10 seat in the Yankee Stadium bleachers. (It was a fifty-five-cent seat, marked up for the Series.) After many hours the haughty players arrived. I was close enough to see the grass stain on Joe DiMaggio's baseball trousers. He was a rookie, having come to the Yankees outfield only that

year from the San Francisco Seals, and people said he was
bound to succeed.

Playing the corresponding position for the Giants that day
was a young man named Jimmy Ripple, never to be so celebrated as DiMaggio, but certainly distinguished on this afternoon, for he hit a home run to tie the score at 1–1 and carry
the Giants to the threshold of hope, where the Yankees broke
the Giants' hearts forever.

Surely they broke mine. In the bottom of the eighth inning
a Yankee player was perched on third base. Frankie Crosetti,
the Yankees shortstop (also a San Franciscan), bounced a ball
off some part of the anatomy of the Giants pitcher, Fred Fitzsimmons. Behind Fitzsimmons the Giants second baseman
Burgess Whitehead struggled valiantly to recover the slow-
rolling ball for the play at first base, but the cause was lost,
the ball was unreachable, unplayable, though Whitehead
wrenched and contorted himself in his effort, and I in the
bleachers behind him assisted him as I could with contortions
and exertions of my own. We failed then and forever. The
winning run crossed the plate for the Yankees, and hope died
for the Giants.

The Yankees were too powerful at every turn, every base,
position for position, subway for subway, then and forever.
They kept getting stronger. In 1937 they accomplished in five
games the subway series victory that had taken them six the
year before. Hubbell pitched the Giants to victory in the only
game they won. Harry Danning drove in two runs where
twenty were needed. The Yankees crushed the Giants 8–1 in
the first game, and as if this were insufficient humiliation,
they did it 8–1 again in the second.

You could see Yankee Stadium from the Giants' Polo
Grounds, walk from one park to the other on a lovely autumn
day across the bridge over the Harlem.

Think how simple the country was then. Big-league baseball went only as far west as St. Louis, whose two major-
league clubs united themselves in one stadium—Sportsman
Park—simultaneous home of the Cardinals and the Browns.
When one was home the other was away.

I was a newsman in St. Louis at the time of the 1944 all–St. Louis—not a subway series but a stationary series. Nobody went anywhere. The two clubs pretended to be traveling as if all this were normal. The Cardinals pretended to be the home team for the first two games, and the Brownies, though they were as perfectly at home as the Cardinals, pretended to be the visitors. Each team then changed from traveling gray to white, or white to gray, and resumed the series on the third day as if they had gone somewhere else. After Game Five they did it again. Back home, so to speak, the Cardinals won the sixth and final game. The Cardinals stars were the brothers Mort and Walker Cooper, pitcher and catcher. (Forty years later the Cardinals and Kansas City Royals played a second all-Missouri classic, coming at things from the eastern and western ends of the state for the Interstate-70 World Series.)

In the final New York subway series, in 1951, the Giants won the first game, as they had in 1936. It often appeared to me that the Yankees tried at the beginning of each World Series to encourage me to think the Giants might win, raising my hopes only to strike them to earth with a rush of late power. In 1936 the Yankees had helplessly bowed to Hubbell on the first day, but they scored eighteen runs on the second and thirteen runs in Game Six.

In 1951, on the momentum of Bobby Thomson's pennant-winning home run, the Giants vanquished the Yankees in the first and third games. Then, however, the Yankees began their bombardment, producing another thirteen-run game, as they had in 1936, featuring hard-hitting by the one-time grass-stained San Francisco rookie DiMaggio, now in his thirteenth year of play. (He had been three years in military service.)

The New York Giants became the San Francisco Giants in 1958. They played their first year in Seals Stadium. I too moved to San Francisco. I wrote an article for the new magazine *Sports Illustrated* on the building of Candlestick Park, which was to be free of the wind or other discomfort, weather-proof and wonderful, and everybody believed everybody else because we were all hopers and believers.

At Candlestick Park the Giants would beat the Yankees, too, wouldn't they? The time was right. Hadn't they beat the Yankees in 1922, the year I entered the world, and wouldn't they beat them again now that we had all come so far west together?

No. East or West the Giants lost to the Yankees, fighting to the bitterest end in the World Series of 1962. At Candlestick Park, in the ninth inning of the seventh game, with two Giants on base and the Yankees leading 1–0, young Willie McCovey *almost* rescued them with a line-drive blast snared at second base by the Yankees' Bobby Richardson. Baseball is a game of inches. The spell of the Yankees over the Giants continued.

Willie Mays was of course the Giants' centerfielder. When he first came to San Francisco the fans treated him badly, viewing him with something like distaste or envy as essentially an alien creation. He had made his reputation in New York. San Francisco yearned for a star of its own.

One day, early in the San Francisco life of the Giants, my wife and I in the grandstand heard a nearby voice we will always remember, a woman crooning softly to Mays each time he came to bat, "Take your time, dear heart." Willie took his time, just as she told him to, and the fans of San Francisco eventually came to his side, claiming him as their own, painting his immortal name on the fence with Carl Hubbell's.

In 1975, in Pittsburgh, I met a man in real estate named Ripple, and I said, "I remember a baseball player named Jimmy Ripple. I saw him play in 1936." And Mr. Ripple replied, "Yes, he was my father." He did not smile. His father had died at thirty-nine. Hubbell, who was luckier, lived to 85. He died in a hospital in Scottsdale, Arizona, a few miles from where I am writing this as I wait to hear whether the Giants will have won the first BART World Series—underwater San Francisco to Oakland, as the subway series sped underground years ago Manhattan to the Bronx. If not this year, then next. Take your time, dear heart.

RECALLING
THE JOY OF
WATCHING BASEBALL
ON THE RADIO

◇ FOR ALMOST EVERYBODY, a game of professional baseball was an image before it was a reality. We heard about it before we saw it. Depending on the year of our birth, it came to us first as a voice through the air into that blind box we called radio. Or it came to us in more recent decades as figures moving on a screen that, in its early stages (I'm remembering the Yankees and Dodgers in the World Series of the early 1950s), often appeared to be men gallantly struggling through a snowstorm.

In time the picture was fine-tuned or cabled, the snowstorms ended, color was introduced and the visual transmission of the game equaled any dream we could have generated out of our imagination. This perfect colored clarity was known as television.

Is television better than radio? Each instrument brings a different kind of satisfaction. Each has different uses and emphases. When radio was all we knew, it was good enough, marvelous beyond telling. One set oneself up with a scorepad and beverage and followed the action without the slightest

144

sense that he was somehow deprived by the fact that he was following something he could not see.

Indeed, he may have seen it better, for he saw it in the stadium of his mind, where nothing intervened, free of the limitations of realism. I saw very vividly in 1932 Babe Ruth's pointing to the fence, hitting the ball over it, and thereby crushing the Chicago Cubs and every National League fan. I saw very vividly, my head poked through the open window of somebody's automobile, the first all-Star Game ever played, when Carl Hubbell for the National League mowed down by strikeouts five American Leaguers in succession.

It does not now occur to me that I did not literally see those things. I saw them as truly as I saw Dave Parker in the 1979 all-Star Game make his remarkable game-saving throw from right field, saw Parker make his throw not once, not twice, but half a dozen times at least by the miracle of instant playback and slow motion. Of playback, nobody had ever heard in 1933. And life itself was slow motion.

The family radio was a luxury, a big item; it occupied a place in the house in the space now reserved for television. A boy of radio days aching to know the score may not have owned a "portable radio." He was pleased enough if somebody posted the line score somewhere outside a shop or hanging on a banner from a window. It was knowledge in depth to know who was pitching, who hit a home run. "How did they get those two in the third inning?" one asked, and someone told how, perhaps accurately, perhaps not.

For details, the fan was required to wait for the seven o'clock sports résumé, delivered once upon a time by a fast-talking sports announcer named Ford Frick, who signed off with "Adios" and rose to become nobody less than the commissioner of baseball. The newspapers carried line scores, but they were often incomplete regarding games in the West (St. Louis, Chicago), and sometimes one went to bed ignorant of outcome, forced to wait for the morning newspaper to tell him who had won and how.

Most of us who are interested in the baseball results choose to watch on television in preference to radio. Some purists among us contend that they watch best by following the television picture and the radio voice—I appreciate that. And a few people scorn television for radio altogether on the ground that the more we see with our eyes the less we truly see in that stadium of the mind where the best excitement dwells.

Radio left things to the brain, to the imagination, and to fantasy. On radio we saw the whole baseball field because we saw it in our minds through wide-angled fantasy. We knew no limits upon our vision. We were our own camera. Pictures arose in our imaginations from the merest hints of things. Our minds were tubes that seldom blew.

This is not to say that radio was better than television, or that one age of mankind was better than another. But that radio was significantly different from television, and not always less efficient, cannot be denied. Radio was awe. The awe was produced by remoteness. No baseball player ever entered my house by radio, as he seems to do by television, staring at me in my own rooms through the eye of the camera, telling me quietly in his soft-spoken voice, through the mediation of an interviewer, how things have been going with him. Television reduces awe. In the days of radio, we scarcely knew the faces of the players, and so they were gods in ways the modern player can never be whose face is familiar to us; whose stance and style we so clearly see; who sweats, who spits, who tugs at his crotch; whose tight-fitting uniform in living color reveals his merely mortal form.

Some baseball announcers in radio days compellingly told play-by-play games they no more saw than you or I. These marvels of communication were somewhere along the line described as "re-creations," but that was a word you almost never heard above the recorded noise.

The voices of radio are no longer the voices of excitement, as they were when they were the *only* voice. They have modulated themselves, striving to be informative, as if they know that they are only holding actions; you will tune them out as soon as you can get to a TV set.

The voice of radio came to us in duet with a roar of the crowd, but radio can no longer hold us on a plateau of indiscriminate excitement. Radio conveyed excitement. Television brings an accurate, hard image out of which everyone may make his own excitement at beckoning moments.

In television the voice of the announcer is not so much provocation to excitement as background to the action. The announcer does not excite us, he informs us. Our eyes now see that scene our fantasies created in the days of radio. Our vision forces modesty, silence and discretion upon the television announcer; only a fool dares to describe what we can see for ourselves.

History has ordained that the pattern of broacast baseball follow from excitement to information. Radio served the fantasizing fan; television serves the viewer watching the game for himself.

Television is closeup. In politics and in warfare in recent years television has cast a cruel but salutary light upon realities. Baseball is neither war nor politics, and whether it required the cruel light of television I do not know. But we may be better off than we were for its having brought us closer to an understanding of the way the game is played afield, and the way it is played by the men and women at every level of enterprise. Truth is better than fakery, and we are better off for having come to the end of the spurious excitement that was radio at worst. We are free to enjoy the act of observing for ourselves the real rhythm of the sport.

Of course, some of the voices of television may irk us, even as some of the voices of radio do. But observers of baseball have options for a kind of excitement different from the excitement of 1932, 1933, the 1950s, days of radio, days of snowstorm television. The voice of the television announcer is low. The voice of radio was shrill, fast. The voice of television is cool. The voice of radio was high and hot.

LADIES' DAY AT THE GAME

◇ EARLY I FORMED a passion for baseball and a passion for the opposite sex, one passion for each, although it was inevitable, as I grew shrewdly worldly, that I should sooner or later have struck upon a happy method of unifying my separate passions.

It was 1939, and it was spring, and I was sixteen, and an unreserved grandstand seat at the Polo Grounds cost, in that golden day, only $1.10. Double $1.10, double railroad fare down from Mount Vernon, add two red-hots, two soda pop, and one score card, and it was four dollars before day was done. It was a vast sum, but my passions were irresistible.

I had estimated my expenses. It was now time to estimate my girls. And it was at this point that I discovered that I had somehow misjudged the nature of things. Girls who had endured me upon other occasions—girls upon whose feet I had danced—simply refused to accompany me to the Polo Grounds. "Yankee Stadium?" I asked, nevertheless chilled by the thought of an alliance with a girl whose loyalty was *there*.

No.

Ebbetts Field?

No. No, it was not the team, not the place; it was the game, the event, it was baseball itself no girl could abide. Since, at sixteen, one never surrenders, I continued my search to such limits that I found myself committed for a day to Hulda Granett, a girl whose reputation was everywhere in question. I did not know why Hulda should have had such a reputation, for she was not, to my observation, the least bit immoral. On the contrary, she was dedicated to the open air, to fresh vegetables, and to a collection of muscle-building apparatus strung from the ceiling in the basement of her house.

To be frank, she was herself a baseball player. On the day of our journey to the Polo Grounds she carried her baseball glove in her purse (she carried in her purse *only* her baseball glove), her intention being to snare balls hit into our section of the grandstand. No balls were hit near us, however, and the glove was therefore superfluous.

So was I. This much I could sense, if not understand. All I understood at the time was that Hulda could not be for me, nor I for her.

Then came Suzanne, and our day was Ladies' Day, so that for all her beauty she cost me only twenty-five cents (plus railroad fare, red-hots, etc.). Once upon a time—in 1883, if it matters—ladies were admitted absolutely free to the Polo Grounds when accompanied by a gentleman, a circumstance that inspired enthusiasts to establish impromptu connections at the gate. Undoubtedly it was a risky social custom, and I am of course pleased to report that it never assumed the status of a firm tradition, but, even so, I could not resist wistful backward glances toward a decade whose women sacrificed propriety upon the altar of enthusiasm. Suzanne was empty of enthusiasm. She possessed neither a sense of the difficulties encountered by the players (Hulda had had all too keen a sense of this) nor the faith to believe that she might, by an exertion of imagination, raise herself to an appreciative level. She asked, from time to time, "What inning is it now?" and between times she bathed her face and shoulders in the sun, first the left side of her face and her left shoulder, then the right, her eyes upturned and closed, while I increasingly lamented her unwilling spirit and my squandered quarter.

Late in the game, the sun having sunk behind the lower tier, she began to applaud, even to cheer, unreasonably, without cause, as ignorant persons will. She applauded the umpire when he dusted home plate, she applauded the bat boy, she applauded foul balls. I could not respect her. She had violated, really, the most urgent item of decorum: Thou shalt not applaud without provocation.

Every girl will learn, with patience and with time, the secret of appreciation. In the meantime a studious silence is preferable to false enthusiasm, and she who cheers without knowing why can command neither the respect of her escort nor the respect of patient women who distinguish between, on the one hand, moments devoid of meaning and, on the other, those moments of critical suspense.

I do not know much about women, but such a tardy effort could not be confused with sincerity, not even by me. Hulda had known too much. Suzanne knew too little. Somewhere I should find a lady for Ladies' Day.

But I never again attended a baseball game on Ladies' Day. It is not a prejudice, merely a fact, although in Atlanta (it was wartime, and the war took me from the big leagues to the territory of the Southern Association) I was myself admitted free. In Atlanta I attended a baseball game with a sergeant of the WAC whose name escapes me but whose hometown, I easily recall, was Parsippany, New Jersey. I have yet to meet a second Parsippanyite, but if I ever do I mean to inquire whether nothing is taught in the schools of that place but arithmetic. My WAC friend, professing a love for baseball, really loved nothing but numbers.

"No doubt you know," she said, "that the distance between second base and home is one hundred and twenty-seven feet and three and three-eighths inches." No doubt I knew, she said, Ty Cobb's lifetime batting average. Did I know the weight of the regulation baseball?

These things she knew, and more, and she told me. Yet while I had often thrown a regulation baseball between second base and home, and while I knew that Ty Cobb was the most competent baseball player in history, the surrounding statistics had never absorbed me. She knew, in a fantastic variety of categories, the most, the least, the longest, the highest, the farthest, but her recital so wearied me that I have trembled ever since at the suggestion of a statistic. I told her—and I have told women since—that statistics must be scorned for the vacuousness they are. No thoughtful

woman, assailed in the sports page and on the air by baseball's numerology, can heed it. To count is not to savor. That
which we love we contemplate but never measure.

Parsippany. Atlanta. The war involved me with the uni-
verse-at-large, quite destroying my boyish loyalties. It no
longer mattered how the afternoon went at the Polo Grounds.

The war over, I entered college and I was grave and I tried
hard to sneer at so irrelevant a pastime as baseball. But even
so, sneer as I might, labor as I might to put my past behind
me, the old dream would not die. During years of high seriousness, even while, to all appearances, I was a sober young
scholar, my secret heart yearned for baseball.

This had its terrors. Would I never grow up, never, as we
said, mature? One may imagine, then, the relief I felt, the
grand sense I knew of release from anxiety, when I came one
day upon that passage in Sherwood Anderson in which he
describes an accidental view of an associate: "The man was in
his house alone," wrote the author of *Winesburg, Ohio,* "and
had become in fancy a baseball player." Watching through the
window, Anderson saw the man racing from side to side
across his living room, heard him shouting encouragement to
other players, saw him fielding, throwing, overturning the
furniture—soothing, in short, his lingering frustration.

Such a state of mind is common, and women do well who
understand that the man beside them at the baseball game is
sometimes not there at all but below, upon the diamond. He
is playing. He is beyond recall. Unless you have yourself attempted to catch high fly balls carried crazily upon the wind,
unless you have yourself attempted to field a ground ball
bouncing wickedly your way, unless you yourself attempted
to bat solidly a tiny white ball thrown fiercely at you by a
pitcher standing sixty feet away (upon a hill!), you cannot
fully appreciate the difficulty, and the danger, of these ma-
neuvers. André Gide has seen it thus: "I recall that Charlie
du Bos, after reading *Si le grain ne meurt* . . . excusing himself for the little interest he took in my account of childhood
games, said: 'But what do you expect, my friend? *I never*

played.' This is the secret of a tremendous lack, which remains invisible to *whoever has never played."*[1]

True! And had I been of greater faith I would have attempted to explain this to my women friends who, like me,
were grave and serious and sober. Lacking this faith, I fixed
upon a solution, a lie. We would attend baseball games, I
said, but we would be more than orthodox fans, not vulgar
folk, not ordinary citizens, but scholars, students of our culture.

At about this time the baseball industry (we preferred not
to call it a *game*) became involved in controversial matters.
There was, for example, the question of the right of baseball
players to organize themselves into a union, and with it the
question whether the industry was or was not a monopoly in
restraint of trade. These questions, we were pleased to see,
were carried upward, away from the ball park, as far, indeed,
as the United States Supreme Court.

Not a moment too soon! For by the time the question of
monopoly was hot the question of the color line had been settled. Only so long as the world of baseball touched upon the
world of loftier issues could I conscientiously escort conscientious young ladies to baseball games. Only so long as we were
not merely *enjoying* ourselves could we justify our attendance
at those absurd spectacles.

Soon baseball descended from the sublime heights of the
Supreme Court, becoming again a mere game, innocent of
controversy. Fortunately, however, my own education had
been advancing, and with it a certain ingenuity, not to say
sophistry. I saw with exultation how, if I was properly persuasive, I could go on and on and on taking young ladies to
ball games forever. There could be no suspicion of self-indul-
gence. *I needed only to know a girl's principal intellectual
interest.*

Was it aesthetic? Then we will view, I said, not a baseball
game but an object of art. Note the color, the symmetry of the
park, the extension of the foul lines to imagined infinity, the

---

[1] *The Journals of André Gide* (New York: Random House, 1956), 11, 82.

play of light and shadow upon the players! Feel the rhythm of the innings! Hear the chorus of the crowd! "It is graphic and choreographic," I said, quoting the learned Jacques Barzun. See how (I produced here Arnold Hano's *A Day in the Bleachers,* itself a song in prose)—see how the game is "a drama . . . obeying no rules of the dramatist," building, building until, like the Greeks, we are purged.

Was she a sociologist? Psychologist? Was she, as I had been at Minnesota, a student of the American scene? "Whoever wants to know the heart and mind of America," I insisted, borrowing speech from Barzun again, "had better learn baseball, the rules and realities of the game." It is all down there before you, I said. See the poor boys playing out the rags-to-riches theme! Sit among the electorate, the common man, who finds here in the ballpark his certainty, his security; nowhere but here do events end decisively, nowhere but here is history complete, tallied in a box score. Here, in clearest relief, the American code reveals itself, for here tradition and law prevail, the rule book is the constitution, the umpire the court.

Here, for the scholar, I insisted, is a laboratory of psychoanalysis, where you may study the spectator wafted by the image of the game back to the remembered serenity of childhood, when all the world was as green as the outfield meadows: the three bases are a trinity, and the fourth is Home itself.

And it was all a lie, and I knew it because she told me so. "Stop lying," she said. "You don't go to baseball games for sociological or literary or historical or political or aesthetic or economic reasons or because it's Greek."

"Certainly I do," I said.

"You go because you like to go," she said. "Because."

"Then why do you go?" I said. She had been going with me for years.

"Because," she said.

"Penetrating logic," I said, which is what I always say when I'm mired in a lie.

She had never played baseball. Sunshine peels her nose. In

the beginning, I suppose, she found the game tiresome, a mystery not worth solving, but she knew also that I was imprisoned by my vice as other men by other vices. What could she do? How escape? Baseball drifted into the house, in print, through the air, and she conquered it by adopting it, by sitting and watching.

She discovered that it is not really a complicated game. Its objectives are simple and its strategy, if somewhat less simple, is swiftly comprehensible; this must be so or the game could not be played by the men who play it, most of whom tend, in their intellectual habit, toward the simple rather than the complex.

Once she grasped the principles, all else followed. Each game, she perceived, is less a contest of teams than of individual men, some in dark suits, some in light suits, young men from farms and towns come to the big cities in search of wealth and fame. It is a struggle we all understand, carried on by young men we seem to know, a gamble against time and chance upon the only battlefield where defeat is never ultimate, where there is always tomorrow or next year.

Baseball, its players stationed far from one another on an expansive site, its rules constant from decade to decade, is the spectator's supreme delight. She relishes it because it is a fair-weather game, never played, as football often is, in arctic hours, never seen through the blue suffocation of an indoor arena.

It serves our minds and our emotions and our hunger for retreat: the ballpark is the safest place in town, and every day is Ladies' Day—for us.

TWO THOUGHTS ABOUT JACKIE ROBINSON

JACKIE ROBINSON
AND MY SISTER

◇ Some time ago the Brooklyn Dodgers signed Jackie Robinson to a baseball contract. That is, they signed him to a Montreal contract. Brooklyn owns Montreal. If Robinson turns out to be a good enough shortstop he will be promoted from the International League and sent to Ebbetts Field.

I scouted around to find out what St. Louis people thought about Brooklyn's new shortstop.

Some people did not have any opinions at all and some said they couldn't blame Brooklyn for wanting to corner the market on infielders.

Other people, however, asked a question instead of answering mine, the way some people do. They wanted to know how I would like it if my sister married Jackie Robinson. They even hinted that such a union was imminent.

Since this is such a popular question I feel it deserves an answer.

I understand, of course, that the matter is not up to me. Robinson says he plans to be married in January to a trained nurse. It would probably be difficult to induce him to change his mind at this point. It would also entail consulting the trained nurse, who is not likely to be any more sympathetic than any other woman in such a situation. Maybe less so, loss of sympathy being an occupational disease peculiar to trained nurses.

Furthermore, he is in South America at the moment, traipsing around with a bunch of norteamericanos, some white and some Negro like himself, playing baseball for their good neighbor aficionados to the south. I cannot see my way clear at this time to run around after him and get him married to my sister before January. And if I don't get them married I won't be able to say how I like it.

Martha, my sister, lives in Mount Vernon, New York, and is in the sixth grade at William Wilson Junior High School. It would not be unkind to say of her that at this time she is not a hot potato. Robinson, at twenty-six, has, by this time, lost all interest in young ladies of twelve.

She last wrote to me just before Halloween, for which she was preparing with traditional enthusiasm.

In her letter, written in reverse slant on blue-lined notebook paper, she hinted that she is now in love with Raymie Carucci. This is not surprising, the Caruccis having always been a lovable bunch. I can distinctly remember being in love with Theresa Carucci off and on during many a school year.

Martha was in love with Billy Pelkus when I was last home. During the winter, however, he smacked her in the eye with a snowball, putting an end to what had been, at best, a one-sided affair.

I do not believe Martha has ever heard of Jackie Robinson. She has never been a student of the sports pages, and I have never known her to follow with any degree of avidity the fortunes of the Kansas City Monarchs, for whom Robinson short-stopped last season.

And I am certain my mother will not permit her to marry before she has completed junior high school.

It does not seem probable that Robinson can be inveigled into marrying my sister before his intended trip to the altar in January.

And my sister's present attachment to Raymie Carucci appears to be a determined thing. If Raymie backs out there's always Billy Pelkus.

The whole thing is out of the question.

EACH GAME WAS A CRUSADE

◇ SOMETIMES ON SUMMER television when I watch a black fellow come to bat during somebody's Game of the Day or Night or Week, I wonder how much he knows about a recent fellow named Jackie Robinson.

Who was Jackie Robinson? I wondered if my students at the University of Pittsburgh knew, so I asked them to scribble me a little answer to the question, "What does the name 'Jackie Robinson' mean to you?" For fun, try it on your own resident student. My students were born, on the average, in 1957. Some of their answers were these. "A very beautiful blonde woman I met in my dental office." "Jackie Robinson—female or male, related possibly to Mrs. Robinson in the movie *The Graduate* & in the song 'Mrs. Robinson' by Simon & Garfunkel. Or is it a baseball player? A musician? I'm guessing."

Yes, baseball player, getting warm. Who was Jackie Robinson? "I thought of a boxer," one student wrote. Another: "He might be a baseball player or a numbers runner." My one black student wrote: "Jackie Robinson is a baseball player. This is a real person, in fact, he played on a baseball team. Not sure what the team was."

The most nearly correct answer was this: "All I know (think) is he's the first black man to play major-league baseball—broke the color barrier."

Take nothing for granted. Hey, you, batter, twirling that stick, spitting that nifty spit (never TV's most appetizing moment), what does the name "Jackie Robinson" mean to you?

In ancient 1947, Robinson, male, a baseball player, a real person, became the first black man to play big-league base-

159

ball, and a lonesome figure he was. In 1947 we had sixteen major-league baseball teams, and every player on every team was white and *that was that*. Except for Robinson, who played first base for the (then) Brooklyn Dodgers of the National League.

If some people had had their way he would have been not only the first but the last. The fact that those people did not have their way is due in large part to Robinson's interior fortitude. But he could also hit and run and field with superior skill at several positions. He had played in four sports at UCLA. He soon became not only an outstanding player but the spiritual leader of his own group (the Dodgers) and a dreaded opponent of all the other groups (the other teams of the National League), whose spirits he often destroyed with his daring and his surprises.

Robinson had been specially selected by Branch Rickey for the pioneer work he did. Rickey, the Dodgers' president, was one of baseball's shrewdest innovators. He had invented the minor-league "farm system" by which big-league organizations developed and nurtured talented young players. Now he was to embark upon a second major innovation: the introduction of black players into organized baseball. The first black player would need to be an extraordinary human being. He would suffer anguish and abuse throughout the cities of the league. The shock of Robinson's presence would not be cushioned in a day.

In 1946, when Robinson was signed to a contract by the Brooklyn organization, a sportswriter in St. Louis assured me that neither Robinson nor any other Negro (that was the proper word then) would ever play baseball against the Cardinals. But after an extremely productive season in Montreal, which was (then) in the International League, Robinson *did* play baseball—for the Dodgers, against the Cardinals, who at first refused to take the field. When at length the St. Louis players obeyed the order of (then) National League president Ford Frick to play or be punished, baseball and America had arrived at a new moment.

In his first game for Montreal, Robinson hit one home run

and three singles, stole two bases, scored four runs. It was only the beginning. He was to be remembered finally, however, not for statistics alone but for incalculable moments when he won baseball games in ways that never enter the box score. He played several positions afield, and he was several persons at the bat; he could hit long balls and he could bunt. He could hit to left or right. He could run very fast and stop very short. He could feint, and he could feint feinting.

He took long, careless leads off base, forcing opposition pitchers into foolish errors. Since he was not only powerful but frequently enraged, he often inflicted injury upon other players in skirmishes along the base paths. His power was sustained by a mission not only personal but historic. Every game, every event, was in the interest of Robinson, of the Dodgers, and of Robinson's equalitarian interpretation of the United States Constitution. During warm-up for an exhibition game in New Orleans he once took time to condemn the black fans when they cheered because a new section of grandstand was opened to them: in Robinson's view, their expanded location was not a gift but a *right*.

He pursued every moment to its absolute end. Possibly nothing can describe him better than his almost unwitnessed action on that famous day, October 3, 1951, when the New York Giants defeated the Dodgers in the final playoff game following a pennant race that had been breathlessly contested for weeks. It was the ninth inning. The Dodgers were leading by two runs, but the Giants had two men on base, and Bobby Thomson was at the bat. Thomson soon stroked a home run more electrifying, more memorable than almost any home run ever struck.

On the field the Giants leaped and tumbled with inexpressible joy. The Dodgers ran dejected and ruined to their privacy. Thousands upon thousands of fans screamed with ecstasy, other thousands upon thousands wept—and Jackie Robinson followed Bobby Thomson with his eyes to be sure that Thomson touched every base. He never stopped playing.

What if the Robinson experiment had failed? Nobody will ever know whether the thing that succeeded was good old-fashioned liberal tradition in its most happy manifestation, or whether the thing that succeeded was old-fashioned dollar pragmatism. Robinson was a winner, and Brooklyn loved a winner, even if he was black. One winner drew a second, and so forth, and their names were Campanella, Black, Newcombe, Gilliam, and they were black, and they all played for Brooklyn during the decade 1947–1956, when the Dodgers won six pennants.

In the American League the Cleveland Indians with a black outfielder named Larry Doby won the pennant in 1948. Doby was the first black *American* League player at a time when I could count on my fingers all the black players. As time passed, my fingers were unable to keep up.

It began with Robinson, Brooklyn, 1947—and radio. In those days—my diary always tells it this way—I "listened to the ballgame." In 1950 I more and more "watched the ballgame," and anyone could see that the hitter's head or the pitcher's head was the size of the screen itself, and sometimes black. It was color television.

Thus the generation of my students, born in 1957 and propped at an early age in front of the tube for the Game of the Day or Night or Year, must have believed from infancy that baseball players had always come in two colors. One never imagined that any such person existed who could be described as "the first black player" any more than anyone could name the first white player. The players came with the game, like artificial turf, the World Series at night, the umpires whose names one never knew, the announcers heard but seldom seen, and the instrument of television itself, even as Adam and Eve had seen it on Opening Day.

The appearance of Robinson and the consciousness he raised among athletes quickened thinking and hastened expectations upon many topics apart from race. He broke more than the color barrier. Robinson meant not only to play the game equally with all Americans but to sleep equally in hotels, and he rallied other black players, often to their discomfort, for they sometimes said to him, "Jackie, we like it here, don't rock the boat." But he had already rocked it climbing in, and the spirit of reform was contagious. White players joined black players to demand unprecedented rights through union organization and other forms of professional representation.

Their ultimate achievement was freedom from the "reserve clause" in players' contracts. In the past, this clause gave the baseball organization or "club" exclusive rights to the players' services. Simply stated, a player was deprived of the opportunity to seek another employer, and therefore he was effectively denied the opportunity to bargain for his own wage. Players now won the right to be "free agents," to own themselves. The odd resemblance of the "reserve clause" to features of black slavery was remote in quality but similar in outline.

So complete, so thorough have been the ultimate effects of this chapter of social evolution that we have difficulty today in distinguishing differences of attitude, if any, between white and black players. From the distant grandstand skin colors merge, nor does anything we see on television betray the ideal of interracial peace.

Robinson made his impact upon literature, too, for when he stirred controversy the game attracted renewed interest among educated classes who could now view the game as both frivolous and meaningful. We have had more serious literature about baseball during the last thirty years than ever before. For myself, Robinson's advent in 1947 inspired my renewed interest in the game. I soon began the first of my baseball novels (*The Southpaw*, 1953), whose heroes include a black second baseman modeled on Robinson and bearing his number 42.

After his playing career ended, Robinson might have become the game's first black manager, but he had never been a truly lovable company man. The front office rejected him. He entered other business, and he made gestures toward politics, but his timing failed, as it never had in baseball; he supported Nixon in 1960, when Kennedy won; and he supported Rockefeller for the 1964 Republican nomination, when Goldwater won.

Family tragedy struck. In 1971 one of his sons, at twenty-four, was killed in an automobile mishap at the end of a long, winning fight against heroin and unspeakable memories of battle in Vietnam.

Robinson's own health failed swiftly thereafter. Red Smith wrote: "At fifty-three Jackie Robinson was sick of body, white of hair. He had survived one heart attack, he had diabetes and high blood pressure and he was going blind."

A good deal of my own perception of Robinson's character and historic uniqueness I gleaned from Roger Kahn's wonderful book, *The Boys of Summer*. When Robinson died, October 24, 1972, Kahn was quoted in the papers. Someone asked him what Jackie Robinson had done for his race. Kahn, a white man, beautifully replied, "His race was humanity, and he did a great deal for us."

BASEBALL PLAYING BOYS

THE MAN WHO HITS TOO MANY HOME RUNS

◇ RICHARD LEE STUART, a handsome twenty-four-year-old baseball player, can do one thing better than nearly anybody else in the world: hit home runs. As he proved last year in Lincoln, Nebraska, and—in spite of a discouraging August slump—seems likely to prove again this season, he not only hits home runs more often than anybody else but also hits them higher and farther and harder with such commanding gusto that fans come from miles around to see him do it. Last year Stuart hit sixty-six homers—and he freely admits that "I'd of hit ninety if the pitching was better."

Since the home run has long been the most spectacular, most popular feat in baseball, and since great home run hitters are widely sought after, it would be natural to expect Dick Stuart to be the biggest star in baseball history, bigger even than Babe Ruth, who had eight years more experience than Stuart before he was good enough to hit even sixty homers in a single year.

But Stuart is not a big star—and it is not because of any lack of opportunity. Since early last spring he has had a chance to play in the major leagues with the Pittsburgh Pirates and in the minor leagues with the Hollywood Stars and the Atlanta Crackers. He failed to make all three teams and is now back where he was last year: with the Lincoln Chiefs of the Class A Western League. In the era of the home run's greatest popularity, this astonishing home run hitter is not a star at all.

Anybody who has ever seen Dick Stuart hit a baseball must at first suspect that the Pittsburgh organization, generally thought to be an alert house of business, has in the present case lost its gift. When Dick Stuart steps to the plate, opposing outfielders retreat to the fences, infielders strategically (and for safety's sake) play deep, and all pray that he will fail. Once, with the bases loaded, a fearful Pueblo, Colorado, pitcher awarded him an intentional base on balls, deliberately forcing in one run rather than risk Stuart's driving in four. At Pueblo, too, one of Stuart's homers traveled 610 feet. "You mean it rolled 610 feet?" he was asked. "No sir, I don't," he said. "It landed on the riverbank and stuck in the crazy mud."

Stuart has a beautiful, rhythmic swing that concentrates all his tremendous power in a smooth, even flow. With this power even a Stuart pop fly is spectacular. The ball goes straight up as though to put out the moon, and as it descends from its unnatural height at a dangerous rate, infielders stagger awkwardly trying to judge its path. Stuart calls them 600-foot drives: "300 up and 300 down."

Nobody is more impressed by Stuart's power than Stuart himself. "Every home run," he says, "gives me the deepest personal thrill, although I've hit droves. Last year at Lincoln I hit sixty-six, yet it was the deepest personal thrill every time I seen that ball flying nine miles out of the park."

At Nashville one of Stuart's line drives, when last seen by witnesses, was still climbing in altitude at a point in space 450 feet from home plate. To a respectful grandstand Stuart blew a joyous kiss as he trotted around the bases. When he hits a home run his spirits soar, his mood lightens and he writes a letter home to his mother and father in San Carlos, California. "Whenever Dick hit one," says Clyde King, who managed him at Hollywood, "it registered his psychology like an electrocardiogram. Coming around third base, he shook my hand so hard I thought he'd drag me clear across home plate."

According to Joe Duhem, a former teammate of Stuart's, Stuart is baseball's strongest man. "And from the tip of his shoulder to the tip of his finger," Duhem proclaims, "he's the strongest man in the whole entire world. We used to arm-rassle, but nobody will arm-rassle with him any more."

Obviously so conspicuous a young man could never have remained anonymous even if he had wished to. "I want to be somebody famous that everybody recognizes, like Ted Williams," Stuart admits. "When Ted Williams walks down the street everybody says, 'Jesus, there goes Ted Williams.' I want to walk down the street and hear them say, 'Jesus, there goes Dick Stuart.' I like to see my name in the paper, especially in the headlines. I crave on it. I *deserve* them headlines. I hit sixty-six home runs—and sixty-six home runs is the Nobel Prize. Jayne Mansfield said to me, 'Hey, how come you get your name in the paper more than me?' I said, 'Hell, you didn't hit no sixty-six home runs in the Western League.'"

This spring when he tried out with the Pittsburgh Pirates in Florida, Stuart was confident of his future. Would he, reporters asked, lead the National League in home runs? "I don't predict," he said. "But I led every league I ever played a full year in, and from what I see of these pitchers down here, I believe I could do it any place I play regular." For autograph hunters he signed eagerly: "Dick Stuart 66."

Yet 1957 has been anything but a good year for Richard Lee Stuart. In four spring-training games with Pittsburgh he clubbed five home runs, but the Pirates' then-manager, Bobby Bragan, decided against keeping him. Stuart was bewildered. "I can't understand the train of Mr. Bragan's mind," he said.

Cross-country he went, to the Hollywood Stars where he hit two home runs on opening day, another the next day, two more the following day. But before the end of the first month he was demoted by Manager Clyde King to Atlanta. "I quit," he said.

Relenting, however—"tears blinding my eyes"—he reported to the Atlanta team and on Monday, May 20, hit a home run. He hit another on Thursday. And on Friday. Saturday, too.

But on June 9 he was benched by Manager Buddy Bates and the next day he was released.

Reassigned to his old 1956 team at Lincoln, he announced, "I won't spend five minutes back in Class A. I'll go home and film pitchers in California." Shortly, however, he reconsidered, and agreed to go back to playing baseball for the Lincoln Chiefs.

It is a perverse trick that baseball history has played on Dick Stuart. In search of money for his pocket and fame for his pride, he had set out as a young man to gain both by playing baseball. Once committed to his career, he chose to be the kind of player whom the game rewards best, the home run hitter. "Money," he has said, "can buy nothing but happiness."

Since baseball history during the last four decades proves that men who consistently hit homers are paid more and therefore are presumably happier, Dick Stuart's logic would seem to be impeccable. Beginning with the days of Babe Ruth much has been done to tailor the game to the slugger. The ball has been "rubberized" and the fences have been relocated in the direction of home plate. The pitcher, thus wounded, has been further demoralized by the outlawing of spitballs, emery balls, and flapping uniform sleeves. These events have cast their shadow upon rule book and paycheck.

Dick Stuart simply tried to conform to history. When he was a little boy swatting rocks with a baseball bat in San Carlos, California, he was the wonder of the neighbors and a menace to their windows. He was known to the police. "By the time we paid for the first window," his mother recalls, "Richard had busted another. And he sure chewed up the bats."

Once, to earn $3.75 for a new bat, Dick Stuart pulled weeds in an artichoke field. He was paid thirty-five cents an hour, and the instant he had earned $3.75 he walked out of the field. "I never wanted to be out in those artichokes," he explains. "What I always really wanted to be was somebody there's not a whole lot of."

When he grew older, he went to play in San Carlos Park,

where there are two baseball fields. The smaller one has a 311-foot left field foul line stretching from home plate to a Boy Scout meeting house. Stuart, a right-handed hitter, peppered the meeting house with baseballs. Soon he was clearing the meeting house, to the horror of tennis players on the asphalt courts beyond. It was not safe, and he transferred his operations to the larger diamond, where the distance to the left field fence is 385 feet (greater than in any major league park). But it failed, as all parks would fail, to hold Dick Stuart. Regularly he lofted baseballs over the fence into Brittan Avenue, and as his skill and strength increased, he cleared rooftops across the street.

On June 15, 1951, after breaking a suitable number of windows all over San Carlos, Stuart graduated from high school with every reason to believe in an abundant future. Two colleges offered him athletic scholarships, but the academic life was not for him. "I never brought a book home in my life. They graduated me because of my .450 average."

Stuart was ready to contribute his bit to baseball history. One week after high school graduation he signed with the Pittsburgh Pirate organization for a $10,000 bonus. He could imagine no serious obstacle to his becoming extremely wealthy. "The man that busts Babe Ruth's record will be a millionaire," he said.

In 1951 there was nowhere to go but up. He played two seasons of minor league ball, collecting "deepest personal thrills" with his home runs, and then went into the army where his military career was distinguished by more home runs for service teams. After his discharge he was promoted to Pittsburgh's Class AA Mexico City Tigers, and here he encountered his first setback. It was Mexican food. "I lost twelve pounds in eight days. I told them send me somewheres else before I vomited my life away." He finished out the year with Billings, Montana, where he collected thirty-two home runs. At twenty-two, counting the one he hit while vomiting in Mexico, he had a grand total of sixty-eight.

It was as nothing. Last year in Lincoln he hammered home his Nobel Prize. On Dick Stuart Night the citizenry showered him with luggage, shirts, fountain pens, wallets, a golf cart, and eighty dollars cash. "Where's the automobile?" Stuart asked. In time people began to turn on the streets of Lincoln, Nebraska. "There goes Dick Stuart," they said.

Then came 1957, and the world of Dick Stuart turned sour. Could it have been that somehow the baseball history he had heard was in fact a deception? Was the home run, after all, not enough? Would Dick Stuart finally be remembered only as the definitive proof that the history of baseball must not be read at a glance?

Not until 1957 had he played baseball where it is played best. And where baseball is played best, the home run—all history and rumor notwithstanding—has by no means rendered all other weapons obsolete. It has charmed fans, captured headlines, and provided the American language with a popular superlative, but neither fans nor headline writers are so intimately bound to the game's necessities as are baseball managers. Dick Stuart has mistaken the grandstand seat for the seat of judgment, the heights of the press box for the heights of critical wisdom.

Psychologically, perhaps, he has *needed* to hit home runs. They have won him admiration, esteem, headlines, and money, but they have kept him from being a baseball player.

In the simplest terms Stuart's chief failure has been his inability to reach first base often enough. He has been content, if he cannot hit a home run, to strike out. Last year he struck out 171 times. At Atlanta this year his eight home runs were accompanied by thirty-one strikeouts, at which rate he would have achieved a fantastic total of 207 by the end of the season. (The all-time major league record in frustration, set last year by Jim Lemon of the Washington Senators, is 138 strikeouts.) Stuart was actually getting to first base little more than once in every five times at bat. It was not enough.

Even when he has two strikes on him, Stuart usually "swings from the tail," still trying for the home run when he should be content to "get wood on the ball," be satisfied to hit it somewhere—anywhere. Where baseball is played best, pitchers are quick to detect a slugger's passion, and as a consequence they lure Stuart into swinging in vain at outrageously bad pitches. Swinging as hard as he does, his prospects for connecting are minimized. To swing more moderately might result in a single or a double or a base on an error, but these fill Stuart with a sense of failure. And he is so appalled by getting a walk to first base that upon occasion, when a fourth ball is called, he turns to the umpire as if to protest.

Yet even these weaknesses would not have discouraged his managers had Stuart given evidence of possessing what the trade vaguely refers to as "attitude"—the will to improve, the flashing desire of every successful ballplayer to correct his own faults. Stuart's attitude appeared to his managers and teammates at Hollywood and Atlanta to respond less to the fate of his team than to his individual success in losing baseballs beyond fences. He had not yet learned to treasure as his "deepest personal thrill" the praise of his fellow players. (It is surely noteworthy that after three weeks with the Atlanta Crackers he still did not know the names of all his teammates.)

It must also be remembered that baseball is played not only at the plate but in the field, and it is here, on defense, with a glove rather than a bat in his hand, that Stuart sometimes offers more aid and comfort to the enemy than to his own club. Pittsburgh ex-Manager Bobby Bragan has called him "one of the worst outfielders I've ever seen." True, Stuart is not a "natural" in the style of Willie Mays, but he does not have to be as bad a fielder as he is. He can, when the spirit moves him, conduct himself on defense adequately if not always with consummate grace. His hands are sure. He is not fleet enough to be a good centerfielder, but he could be effective in right or left field, and he has a wonderfully strong and accurate throwing arm.

Unfortunately, however, Stuart afield tends to become a study in dejection. His natural endowment goes largely to waste because he is busy thinking about the last home run he hit, the home run he failed to hit, or the home run he hopes to hit just as soon as he can return to the dugout and exchange his glove for his beloved bat. Manager Bates at Atlanta, who experimented with Stuart not only in the outfield and at first base but also at third base, was inclined to ask himself not where Stuart could do the most good but where he could do the least damage.

Manager Clyde King of Hollywood remembers: "Dick and I, we conducted a regular debating society. 'Skip,' he said, 'Wouldn't you ruther I hit two home runs than five singles?' 'Dick,' I said, 'No, I ruther you hit the five singles.' 'Skip,' he said, 'I'm not really as bad in the field as they say.' 'Dick,' I said, 'in the field you're not concentrating. You're losing me more ball games through the middle of your legs than you're winning me with your bat.' 'Skip,' he said, 'I *am* concentrating.' 'Dick,' I said, 'I *know* you're concentrating because I know it's not possible a man's mind will be blank when he's awake. But what are you concentrating *on?*' 'Skip,' he said, 'what am I basically doing wrong?' 'Dick,' I said, 'what you're basically doing wrong is you're swinging at balls and missing them.' "

When Dick Stuart was benched in Atlanta, his replacement was not a still more luminous home run hitter but a thirty-three-year-old journeyman baseball player named Sammy Meeks. Meeks cannot hit a ball as far as Dick Stuart can, and he cannot throw as hard. Hardly anybody has ever bought a ticket to a ball game primarily to see Sammy Meeks play.

But less than four innings had passed on the day Sammy Meeks replaced Dick Stuart when the difference between the two men became evident. The score was 0–0, and Atlanta had a man on first with one out when Sammy Meeks came up to bat. Manager Bates signaled for the hit-and-run, the man on first to run with the pitch, and Sammy Meeks to make every effort to "get wood on the ball." As it happened, Meeks did hit the ball, it was fielded by the second baseman, and Meeks was thrown out at first. But there had been no chance to get the base runner, who wound up on second in scoring position. When the next batter singled, the runner scored what proved to be the day's winning run.

There was no headline in the next day's newspapers: SAMMY MEEKS GROUNDS OUT TO SECOND BASE. But his sacrifice of himself in the interest of his team was fully satisfactory to the other players and to the manager. Calculating their art in terms of the strenuous necessities of a 154-game campaign, they prefer just such quiet victories to explosive but futile glory.

Back in Lincoln, Stuart resumed his familiar pattern. In his first game for the Lincoln Chiefs this June he clobbered a home run with the bases loaded. In a doubleheader against Amarillo he hit three more. Within seven days he had hit six, within a month ten, and by the beginning of last week a total of twenty-four. Counting his exploits at Hollywood and Atlanta, he now has thirty-eight.

"I can make it with home runs," he has always claimed. But his quick intelligence may soon persuade him that Paragraph 1.01, the very first in the rule book, retains all its hoariest validity: "Baseball is a game between two teams of nine players."

Possibly his disappointments have begun to direct Stuart toward self-fulfillment. That he may one day be a ranking baseball player nobody denies: the Pittsburgh Pirates, who once gave Dick Stuart $10,000 for his autograph, have by no means abandoned hope.

Baseball is not arm-rassling. Brute force counts for little. Defense is still at least half the game, while the vital offensive element is still that steady fellow who in some manner reaches first base. The run he scores counts equally with the nine-mile catapult, and it happens more often.

Stuart may soon discover that the star system does not operate in baseball, that the game remains one of precise and painstaking skill. Baseball has never capitulated to the slugger. If it does, it will no longer be baseball, and the men who play it will not be baseball players but home run hitters.

If, before another season passes, Dick Stuart transforms

himself from a home run hitter into a baseball player, he will become a very fine baseball player indeed. But he will then no longer be the Dick Stuart who hit sixty-six home runs last year—and who cannot quite forget that immense misfortune.

AN OUTFIELDER
FOR HIROSHIMA

White are the trodden paths
Of baseball,
Among the tall grasses
Of summer.

Far, and beyond
The summer grass,
The baseball players are seen.

—SHIKI MASAOKA (1867–1902),
translated from the Japanese
by Nobuyuki Yuasa,
University of Hiroshima

◇ THE MOST PORTENTOUS resident of the city of Hiroshima
(pop.: 400,000) is the twenty-eight-year-old Californian who
plays in the outfield for its major league Carp. The city's fans,
who in 1958 will pass in record numbers beyond the ticket
takers at the brand-new Hiroshima Citizens' Ball Place, call
him "Hweebah," which is the way the Japanese deliver "Fibber," which in turn was his father's version of "February," the
month of Fibber's birth, in Fresno.

If nobody has ever called him by his proper name, Satoshi,
which means, in Japanese, wisdom, and which much more
accurately defines his character than Fibber, he has not complained. Indeed, although he has borne through life his full

share of small disappointments, and—once at least—a measure of pure injustice, he has confounded fate as he confounded the rivals of his football days at Fresno State College, most of whom outweighed him by fifty pounds. "Nobody," he recollects, "ever hit me real solid."

Of Fibber Hirayama's spiritual past, however, the citizenry of Hiroshima hears nothing. His memory is notably weak in the matter of his own considerable achievement. To his father in Lindsay, California—Tokuzo, called George—and to his wife Jean in Hiroshima he has delegated the task of pasting up his scrapbooks, while Fibber himself, in the language of Carp manager Katsumi Shiraishi, "plays baseball *like* baseball."

Therefore, the city's copious affection for him can only be ascribed to its conscious appreciation of his present talents. For three years he has been the Carp's gracefully aggressive right fielder, lead-off batter and spiritual focus, and in this year of promise he continues to be its vital center, as the Carp, who have never finished higher than fourth in the Central League, point their hopes toward the top brackets.

But this conscious appreciation, like all activity in a city whose devastation is so recent to memory, is in fact an expression of Hiroshima's profound necessity to achieve something much more ennobling than a mere pennant at baseball. Thorstein Veblen might have been describing the aroused temperament of this historic community when he spoke of a people "brought up against an imperative call to revise their scheme of institutions in the light of their native instincts, on pain of collapse or decay."

A way of life is sought which shall be more humane and democratic than the feudal pattern of the Oriental past. Yet it can be nothing so simple-minded as the blind adoption of all things American. In the person of Fibber Hirayama, whose ancestry is Japanese, whose techniques are American, and who contains in fine balance within himself his double heritage, the humiliated but emergent city of Hiroshima glimpses an ideal fusion of West with East.

Three years ago, when Fibber Hirayama arrived with his

bride in Hiroshima, he was greeted by 10,000 persons. He paled. "It was something *terrible.*" Informed of the possibility of a small welcoming committee, he had earlier requested translation into Japanese of a speech which he had rehearsed upon the train from Tokyo and which, when silence was established, he delivered at Hiroshima station. When 10,000 people hallooed with laughter he was appalled. In beginner's Japanese he had attempted to say, "I am Satoshi Hirayama. I will do my best," but he afterward learned that he had committed the ludicrous error of misusing a word, which caused him to say: "I am Satoshi Hirayama and a splendid fellow."

His Carp teammates, still made merry by that incident, console him for his ignorance by reference to his primitive origins: he is only, they say, a piteous California farmer from a woebegone place called Fresno. "Hirayama," they sometimes inquire, "is it true that Fresno will soon have electricity?"

But he has done his best, as promised. Fibber Hirayama, according to the testimony of Takeo Yagi, chairman of Carp Fans (19,600 of whom have thus far this year contributed 200 yen apiece to their club, and who in the dark days of the Carp's infancy paid the team's salaries by public subscription), has become "famous for his constancy and sincerity," which is only to say, of course, that Fibber plays baseball as he learned to play it at Fresno.

At first glance, Fibber's resemblance to an athlete is by no means pronounced. Afflicted by nature with near-sightedness and a slight astigmatism, he wears tortoise-shell eyeglasses, exchanging those when in baseball uniform for silver-rimmed unbreakable lenses which he habitually polishes with a bar of dry soap. Elevated by nature to a height of only five feet three inches (5.22 Japanese *shaku*) he is sometimes indistinguishable from the bat boy, and even in Japan, where folk stand upon the average nearly a *shaku* shorter than Americans, he presently is the smallest Carp of all.

On the other hand, if he is vertically Japanese he is horizontally American. Nourished upon eggs, meat, and milk ("Hirayama drinks milk like water"), he is broad-shouldered and full-chested, unlike most Japanese baseball players, whose power is predominantly in their legs. In a recent soliloquy in one of the two Hiroshima magazines entitled—one in English, one in Japanese—*Carp,* an essayist arrived at the somewhat metaphysical conclusion that Fibber has the "strongest shoulders" of any Carp. And it is a tangible fact that he is the only Carp who can throw to home plate from the farthest reaches of the Ball Place. In a game in Honolulu on a 1951 tour with the Fresno State College baseball team, Fibber retired a runner at home with a heroic throw which moved sportswriter Wallace Hirai to maintain that "other than Joe DiMaggio, no player has come through with such a perfect strike from the outfield in the twenty-five-year history of the stadium."

Fibber attributes his compact power to "real good wrists" and abundant sleep ("I sleep rather well. Just so I can get sideways I can sleep") and a mystic quality he calls "quickness." Characteristically amiable with regard to fine verbal distinctions, he allows "quickness" to mean "timing" as well. "Like in football," he explains, "being able to hit the hole at just the right time, cut back, cut out, in one or two strides I can make my cut."

From the moment Fibber became a Carp, according to veteran second baseman Jiro Kanayama, he "took charge." Kanayama recalls his astonishment at the discovery, returning to the dugout between innings, that Fibber, running in from the outfield, was already sitting on the bench. Thereupon Kanayama too began to run. Contrary to Japanese custom, Fibber also runs swiftly to first base in spite of the depressing effects of a ground ball weakly hit to the infield. In Japan, as in America, he has betrayed a dangerous but somehow inspiring tendency to crash into outfield fences in pursuit of fly balls, a form of behavior which resulted last year in a painful rib injury but which has contributed to the Carp in that magical way in which the contagious passion of a lone player often uplifts an entire team.

The Carp have openly emulated him, especially at those points at which his deportment afield is imaginative rather than theoretical. He sometimes scores from first base on a single, or from second base on an infield out. He has introduced to the Carp the bumptious but perfectly legitimate Occidental custom of foiling a double play by sliding into the relay. The unhappy Carp tendency to miss a signal because it was not anticipated is fading in an atmosphere conditioned by Fibber's conviction that strategy ceases to be strategy when it reduces itself to ritual. And some Carp, immobilized in former days by edifying visions of their own dexterity at one-handed fielding, have observed that the truest esthetic calls for Fibber's practical habit of speedily throwing the ball to the appropriate base.

It is natural enough that members of the Carp, being Japanese, have learned to play baseball as it has traditionally been played in Japan. This is not quite equivalent to playing baseball like baseball, although to the casual eye an afternoon's transaction at the Hiroshima Citizens' Ball Place looks like baseball. The diamond lies below in its American dimensions. The ball itself is the American ball in every essential stitch. The teams perform in American whites and grays, their names written in English across their shirts, their nicknames borrowed, as in America, from the kingdoms of beasts and demons—Giants, Tigers, Dragons, Lions, Whales, Hawks. It is the American stadium, complete with vendors, flags, fenceboard advertising, scoreboard, peanuts, soda pop, and a raincheck—everything except, for some inscrutable reason, the seventh-inning stretch. Now and then it is Ladies' Day. On Sunday there's a "dubburuhedduru." There's a Most Valuable Player. The Central League opposes the Pacific League in an annual all-Star competition in July and in a Nippon Series in October. The "peetcha" (he may be a "souspaw") throws "carvus" and "droppus," perhaps a "nukkuruboru." or in temper a "binbol," the "battah" runs to "farst-o" on a "hit-o." "Get two," the players sometimes call, and when they do the umpires cry "Out-o." The "catchah" wears the protective equipment designed in America, and the players jogging in from "left-o," "right-o," "second-o," "short-o," and "sardo" now carry their gloves with them—as they saw the touring San Francisco Seals do in 1949.

Into this perfectly persuasive Ball Place the Japanese player carries not only his bat and glove but his culture. And Japanese culture has inhibited the free growth of baseball in a variety of subtle ways. For example, the Hiroshima Carp whom Fibber Hirayama joined were committed as truly as any group of Japanese workers, whether in industry, the professions, or education, to the firm tradition of *senpai* and *kohai*. A *senpai* (superior) is bound in honor to advance the interests of some younger man (his *kohai,* inferior) with whom he is identified by virtue of their having attended the same high school, or because they originate from the same native town. In turn, the *kohai*'s first loyalty is to his *senpai.* It is a paternalism whose beneficence is apparent in many areas of Japanese life, but to a baseball team it is crippling. It results not in unity but in fragmentation, and it hampers a learning process especially important in Japanese baseball, where that Harvard and Yale of American ballplayers—the minor league farm club—does not exist. The young *kohai* shortstop whose native place is Yamaguchi will disastrously offend his *senpai* (a catcher whose native place is likewise Yamaguchi) by seeking tips on shortstopping from another shortstop whose native place is unfortunately Sendai. The free interchange of criticism and information among players, which circulates upward and downward and across all lines of age and place in America, may travel only within sensitive limits in Japan.

An outsider, untrained in America to honor a *senpai* or shelter a *kohai,* Fibber Hirayama, in the intimacy of railroad cars, baths, and hotels, has behaved for three years as if all Carp were created equal. Response to this novel conduct has been especially quick among those younger Carp of a postwar generation already hopeful of loosening *senpai* ties, which control even the choice of a wife. Now that Fibber himself has assumed a senior status (he is the sixth-oldest player on the youngest roster in the Japanese major leagues), the cultural impulse has been diverted in his direction. But since he will be nobody's *senpai,* the impulse dissolves, and the team as a whole moves toward a unity unprecedented among Japanese baseball clubs.

When the atomic bomb burst over Hiroshima, at a point almost directly above the dome of the Industrial Promotion Building (which alone survives today as a monument to the blast), Fibber himself was playing baseball in Arizona sunshine at Poston Relocation Center Two. "There really wasn't too much else to do. The nearest town was twenty miles away, and we weren't allowed to go."

He was fifteen. Three years earlier he had been evicted from Exeter, California by an anxious U.S. government, which had somehow mistaken Fibber, pedaling his bicycle over the highways of Tulare County, for a potential enemy. With his father and two brothers (it was the year his mother died), their home and other possessions sold, he entrained to take up life in a single barracks room at Poston Two. And when, a few days after the dropping of the bomb—the "catastrophe," as Hiroshimans call it—the Hirayamas were permitted to return home, there actually wasn't, as Fibber now perceives, "too much to go back to."

But if the prospect was dark he hadn't noticed. Or possibly he said, in the Japanese mood, *"Shikataganai."* In the home where Japanese foods had sometimes been prepared, where he had heard the language spoken by his mother and where he had bathed all his life in a woodburning bath modeled upon the magnificent tubs of the old country, it was inevitable that he should have been a little bit shaped by the philosophy of *Shikataganai:* "It cannot be helped . . . it is Nature." A household word in Japan, *Shikataganai* describes the ancient Japanese habit of submitting to fate, blending with the landscape: the Japanese mountain road winds its way not over nor through but around. If it was the nature of the U.S. government or the citizens of California to view Fibber Hirayama with suspicion or mistrust, very well, *Shikata-*

ganai. But at Exeter High, where he was the only Oriental boy, he discovered that it was also the nature of Americans to admire athletic skill. Devoting himself with all earnestness and all joy to games, he proceeded toward redemption, and on the playing fields of America, as afterward in Japan, he soon won not only acceptance but distinction.

At Fresno State College, with a tuition scholarship and fifty dollars a month as wages for "art work" and other exhausting duties, he studied physical education and health education (he hopes to coach high school athletics in California), intellectual disciplines embodying tumbling, boxing, wrestling, and hygiene. He played football in the autumn and baseball in the spring.

Weighing 150 pounds fully armored (18.13 Japanese *kan*), acclaimed by the Fresno press as "pound for pound" the best halfback on the Coast, he threw passes, ran the ends and squirmed and squirted through holes in the line which a larger man could never have maneuvered. On defense he was notably adept at intercepting passes, but his principal charm from the spectators' point of view perhaps was his finesse in upending competitors whose relative bulk might have awed him had he paused to calculate the risk.

The Fresno State College baseball teams of 1950–52, twice captained by center fielder Fibber Hirayama, were among the strongest in the nation. The 1951 team won thirty-six games in forty starts, ten more in a thirteen-game postseason tour of Hawaii where, in addition to his memorable throw, Fibber typically distinguished himself by being twice hit by the opposing pitcher in a single game (once in the head), each time rising, trotting to first base and subsequently scoring. In 1952, against such major college competition as the University of California, USC, Stanford, UCLA, and Oregon State College, the Fresno team won thirty-one games and lost nine.

Perhaps of even more significance than his ability to master the nature of baseball was the singular fact of Fibber's personality, which seduces people, wherever he goes, to accord him honors he never seeks. As he was twice captain of the Fresno Bulldogs, so was he also twice voted most popular player at National Baseball Congress tournaments in Wichita. Voted in 1951 Nisei player of the year, admitted to the 1951–52 edition of *Who's Who Among Students in American Colleges and Universities,* he was also elected campus king (queen Norma Morrison was slightly taller), in which capacity he proclaimed a holiday, reigned over a carnival and led a grand march down a dance floor dominated by plaster figures of a prince and princess eighteen feet tall.

If ever a man had rejoined his community, Fibber Hirayama had done so. The U.S. government, which had exiled him from his home a decade before, now reclaimed him, and he found himself, in January 1953, once again in a barracks, this time at Fort Ord, California. Here, in addition to military duties, he batted .300 for the Fort Ord Warriors, 1954 all-service champions. Discharged from the Army in October 1954, into a world in which, from the point of view of American baseball, he lacked *shaku* and *kan,* Fibber was fearful, at this time, that his race disqualified him for coaching jobs on the West Coast.

It was then that he was encouraged by his good friend Kenichiro Zenimura of Fresno to hire out to the faraway Carp. Kenichiro—whose name means Health One—was born in Hiroshima, where a son Kenji—Health Two, called Harry —now lives, and where Kenso and Kenshi—Health Three and Health Four, called Howie and Harvey—played for the Carp for varying periods between 1953 and 1956. "I realized that I wouldn't be able to go anywhere as far as pro ball in the States is concerned," Fibber says, "and there's no place to go unless you can play in the big time. I decided to take a chance."

Lured, too, by the opportunity to visit Kumamoto, where generations of Hirayamas have raised rice and green tea, he was supported in his intention by Jean Doi, whom he had first pursued in aggressive American fashion down a corridor of the Administration Building at the campus in Fresno, and to whom he was married on February 12, 1955 in the First Congregational Church. ("I like whatever country my husband is in," she was afterward to say.)

On a wedding trip to Nevada and a visit to relatives in Los Angeles they spent a portion of their savings in American dollars, and on March 7, with tickets purchased in yen by the Hiroshima Carp Limited Companies, they departed San Francisco by Japan Air Lines. Two evenings later they dined at a Chinese-style restaurant in Tokyo, where Fibber was alarmed to discover a coeducational lavatory. On March 11 they arrived at Hiroshima Station.

To the land of *Shikataganai* the poet-reformer Shiki Masaoka, explaining baseball as long ago as 1896, stressed that the game continues for nine innings, after which "the total number of points are compared, and those who have more points are considered to be the winners. For example, 8–23." But Japanese baseball players have been accustomed to capitulate in early innings to the nature of a losing day. Moreover, when they do so they smile, since to reveal one's own humiliation is considered un-Japanese.

Fibber Hirayama, who smiles easily, has nevertheless been unable to take a long, philosophical view of a bad day. Fresno State College baseball coach Pete Beiden recalls that during a period when Fibber went hitless in forty-two attempts "he lost his sense of humor in the situation." He does not conceal emotions of disgust when he errs nor emotions of humiliation when he is outwitted by an opposing pitcher, nor has it ever occurred to him to consent to defeat until nine full innings have been played.

Was the smile better? The surrender to Nature? Deference to authority? Does Hiroshima need baseball at the expense of its mellow code? But it is a city whose recent convulsive history forces it to choose with unnatural haste a symbol of its intention. It must choose between the bombed dome and the Ball Place.

Significantly, its initial reception for Fibber Hirayama, followed by a fifty-car parade, has recently been equaled by its reception for only two other individuals: India's Nehru, whom the city views as a principal spokesman for world peace, and Helen Keller, the American woman who has defied nature in her conquest of physical handicap. *Shikataganai* no longer serves.

In their support of their baseball team, the citizens of Hiroshima have enjoyed their first sustained opportunity to condemn a past which brought them to the edge of extinction. Never have citizens representing every economic level and every social distinction shared so clear a stake in a common endeavor. The Hiroshima Carp, organized nine years ago on a shareholding basis, is the only Japanese big-league team popularly bearing not the name of an industrial sponsor but the name of its city: of the other eleven teams, six are owned by transportation companies, two by newspapers, one by a motion picture company, one by a fishery, and one jointly by a newspaper and a motion picture company. This is a point of pride to Hiroshimans, who wish the world to know not only that their city fell but that it picked itself up again.

Last year Carp fans recorded a home attendance of 746,000, although the new 31,000-seat Ball Place was not put into use until late August. This year an attendance of 850,000 —more than twice the city's population—is assured, a rate which will be nowhere approached in Japan and exceeded in the U.S. only at Milwaukee. In 1958 the Carp will show its first profit in yen. Long before opening day, April 5, interest was high: in mid-February 20,000 people attended an exhibition double-header, while on March 2 an equal number viewed games in cold which turned to snow before the afternoon was over.

The carp, in Japanese lore, is a fish which swims upstream, even over waterfalls. The Carp, in Japanese baseball, must struggle upstream against the formidable Central League empires of Tokyo (three teams), Osaka and Nagoya, whose millions in population provide a financial basis unavailable to

Hiroshima and whose teams recruit the outstanding college players. The Carp cannot pay, as the Yomiuri Giants recently did, a bonus of twenty-five million yen for a rookie third baseman.

Basically, if the Carp are to win, they can do so only by playing baseball like baseball, avoiding the mistake of confusing form with function: for baseball is more than a form. It is a spirit made in America and therefore, for better or for worse, the antithesis of *Shikataganai.* At the Hiroshima Citizens' Ball Place, accelerated by history and with an assist by Fibber Hirayama, the secret of that spirit is in the process of revelation.

Yet Fibber did not come to Hiroshima to instruct. He came as a workman, hired out to the Carp, as counterpart workmen in the U.S. hire out to the Red Sox or the Dodgers. On his new job he troubled himself to learn the language of his fellow workers; which he speaks in a frontal style, lopping from his speech that great variety of polite attachments of which Japanese is capable. He sacrificed meat and milk when necessary for rice and fish, although he deplores fish, especially raw, and once became morbidly ill on sardines. He has consistently rejected the special treatment Japanese hospitality daily offers the foreigner. He has asked neither privilege nor favor. He has given all he knows.

Although "a real good book reader," he has not yet encountered Fielding's *Joseph Andrews,* but he has somehow known —his name, after all, is Satoshi, wisdom—"that examples work more forcibly on the mind than precepts."

For his pains he has been rewarded. In the night, traveling through the sleeping countryside, a fellow player calls: "Hirayama, California farmer, look out the window," and Fibber, peering into the darkness, sees swiftly receding the lonely lights of a desolate rural station. "That," say the Carp, "is Fresno."

Less than profound, it is the baseball player's universal method of asserting affection. It is an affection earned. For his team, and for the city in which he has chosen to live his life so long as he can play baseball like baseball, Fibber has been an example working forcibly on the mind. It is much to have accomplished for a young man whom nature gave short supply in *shaku* and *kan*.

YOU CAN'T SCOUT DESIRE

◇ Fᴏʀ Yᴀɴᴋᴇᴇ ꜰᴀʀᴍʜᴀɴᴅ Edward James Cereghino, sitting chewing eighteen-cent Beech-Nut tobacco in the San Francisco suburbs, winter was a season devoted to the diagnosis and cure of a case of benign schizophrenia, aggravated by a compound fracture of the ego and recurring attacks of acute conscience.

Sometimes he thought maybe he could write it down. At three o'clock on winter mornings, "free as a breeze," his best ideas flowed, and he wrote them down in longhand. When daylight came he typed them up and put the commas in.

Sometimes he walked alone on the diamond at Daly City's Jefferson High, where in June 1951 he had graduated. A week later the New York Yankees had paid him $74,000 for his autograph. "I like to go over there and walk around. There's something about a ballpark when there's nobody there. Really peaceful. You know, maybe that's what it was— maybe that's why I didn't cut it—the competitiveness."

In Daly City, principal Glenn South of Westmoor High, who had coached Cereghino at Jefferson, strolled out for a haircut. He was asked, "Whatever happened to Ed Cereghino? How come he never made it?" It wasn't a question he could answer offhand in the barbershop.

But South thought about it, and sometimes the farmhand himself dropped in for a chat. "I want to know where I went wrong. I'd like to know some reason. There has to be a reason. I like baseball. I've thought of this and thought of that, I've heard this and that. It doesn't seem right that a kid can get that kind of money for producing nothing. Still, it wasn't money that made me complacent. I've heard that before, but

190

I'm close enough to myself to know better. I worked harder and harder. I tried. Maybe trying isn't enough."

By winter's end he had made at least one decision: When his contract came from the Yankees he didn't send it back.

His future decided, his past was still unclarified. Why had he failed?

Every Sunday, with his mother, he attended 6:30 mass at the Church of Our Lady of Perpetual Help. He busied himself around the house. He spent a week with *Doctor Zhivago*. His wife Janet was pregnant with their fourth child. His father, who is vice-president of the Pacific Pump and Supply Company, installed new bookcases in Ed's house, "clear to the ceiling," while the farmhand and his mother now and then amused themselves with *Pickwick Papers* on the telephone.

In an essay for a class at San Francisco State College, Cereghino (say chair-a-*gee*-no) was writing: "If man persists in his competitive patterns which serve at present to enhance only his materialistic cravings, he is surely leading to a very lasting destruction. He can remedy this situation by calling forth a constructive competition, a new competitive feeling to be applied to the betterment of mankind."

His own materialistic cravings had led him into the error— he now felt—of possessing an Oldsmobile, so he bought a 1941 Plymouth. It was the car he had owned before he owned the $74,000. Maybe it would revive the memories. There had to be a reason. He tried to walk it out, to talk it out, to write it out.

The winter baseball news was full of hints of competitive patterns—hiring, firing, deal, and swap. In San Francisco the Giants were preparing to abandon Seals Stadium, where the farmhand had played his first game of professional baseball. Lefty O'Doul, who was the farmhand's first manager, and Charlie Silvera, who was his last, were competing in the DiMaggio Invitational at nearby Lake Merced. Dominic DiMaggio, in town for the event, announced that the American League was "stagnating." Branch Rickey, arriving for a visit with his daughter in Los Altos, said the minor leagues, too, were stagnating, and blamed it on the "incredible stupidity" of the majors. In the East, Joe Cronin, who had struggled upward from San Francisco sandlots (he was tapped for the big leagues by scout Joe Devine, who also signed Cereghino), became president of the American League, and Casey Stengel was saying that Mickey Mantle could earn $125,000 if only he'd straighten up and fly right. Yankee farmhands at the Richmond affiliate were threatening to strike for pensions, but the Yankee front office appeared unworried. Said one Yankee executive, "They'll all be hungry in March."

The farmhand wrote: "I enjoy reading a well-written essay. I like to sit in my study, shut away from the toils of the world."

And maybe it was his mother whose answer came closest. "There's an Irish expression," says Eddie's mother (she was a Quillinan), "where we say of somebody that he's got the wee bean in his tail. Somebody that wants to haul the whole sheboodle somewhere else, somebody that can't stay put, always moving, always traveling, then you've got the wee bean in your tail. That's what it meant in our house."

In baseball the nearest equivalent is "desire," the relentless will to succeed and to win from baseball the rewards the game can bring. The word is commonly employed by baseball scouts, but although they can name it they have never been able to scout it. Hollis Thurston, who bid for Cereghino on behalf of the White Sox in 1951, has said: "Eighty percent of it is desire. You can't scout that." It cannot be weighed or measured or computed or entered into columns of statistics. Desire is invisible, the wee bean that may have been there, or may not, or maybe was there and went away.

When bonus baby Cereghino was seventeen he was nothing but desire. When the New York Yankees passed $74,000 into his hand they bought a 200-pound right-handed pitcher whose control was good, who could field his position ably— though he was no "cat"—who was diligent in backing up the bases and who was also reasonably effective at bat. In the language of the craft, he was "sneaky fast," which is to say that his fast ball was deceptive, as opposed to overpowering:

He depended for effectiveness more upon the motion with which he threw than upon the actual speed of the ball.

He was the last prospect to be signed by Joe Devine, who died soon thereafter. Devine, perhaps the game's most renowned scout, had been prohibited by baseball law from talking terms with high school athletes, but nothing had prevented Devine, a San Franciscan, from forming a warm friendship with the Cereghino family and observing Eddie at the legal distance. The boy appeared to have his heart set upon a career in baseball. He played ball all day on the school grounds at Jefferson High, half a block from the Cereghino residence (sometimes between innings he came running home for lunch), his personal habits were admirable, his family life was serene, and his record of performance was infinitely encouraging: In 158 high school and sandlot games he had pitched seven no-hitters. His overall ERA was a phenom's 0.080. Once, in a single game, he struck out twenty-two, once twenty-one, and three times he struck out twenty. In his final year at Jefferson High he won thirteen games, lost two.

Beginning in Eddie's sophomore year the scouts had been gathering together in the grandstand at Jefferson High. When graduation day came and Eddie was legal, they gathered together on his doorstep. Branch Rickey Jr. was there for the Pirates, Hollis Thurston for the White Sox. The Red Sox and the Phillies were there, the Tigers and the Indians, the Braves (then of Boston) and the Giants (then of New York). "Listen to their offers," Joe Devine advised the Cereghinos, "then phone me."

On June 8, 1951, six days before graduation, Eddie had pitched and won a high school all-Star game at Seals Stadium. He also hit a home run. Voted the game's outstanding participant, he was awarded a free trip to the World Series, and the price of his signature was said to be $100,000. The scouts scoffed. Even so, when Eddie pitched a week later at Funston Field—in the DiMaggio neighborhood—the scouts were there. Playing for the Pomona Tile Company, he set down Johnny's Billiards 7–1, struck out twenty-two, and gave up only one hit. His price was now said to be $200,000. "Now look," said the scouts, "the lights weren't so good out there, you're not overpowering fast, you're only sneaky fast, you're no cat, the high school competition you played against wasn't the best, your legs are heavy and you're vibrating with baby fat." They retreated to obscure corners of the city.

The bonus baby had learned something about competitive patterns. With his dad, he also retreated, emerging after three days of seclusion at the summer home of relatives to discover that the offers now were firm. After he had heard them he telephoned Joe Devine, and Joe topped the best.

Bonus baby Cereghino said, "Being a Yankee? That's the best deal of all."

"I'd advise against a Cadillac," said Joe Devine, who thought it was *nouveau riche* and un-Yankee, and the bonus baby traded off his 1941 Plymouth for an Oldsmobile 88. "What would you say," asked Devine, "if instead of starting out somewhere down in C ball you were to start right here with the Seals?"

"I'd say I'll give it a try," the bonus baby said.

The proposal appealed equally to the treasurer of the San Francisco Seals, for when Cereghino showed up for the ball game on Sunday, July 1, more than 12,000 fans were there. It was the season's largest crowd (the Seals were in the cellar). His dad and his mother and his girl Janet were there. Everybody he had ever known was there. He kissed his mother at the rail beside the dugout, and he took the mound. The enemy was San Diego, and when Eddie hitched his pants they called from the bench, "Attaboy, Mr. Brinks, hike up them moneybelts." One out away from victory, he lost. He drank root beer in the clubhouse afterward. Manager Lefty O'Doul sent him to MacIntosh for a $155 suit of big league clothes.

Next Sunday the crowd was 14,000, and the bonus baby, pitching the distance, snapped Seattle's winning streak at nine. By August he was a regular starter, and when the season ended on September 9 he owned a very decent won-lost record of 4–6 with a club which finished in last place, twenty-five games from the top. Lefty O'Doul was fired.

In his new green Oldsmobile 88, bonus baby Cereghino rolled on down to Los Angeles, where he distributed $500 in two weeks, part of it in wining and dining a girl named Christine Reed, whose photograph he had admired on the cover of the August issue of the *Ladies' Home Journal*. He installed the name Chris in chrome on the side of his Oldsmobile. In a postcard from Catalina Island to his friend Milton Tromborg, Cereghino described the ease of life in southern California. Tromborg, whose desire it was to become a journalist, caused an item to appear in the public prints to the effect that Cereghino's four-year romance with Janet had now "faded into obscurity."

Later in the month he left by Western Pacific for his free trip to the World Series. He had never been out of California. In New York he was housed at the Biltmore, bought a sixty-five dollar set of electric trains and saw Bobby Thomson hit his historic home run. He was a guest in the Yankee clubhouse. At the Series, when Lefty O'Doul asked him if he'd care to tour Japan, he said he would. Yankee physician Sidney Gaynor pumped his arms full of overseas shots, and he was soon aboard Pan American, Orient-bound. His traveling companions, in addition to O'Doul, included such hitherto remote and mythical heroes of the Western world as Joe and Dominic DiMaggio, Eddie Lopat, Billy Martin, Ferris Fain, and Mel Parnell. In Tokyo, General and Mrs. Ridgway requested the pleasure of Eddie's company for cocktails at the embassy, and he bought silk, lamps, cedarwood, chinaware, more electric trains, and cigarette lighters that never lit. Anyhow, he didn't smoke. There were lots of pretty girls on the Ginza, and his fellow players dubbed him "Ginzateer." Lefty O'Doul donated 100,000 yen to a private school for mentally retarded children.

Thus, within five months of his high school graduation, he had become rich, he had traveled internationally, and he had seen heroes in their underwear. To a quick-witted boy it may have seemed that he had seen enough, even so soon, of cash and fame. At any rate, when he returned to San Francisco he removed Chris from the side of his automobile, "touched it up," and bought a diamond ring for Janet. The bulk of his fortune he invested in nonspeculative stock: "Widows' and orphans' stock," he calls it, and he still has it.

How soon would he be a Yankee?

"There's no man alive," Devine had once remarked, "who can say just how any player is going to develop. Who can tell how Cereghino's legs are going to be or what he'll grow into? Not me, and I just paid out a lot of the New York Yankees' money to sign him. I'm taking a gamble, that's all. Some of these guys will tell you they can see whether the pitcher shows the seam of a ball on his curve at night. At night I can't even see the pitcher's glove, much less the ball he's holding. There's nobody that sharp."

The record books reveal that on the following July 12, with a seven-hit victory over the Columbus Redbirds, bonus baby Cereghino won his tenth consecutive game for the Kansas City Blues, a Yankee farm. But throughout the rest of the season he did not win another—he lost eight. Back in 1953 for another try in Triple-A he had won two and lost four by June, when he was shipped down to the Binghamton Triplets in the Class A Eastern League. An 11–3 record here earned him, in 1954, a new Triple-A test. At Kansas City again, he defeated the heat, which had troubled him, and the mosquitoes ("If you didn't keep moving they'd carry you off"), but he couldn't defeat rival clubs more often than they defeated him—he was 11–14 on the season. "Then they started moving me around from club to club. I can't blame the Yankee organization; I was the productive factor but I wasn't producing. It was a bad sign for a fellow. It was becoming nothing but picking up and running, my trunk was always packed, I told myself Always Be Prepared." By midseason 1955 he had won two games and lost five in relief for Sacramento. He was sent to Toronto. "By the time I got up there, Toronto didn't need a pitcher." He was assigned to Denver, where in the season's final month he appeared in four games, pitched three innings, struck one man out, walked nobody, and neither won nor lost. In 1956 at Richmond his ERA was 4.39 (three won, nine lost). In 1957 he pitched a total of only seven innings. Last year, in

Double-A baseball at New Orleans, he won nine games. He lost sixteen.

Then if it wasn't heat and it wasn't mosquitoes, what was it? Desire?

It wasn't that he didn't develop. Catcher Roy Partee, who played at Kansas City, recalls that Cereghino developed "a real good curve ball" to go with his sneaky fast. But he couldn't win with it. "He worked hard," says Partee. "He was out there running every night."

There was talk, when he won ten straight in 1952, of his going up to the big show, but although the call never came he worked spiritedly ahead. It was never charged against the farmhand that he dogged it, that he didn't hustle, that he wouldn't listen, or that he couldn't learn.

Nobody ever said he lacked "tools." "What impressed me," Devine had said after Funston Field, "was his coolness. There were 3,000 people watching him, and more than a dozen scouts. That could have flustered a lot of kids. He's big. That's good, too. He has fine control for a youngster, a fine type of boy, goes to church, has a good disposition. Those things are what want to make you gamble."

Nobody ever said he lacked "attitude." "All ears and eyes," said Lefty O'Doul after Seals Stadium. "Quick on the uptake. He watches the game. He doesn't stand with his hands on his hips. He's not too dignified to stoop for a bunt. He calls me 'Mr. O'Doul,' though he doesn't bow and scrape. They tell me he rated A's and B's on his report card, and I can believe it. He doesn't roll his eyes in space."

He listened to O'Doul, to Partee and Mickey Owen at Kansas City, to the late Phil Page at Binghamton, to Eddie Lopat at Richmond, Ralph Houk at Denver, and Yankee tutors in Florida for seven springs.

Last summer, at New Orleans, he shared an apartment with Walt Kellner (brother of the Cardinals' Alex). Kellner cooked, Cereghino washed the dishes and when they laid aside their aprons Cereghino read aloud—"hour on hour at night"—from *A History of Civilization* (Brinton, Christopher, and Wolff, volume two). "Then we'd discuss it, and Walt would ask me things, piercing questions I couldn't answer. I hate like hell when people ask me questions I can't answer." Toward the end of answering some of their own questions they planned to erect a chart on their wall, an outline of the major causes and battles of World War I. "Walt was going to take the battles, I was going to take the causes. He didn't care too much for the causes."

Unfortunately, before the project was far advanced, Kellner was shipped to the Texas League. Manager Charlie Silvera quit. And Ed Cereghino, his mind turning upon causes, returned to San Francisco and to his winter of review.

He remembered—now that he set about to stir up the memories—that as early as 1953, before he was twenty and before he had yet really had a bad year, he found himself carrying books with his gear. In that year it was Burns's *Western Civilizations,* a thousand-page volume which he intended to outline, although precisely why he thought it needed it he cannot tell. He had bought it in the bookshop of San Francisco State College, but why he had been on campus he cannot tell. "I went up there for no reason at all. I walked through the halls and wound up in the bookstore, and I bought it and took it with me. It was the unrevised edition." In June, in Kansas City, in an examination proctored by a high school principal, he won entrance to San Francisco State. A few days later he was farmed to Binghamton, helped to pitch the Triplets into the playoffs, and as a result was two weeks late for the beginning of the autumn semester.

"I didn't know where to start. I didn't even have a program planning sheet. Everything was jammed. I wasn't going to go to college if it was going to be this much trouble." Aware that an entering freshman was required to complete Biology I (Human Biology and Health), the farmhand wandered into a classroom conducted by Prof. Jack Hensill, who found him an empty seat. "I popped into it. I believe to this day that if it hadn't been for Dr. Hensill I wouldn't have stayed."

After that first session, Professor Hensill, by telephone, found other empty seats for Cereghino—in English 6.1; in Personal, Social, and Occupational Development ("a one-year introductory course dealing with basic concepts of psychology and stressing their applications to life problems and to occupations"); and in Culture and Society ("dealing primarily with functional and historical aspects of man as a social being"). Student Cereghino received three grades of B and one C.

Of more significance than his grades, one of his first classroom exercises reveals his unconscious attempt, in writing, to locate his truest desire. In a story entitled "The Case of Tommy Baron" he created a boy engaged in a quest for suitable labor. Tommy, who attended church regularly, decided he would be a priest in spite of all opposition. "He packed his belongings and departed. Within six months Tom was granted an entrance expense from the order of his choice. To summarize, I would like to say that Tom was a very lucky boy. Many boys in the same situation would have turned to a life of crime. Tom had the determination and has now realized his dreams. I know that if my children have a strong desire to enter a certain vocation I will be one to encourage them." For this first excursion into fiction, student Cereghino won from Prof. Sinclair Kerby-Miller, an Oxford scholar, a grade of B minus.

Every spring he went away to play baseball, and every autumn he returned to college. He had always been diligent. "When Eddie was a boy," his father remembers, "he studied by the hour. One time a teacher said something concerning his lack of penmanship, and he came home and went in that room and he didn't come out until his penmanship was perfect. After that, if there was anything the teacher wanted saved on the blackboard it was Eddie's job to write it up."

"Normally," says Principal South, stirring up the memories, "I wouldn't have expected a boy so wrapped up in baseball to have been so wrapped up in his studies. I also had Don Mossi at Jefferson. I never would have believed Don could make it in baseball, but Don made it and Eddie didn't. You never know what's inside a boy's head."

San Francisco State College, a thronging, tax-supported "streetcar college" pleasantly situated a long throw from the ocean beach, has a student population of about 11,000 and a tuition of forty-four dollars a year. Its sixty-year life has been distinguished by pioneer work in teacher education, while in the past decade it has earned a national name for audacious work in the arts. Its football coach is paid a professor's wage.

At first Cereghino felt himself to be an outsider. Since he attended classes only in half-year swoops he was continually falling behind his friends. He was older than most students and richer than most professors. All through his teens he had been led to believe that his future lay in baseball, and as a consequence it was difficult for him to visualize himself in the role of student. But the process of discovery sustained him. When, for example, the Poetry Center sponsored a reading by Marianne Moore, Cereghino recorded his own relationship to the occasion in an essay entitled "An Hour Well Spent": "Notwithstanding the inefficiency of the microphone, Marianne Moore's reading was positively exhilarating . . . I had never attended a poetry reading, for I thought these recitals were for other people. A fellow student told me, 'You do not want to read her poems, for they are too difficult to fathom.' Nothing could be farther from the truth." And when she read her "Hometown Piece for Messrs. Alston and Reese" he praised the eloquence with which a mere lady poet spoke to his own condition: She revealed in her lines, he wrote, "an understanding of the tortures and anxieties . . . of the ballplayer."

The college traditionally has placed a heavy emphasis upon close working relationships between student and teacher. Professor Hensill's hospitality was actually routine enough. "I was there, so I helped the guy. Everybody does this sort of thing for a lot of kids. In Eddie's case it was nothing special. If he thinks it was, it's only because he happened to respond to my particular brand of malarkey."

Student Cereghino was reluctant, in the beginning, to raise his voice in class, although at home, in his study, with his tobacco in his mouth, he was fluent in a manner somewhat at variance with his appearance. To Prof. Leo Cagan, onetime research scholar at the London School of Economics and Political Science, Cereghino "seemed to me at first like a C or

C-plus student. In the seventh week of the course he turned in a paper that was so advanced I told him I couldn't believe an undergraduate had written it. He was more hurt than indignant. But his later work was so good that by the end of the semester I had no doubt that paper was his."

As time passed, his confidence increased. Prof. Eleanor McCann, his instructor in English last fall, describes him as "a leader in the class. He has a lot to offer. He's a philosophical person, and he's an exceptionally nice person." And she characterizes him with the very words of Joe Devine. "Cereghino," she says, "has poise."

"Right about now," says student Cereghino, "I've got the same confidence I used to feel playing ball. I always look forward to going to school, the way I used to look forward to going to the park." On February 9, when State's spring semester began, Cereghino was enrolled. He had attended six previous semesters, but never before in the spring.

The case of Ed Cereghino—"The Case of Tommy Baron"—of course underscores a general problem facing the baseball industry. If the industry cannot scout desire, it must learn to do its scouting in terms of the impact of an era whose young men are free to select between the perils of a baseball career and the relative security of higher education. Baseball, at best, was always a risk, a dream, a gamble for glory, but the risk has proportionately enlarged. College is not only an economic necessity, but it is a force which often subdues the kind of desire baseball demands.

When Ed Cereghino found himself pursuing required academic units in Introduction to Geography (planetary geography, "maps and earth measurements") it may have begun to appear to him less and less urgent to win at baseball by rocketing a rocklike object at another man's head. Men, values, and horizons are becoming increasingly familiar to sons whose fathers never measured the earth. Last fall, for Professor McCann, Cereghino wrote: "One experiences a certain . . . exciting feeling while browsing through a library. It is a delight . . . to wade back through the ages into societies which differed so much from our present one."

Joe DiMaggio was the child of immigrants. Ed Cereghino was not. Lefty O'Doul is a restaurateur. Ed Cereghino thinks he would like to teach school. The late Tony Lazzeri, when San Francisco friends visited him in New York, flung open his closet door and exulted: "How many people you know owns this many suits!" But Cereghino's desire, a quarter of a century later, has become something else. "I want to live on a flat street with a view, and I don't want my kids running to me with questions I can't answer. I don't want to knock the world over. I don't want to fight the guy next door. I used to think an Oldsmobile was what you needed to show people something, but maybe all it shows is you're a damn fool working sixteen hours a day to pay it off."

If Ed Cereghino had never received his bonus he probably would have arrived at his decisive moment two winters earlier. Out of a sense of obligation to the New York Yankees organization, he lingered. But his quitting, at whatever point, strikes a note both sad and prophetic: he is twenty-five and he likes to play baseball, and there is no place to play.

As matters stand, when a man's desire falls short of passion there is no roster to accommodate him, for it is one of baseball's assumptions that the smaller cities of the nation can usefully exist only as way stations to the big time. And yet it is reasonably clear that the poverty of the minors has paralleled their absolute conquest by the farm system. A local public has numbly learned to resist baseball games conducted in an atmosphere increasingly barren of continuity from one impersonal season to the next. Can baseball, like some disembodied monster, survive only at the top?

The result is not simply the withering of local baseball, but a forecast of the death of the game itself. If there is to be a great poetry, said Whitman, there must be great audiences, too. Why not, then, the aggressive encouragement of a midsummer season? The fans of smaller cities, where baseball wanes, may happily cultivate enthusiasms for familiar returning faces, for college boys encouraged by local applause to play well—and who will do so in spite of B's and C's on their big league report cards. Fans have never bought tickets so much to see skill as personality, and they will form affections for ballplayers who, like student Cereghino, drive Plymouths without shame—even for players who, if they do not become so rich as Mickey Mantle, at least weren't hungry in March.

LOU GEHRIG—THE IRON MAN

◇ No HERO WAS ever so silent. No handsome, beautiful, rugged, muscular man was ever less susceptible to romance, less vulnerable to scandal. No man ever lent himself less to publicity or controversy, and no man ever played baseball more earnestly for its own sake.

Gehrig never spoke a memorable sentence until his doleful end, standing up dying before 60,000 baseball fans, and then he spoke two. He said first, "Though I may have been given a bad break, I consider myself the luckiest man on the face of the earth." One remembers the lone voice echoing against the girders among the silent thousands on that Appreciation Day. If we do not remember the voice first-hand, we remember the voice of Gary Cooper in the motion picture *The Pride of the Yankees.*

As a ballplayer his skill was incomparable, and he was lucky enough to play all his major-league career for baseball's biggest winner. It was easy, it was fun, he was rich, he was famous, and he said to a sportswriter on Gehrig Appreciation Day, "It's going to be very hard to leave all this." That was his second memorable sentence.

Gehrig played baseball across two decades and never made an enemy. One historian has written with probable truth, "Gehrig never yelled a bad word at anybody in his life." The Baseball Writers of America in a moment of unprecedented consensus and speed voted him into the Hall of Fame within weeks of his retirement.

In their own way the owners of the Yankees loved him well. In 1927, when the Yankees paid Babe Ruth $70,000, they paid Gehrig only $8,000, although Gehrig was Most Valuable

Player in that very year of Ruth's sixty home runs. But nobody, after all, paid to see *him* play—it was the Babe who drew the thousands; Yankee Stadium was "the house that *Ruth* built." "Not Babe Ruth but Lou Gehrig was the most productive hitter in Yankee history," sportswriter Jack Mann has written. "Lou Gehrig was a great baseball player. But never in baseball history have so many been so unexcited about so much."

Everyone merely *expected* Gehrig to be there, and to do well. He played every day. As a boy he had never missed school, and as a man he never missed a day of baseball. When he withdrew himself in 1939 from the Yankee lineup, he had not missed a game in fourteen years. He was called "The Iron Man" by newsmen—sometimes "Iron Horse" (Babe Ruth called him "The Dutchman")—and nobody had ever been so regular, so sober, so faithful to his wife, so deeply in love with his mother and his father.

He was an Establishment rock. By 1939 he had been suffering off and on for several years from "lumbago," as he preferred to call it. His affliction was in fact lateral sclerosis, a disease that causes degeneration of the spinal cord. Had he played less regularly, with less fidelity to his employers, he might have lived into comfortable retirement. Instead, he died at thirty-eight.

Gehrig's story was the American immigrant tale writ large, Horatio Alger on the hoof.

Henry Louis Gehrig was that rarity—a New York Yankee from New York City. He was born in 1903 in the Yorkville section of Manhattan, child of German immigrants. June was his month: born in June, he first reported to the Yankees in June (1923), broke in as a regular player in June two years later, and died in June of 1941. His father was an ironworker, soon ailing and unemployed. Early in life Gehrig learned that economy for which Babe Ruth razzed him for ten years. Ruth's second wife wrote afterward, "Surely Babe was ridiculous when he left a ten-dollar tip where fifty cents would have been generous. But Lou's dimes were just as silly."

In Manhattan, for the High School of Commerce, Gehrig

played football and soccer as well as baseball. He was a member of the championship Commerce High team that journeyed to Chicago for an intersectional game with Lane Tech. In Chicago, playing at Wrigley Field, Gehrig walloped his first home run in a big-league stadium.

As a high-school boy Gehrig worked with his father and mother as housekeepers and kitchen crew for Sigma Nu fraternity at Columbia University. The diligent boy did his homework on streetcars. But perhaps because of this experience Columbia became a reality to him—a great university was only people, after all. Gehrig became a student there, and on the college baseball team he played first base, outfield, and pitcher.

Now occurred the only clouded moment of his life. During one summer Gehrig played semiprofessional baseball in Hartford, Connecticut, under the thin disguise of the name "Lewis." His amateur standing was threatened. Gehrig pleaded ignorance of the rules (why then had he assumed a false name?), showed how he had momentarily come under bad influences, sought forgiveness, and was soon reinstated by the Columbia Athletic Council. It was his only known wickedness, although it is also true that after he had become a Yankee, he and other young men were detained by police one night for playing ball noisily on a residential street.

At one point Columbia Lou Gehrig tried out for the New York Giants. The Giants were then the dominant New York team, and it is possible that they would have remained so had manager John McGraw seized Gehrig on the spot. Legend has it that McGraw was prejudiced against college players. At any rate, he was unimpressed by Gehrig. "Get him out of here," he said. Gehrig, for his part, expressed disgust with McGraw's obscene language. "I wouldn't want to play for him," the young man exclaimed.

When Paul Krichell, scout for the Yankees, signed Gehrig, he told Yankees business manager Ed Barrow, "I think I've found another Babe Ruth." At the Yankees' training camp in New Orleans, Gehrig was so depressed by the low state of his cash that he was even on the verge of taking a part-time job as a waiter when a more worldly teammate warned him against subjecting himself to the ridicule of his fellow Yankees. The plight of his parents worried him, then and always. He was subject to fits of homesickness. He missed his mother's pickled eels.

But he persisted. He was assigned by the Yankees to the Eastern League, where he played two years for Hartford, city of his former crime. In the spring of 1925 he traveled north from training camp with the Yankees as their reserve first baseman. The club's regular first baseman was Wally Pipp, a fourteen-year veteran who had twice led the American League in home runs.

On the first day of June, Gehrig pinch-hit for shortstop Pee Wee Wanninger, and on the following day manager Miller Huggins thought to give Pipp a day's rest. Gehrig played the whole game. The new young man delivered three hits in five times at bat. He had now played for the Yankees in two consecutive games, and he was to continue to play for them every day until his body could play no longer. He played 2,130 games without rest.

Once, when Gehrig was ill, he batted as leadoff man and withdrew from the game, keeping his record intact. For that half inning of his life he was officially listed as shortstop. (Another Yankee shortstop, Lyn Lary, once deprived Gehrig of a home run by wandering from the basepaths while Gehrig was running out his homer. Gehrig was ruled "out" for passing Lary, who explained that he thought the ball had been caught. What was one home run more or less? In his career Gehrig struck 493 regular-season home runs.)

If it is true, as Mr. Leo Durocher has asserted, that nice guys finish last, why did Lou Gehrig so often finish first? Did some ferocious aggression lurk beneath his apparent serenity? Lou Gehrig was unblemished; he was iron until he fell; he earned a good living playing baseball every summer; he played in seven World Series; for ten years he batted after Babe Ruth, whose excesses and appetites for food, drink, women, money, and public exhibition Gehrig viewed without comment; he himself was wild about fishing; he succeeded Ruth in 1934 as captain of the Yankees.

We know that he played in pain without complaint. His body appeared supreme. He was Adonis. Gehrig's perfection of form suggested a perfection of technique. He was one of the mightiest batsmen of the century, but he was also a graceful first baseman and a fast, alert runner on the bases. Those of us who grew up with the New York Yankees of the 1930s imagined that he was indestructible. But Adonis was slain in his youth.

BASEBALL'S ONE-LINERS

◇ IMAGINE THAT YOU are a boy playing baseball. Imagine that your name is Jimmy Butterman. You live in Middle America in a small city called Zygmont. You are eleven years old and already a kind of veteran of baseball, for you have been playing the game since you were three, when your father began to coach you. You are in sixth grade. You are a first baseman on your Little League team. People in Zygmont tell you that you are an excellent player and that at the rate you are going you will certainly be an asset to the team at Zygmont High. Coach Ripley himself comes one day to Little League Field to see you play. He keeps his eye on you thereafter.

In the spring of your first year in high school you "try out" for the baseball team. This trying-out is rather a formality because coach Ripley has known all along that you are going to be his first baseman and he is very happy. This is a problem solved for him.

At Zygmont High you set several records. During your last two years you lead the county in slugging percentage. You are a classy fielder, too—you really know how to cover that base. You are twice all-County.

You bat left-handed. Coach Ripley has strongly suggested that you might be smart to try batting right-handed, too, and you have tried it but you feel awkward and insecure. You think, *Forget it, everything's been working so far. Why fix it when it ain't broke?*

You were never one of the grammatical crowd. You were good at arithmetic. In one of those Aptitude Tests you came up Banker. You began to have the feeling, though, that you were never going to need grammar or arithmetic. Everyone told you your future was baseball, which seemed to describe the situation shaping up. You received fourteen college scholarship offers to which you replied with a letter of intent to Southwest.

You choose Southwest because the desert climate down there permits the university team to play an eighty-game schedule. When you are a freshman you play in twenty of them. When you are a sophomore you play in forty. When you are a junior you play in every game but two: you sit out two games with a sprained back. You bat for a high average and you crack out many extra-base hits. You run good. At your base you are both stylish and aggressive. You were never afraid of getting in front of the batted ball: all your life you carry the bruises to prove it.

Hey, why play senior year at all? The sooner you turned professional the sooner you'd start making a little money, and the sooner you made a little money the sooner you'd make a lot. Coach Skinner at Southwest thought you were making a mistake dropping out without playing your senior year, and you thought the coach had, after all, his own motives in wanting to keep you. You were beginning to observe that people weren't looking out for you as they had when you were younger. You were no kid any more. You were nineteen. You had to begin to look out for yourself.

You committed yourself to a major-league organization. You played in an instructional league and in a low minor league. You knew that although the stands were empty people were watching you, as coach Ripley had been watching you even before you entered high school. Your manager said you had a good attitude, and he sent word ahead that you also had a good bat and a good glove. You improved steadily, as you always knew you would. During your second year in professional baseball you did far better in AA than you had done in A, and in your third year, when you went up to AAA, you knew that you were three times the ballplayer you'd ever been.

Your AAA manager was a one-time big-leaguer named

Ernie Taglia. You had never heard of him. You looked him up in *The Baseball Encyclopedia.* Now that you were getting to know him you saw what a smart baseball man he was. He was terrific.

You were twenty-two years old and everybody in Zygmont was rooting for you to go the next step to the biggies. One eventful weekend your mother, your father, your sister, and your girlfriend came to watch you play and to be proud of you. Of that day you remember one moment especially. You were standing for your photograph with your family and Ernie Taglia when your dad said to Ernie, "Everybody back home is pretty sure my boy is going to make it to the big leagues." You thought so, too, and you waited to hear Ernie say so, but he did not. He slowly said to your dad, "Jimmy does everything a boy is supposed to do." Ernie had not said No but he had not said Yes, either. This was your first doubt about yourself. Not until this moment had you imagined the possibility of your not making it to the big leagues.

Up you went for the September call-up. They wanted to look you over. Maybe you'd actually get into some games, maybe you wouldn't. You mingled with big-name players. You had known a few of them in the minors when they were on their way up, and you were yet to meet some of them in the minors on their way down. They seemed glad enough to see you and to tell you what they knew. Beyond that they had a kind of Ernie Taglia reticence about them, as if they knew too much about the nature of reality to say anything for sure. Wished you luck. They did not tell you, as people in Zygmont had been telling you, that you were sure to graduate to the big leagues—wished you luck, that was as far as they'd go. Not every player on the club was friendly. If you made it up here you were going to take somebody's job.

You felt good taking batting practice. You knew what you were doing, you were never more at home in your life, never more confident of yourself than when you were standing in there with the bat hitting hard curving line drives down the right-field line and up against the fence and now and again into the seats. You had never seen such a long right-field line.

You sat on the bench until the middle of September, wondering if the skipper was ever going to send you out there so you could show him what you could do. Was the seat of your pants wearing the bench smooth or was the bench wearing out the seat of your pants? Well, you couldn't blame the skipper. The club was fighting uphill for the division and you couldn't expect them to—well, you couldn't expect them to depend on an untried factor like you, could you? But then! It is the skipper's voice. He gets your name wrong but you know who he means. "Butterfield, go play the base." You think he's mad to send you in at a time like this.

In you go. It is the bottom of the eighth inning. Two men go out. Now somebody hits a ground ball to your third baseman and your third baseman throws it to you. You have made a big-league putout. May you make ten thousand.

Soon comes your batting chance. The tying run is on first base and you are at bat. Wouldn't it be great to hit a home run down that long right-field line? Not that you were thinking those thoughts at that moment. You were going to have plenty of time to think those thoughts and many more. You never knew the name of the pitcher. It was only one more time at bat after hundreds of times at bat from Zygmont Little League to this moment, and you had no reason to believe this moment was special or pivotal to your life.

You remember only one thing. You remember that you whacked the ball pretty hard and sent a high drive to right field. You thought it was over the fence. In every park you had ever played a ball hit that well went over. No such luck today. The right-fielder caught the ball, his back against the fence.

Hey, what the hell, right? Tomorrow's another day.

But tomorrow never came. Before the skipper ever sent you scampering again into a game September was over.

In the final month of the next season you were called up again, but you did not play.

One year later you would certainly have been summoned for the September call-up but you were suffering an injured back. Your back had not troubled you since your junior year at Southwest.

You turned twenty-five. Back home in Zygmont, where you were working winters in First Town Bank & Trust, lots of people were saying to you, "It's going to be next year for sure. We know you're going to make it." You remembered that people had said the same thing the year before. You could tell when one of your bank associates was talking about you, looking your way, impressing a new customer, "He's in the big leagues, you know—almost."

On your AAA club you were now one of the veterans. You had given the organization a good first base, but you had given it all in AAA. One big-league PO! One big-league fly ball! Time was running out for you. Even as your chances lessened, your skills improved. You really and truly knew how to play baseball. You were all-around as good as the other first basemen in the organization, but somebody always had something you did not. One day in batting practice you tried hitting right-handed, as coach Ripley had advised in high school. But it was late for that.

The longer you remained in AAA the more deeply you established your identity there. You were an AAA ballplayer. You would never become anything else. These realities seemed to be governed by a timetable known to experienced men of baseball.

When, at the end of the following season, you were not selected for the call-up, you quit. No, no, no, no, that's the wrong word. You did not *quit*. You had given everything to the game over the course of your young manhood, and you had the bruises to prove it. You had been six years a professional player, and by the end you knew how to read the timetable as well as any other baseball man.

Jimmy Butterman, the imaginary first baseman from Zygmont, took his lifetime place as an item in the 3,000-page *The Baseball Encyclopedia*—"The Complete and Official Record of Major League Baseball . . . Revised, Updated & Expanded."

The Baseball Encyclopedia was first published in 1969 after intensive research, usually dependent upon computers, designed to capture a record of every person who had ever appeared in a big-league baseball game.

Organized baseball is more than a century old. For many early players the records available were necessarily fragmentary. For more recent players the records were easily accessible, but often brief. Many recent players played only one year or less. Their records, therefore, given the format of *The Baseball Encyclopedia,* could be contained in a single line. One year, one line. Ten years, ten lines.

Our imaginary first baseman from Zygmont would appear in the *Encyclopedia* as one of thousands of baseball one-liners, and he wouldn't really like to look at it. Its eternal unalterable starkness would depress him. Nevertheless, here he is:

BUTTERMAN, JAMES W. BL TL 6'3" 190 lbs.
B. Jan. 12, 1963, Zygmont, Middle America

	G	AB	H	2B	3B	HR	HR%	R	RBI	BB	SO	SB	BA	SA	PINCH HIT AB	PINCH HIT H	G	BY POS
1985	1	1	0	0	0	0	0	0	0	0	0	0	.000	.000	0	0		1B-1

Anyone with access to *The Baseball Encyclopedia* may amuse himself by choosing from thousands of eligible players his or her Major League all-Star One-Liner club. Here are my candidates, and a player pool from which the manager can develop his roster.

Manager. Baseball has produced so many one-line managers we have the luxury of choosing among men who never lost a game. Ken Silvestri managing Atlanta in 1967 won three games. His coaching staff will be Bill Burwell, who won one game as manager for Pittsburgh in 1947, and Rudy York, who had an identical record for the Red Sox in 1959.

Pitcher. Tex Hoyle's distinction is the brevity of his career. He pitched two and one-third innings in three games for the Philadelphia Athletics in 1952. He gave up nine hits. His ERA is a distressing 27.00. Earl Huckleberry won one game and lost none for the Philadelphia Athletics in 1935. He started one game but did not complete it. Huckleberry's distinction may be his position in *The Baseball Encyclopedia* between Carl Hubbell, who won more than 250 games in sixteen years, and Willis Hudlin, who won 158.

Frank Wurm walked five batters and gave up one hit and four runs in one-third of an inning with Brooklyn in 1944. His ERA is 108.00. His teammate Albert Myron Zachary fared somewhat better in the same season, giving up ten hits in ten and one-third innings, figuring in two decisions and losing both.

Catcher. Pat Kilhullen came to bat once without distinction during the game he played for Pittsburgh in 1914. In *The Baseball Encyclopedia* his entry precedes Harmon Killebrew, who played for twenty-two years. Kilhullen's record is exactly duplicated by Tom Yewcic, who came to bat once while catching in one game for Detroit in 1957.

First Base. Walter Alston struck out in his single appearance at bat in the game he played at first base for the St. Louis Cardinals in 1936. He was elected to the Hall of Fame forty-seven years later, however, after twenty-two years as manager of the Dodgers in Brooklyn and Los Angeles.

Second Base. Steve Biras batted 1.000, smacking out two hits and driving in two runs during two games for Cleveland in 1944. Tom Kane walked twice in four appearances at the plate for the Boston Braves in 1938. His inevitable nickname was Sugar. Skeeter Kell batted .221 in seventy-five games for the Philadelphia Athletics in 1952. His brother, George, played fifteen years in the same league and was elected to the Hall of Fame in 1983.

Third Base. Jim Stroner's career with Pittsburgh was sensational but short. In six games he batted .375 and drew a walk. One of his hits was a triple. Bill Doran, playing for Cleveland, batted .500 in three games in 1922. Bob Rothel, playing for the same team twenty-three years later, drew three walks while batting .200 in four games.

Shortstop. Bucky Guth scored one run in three hitless times at bat in one game with Minnesota in 1972. In 1919, Jesse Baker, playing for Washington, batted in one run with a sacrifice in his single appearance at the plate. Tommy Irwin hit once, scored one run, struck out once, and drew three walks, batting .111 in three games for Cleveland in 1938.

Outfielders. Stump Edington batted a smart .302 with sixteen hits in fifty-three times at bat for Pittsburgh in 1912.

Moonlight Graham played half an inning in right field for the New York Giants in 1905. He never touched the ball. He never came to bat. Graham was portrayed by Burt Lancaster in the film *Field of Dreams,* adapted from W. P. Kinsella's fiction *Shoeless Joe.* In Kinsella's book Graham relates his half-inning: "I'd practiced in the outfield all the time I'd been with the Giants, but it was a different matter to play it. It seemed like a mile to the infield, the batter looked like a midget, his bat a toothpick. I tried to take deep breaths and calm down, wondering what I'd do if the ball was hit my way, hoping it wouldn't be, and at the same time hoping it would . . . I kept telling myself, this is it. You've hit the top. The major leagues. You can say for the rest of your life, 'I played for the New York Giants.' . . . I bet I wasn't out in right field more than five minutes."

George Halas played six games in the outfield for the New York Yankees in 1919. He hit safely twice in twenty-two times at bat. He was afterward founder and long-time coach of the Chicago Bears football team and founder of the American Professional Football Association, forerunner of the AFL.

Drungo Hazewood drove in a run but was hitless in five times at bat in six games for Baltimore in 1980. Lou Scoffic

retired from baseball in 1936 with an impressive career aver- ·
age of .429: in four games for the St. Louis Cardinals he hit
safely three times in seven plate appearances.

But the principal trouble with one-liners is their way of making success look like failure. They make the end of a hard
struggle look like quitting. They make the player appear as if
he had been less than good—a vain, deluded fellow who
should have known better than even to try.

This is far from accurate. Regarding the multitude of one-
line players comprehending observers and baseball fans re-
tain the essential fact that these men were good baseball
players. They played a hard game well. Like Jim Butterman,
they had worked for a long time, beginning as children, to
perfect their style of play.

Then, one day they almost made it. They were there. They
were playing in the big leagues, if only for a moment, if only
Moonlight Graham's five minutes, one game, ten games, half
a season. At that point something had failed them. Perhaps
even the decision-makers who judged them were mistaken:
some One-Liners may have been judged too quick too soon.
Whatever the case, Fate and Chance stepped in. The day had
come but the hour was wrong.

My consultant, model, and inspiration for this study of the
baseball one-liner is a man who knows the feeling. Larry
Yount walked out to the pitching hill at Houston on September 15, 1971, to play in relief for the home team against Atlanta. He was twenty-one years old. In this, his first major-
league game, he was to be confronted at the bat by Ralph
Garr, Earl Williams, and Henry Aaron.

Yount threw his warm-up pitches. Then something went
wrong. His elbow "popped." Why? Perhaps he had come back
into action too fast, too soon, after a period of idleness. He
could never be sure what he had done wrong, if in fact he had
done anything. He left the game before facing the leadoff batter. However, his having been announced made his appearance official. In that moment he stepped into the record book:

his height, his weight, his handedness, his birthdate, and his birthplace pursued by a succession of expectant, waiting zeroes.

He did not appear for Houston again that year. He began the following season with Houston's AAA team at Oklahoma City, and he did very well, to begin with. He won his first four games, whereupon, for no apparent reason, "I just lost it." He continued to pitch in AAA baseball for four more years, but he was never to return to the major leagues.

Yount retains close ties to baseball as president of the Phoenix Firebirds, AAA affiliate of the San Francisco Giants, and through his working association with his brother, Robin, who has played since 1974 with Milwaukee. If at moments Larry Yount may be wistful about his vanished dream, he recognizes in his youthful experience the fundamental truth of the work ethic. "You worked hard to get there," he says. "The work ethic carries you into the other life."

And so it was over, sooner than they had hoped, for all the Jim Buttermans of America who had made a run at it, given it a try. Yet it was not as if they had not been good ballplayers, as if they had wasted our time or theirs, or as if they had been fakes or pretenders.

They ended their baseball careers "even-Steven" with the world, in a situation expressed in connection with the fictional character called Squarehead, who played so very briefly for the ball club called the Mammoths and the manager called Dutch in the novel *The Southpaw:* "Dutch give him all the chance he dared, and the record reads 10 times at bat, 1 hit, 1 home run, 1 run drove in, for a .100 average. Dutch played him 1 inning afield, and the record reads 1 putout, 1 assist, and 1 error, and the error cost a run, and the run canceled out the 1 run Squarehead batted in. So Squarehead left the Mammoths no better and no worse than he found them, even-Steven."

BAD DAYS
IN BASEBALL

TRAGEDY AS PLEASURE: GIAMATTI AND ROSE

◇ Now, LADIES AND gentlemen, let me ask you this: Why was Giamatti made commissioner instead of me? How was he prepared for that job in ways that I was not? Anything he could do I could do, too. I was the obvious choice. My general appearance could easily have lent itself to the media image of the incorruptible scholar who by temperament is also warm and jolly. I was photogenic. I could have grown a little beard like his. I too was a teacher of English. I knew the history of the baseball scandal of 1919 and I would see to it that it never happened again. I had played baseball from an early age— never a great player, to be sure, but I would have shown sufficiently good form throwing out the first ball on Opening Day. Giamatti stole my game from me, he took it away, he lived my dream.

I hit the baseball squarely and ran to the base and was praised for having done that thing so well. I remember it clearly because it was only sixty years ago on a dusty rock-strewn sandlot behind the Sheridan Gardens Apartment House in Mount Vernon, New York. I remember the fact of my having now and then hit the ball so solidly I glowed with achievement.

The rules of the game were inflexible. I soon learned them, as most boys did, by the same process all boys (and now girls, too) learned the same rules governing the same game in far-flung places, just as Peter Edward Rose, one of the most fabulous men of baseball, learned them in Cincinnati, and Angelo

221

Bartlett Giamatti, once professor of English, once president of Yale, once president of the National League, finally briefly commissioner of baseball, learned them in South Hadley, Massachusetts.

The game was over for me when I was a boy and put away childish things and took up the practical future. I was supposed to become something better—accountant, bookkeeper, lawyer, doctor, mortician, mad scientist, something admirable like that, following in the steps of industrious men of Mount Vernon who had figured out how to become something.

Dr. Giamatti (Bart, as I hear him called), two states north of me, sixteen years behind me, like me a baseball boy, fantasizer of heroic home runs struck in behalf of the Boston Red Sox, soon left the game and followed in his father's steps into teaching. The elder Giamatti taught Italian and Italian literature at Mount Holyoke College in South Hadley, Massachusetts. He had studied at Yale. His son Angelo became a student of literature at Yale, a teacher thereafter for two years at Princeton, returning to Yale in 1966 as an assistant professor, and in twelve years—almost no time at all, as such things go —he had become president of Yale University.

Imagine this, assistant professor to president in twelve years! And this is not West Skidoo College we're talking about. A writer named George Vecsey of the New York *Times,* who seems to have taken a dislike to Giamatti, has spoken of his "flair for power." I wondered about that—president at forty when he should have been, say, associate professor. Whom had he been cultivating while honest scholars did their work?

But in fact Giamatti, whatever his extraversion at Yale, provided literature with a prodigious body of scholarship as sound and as ambitious as a man might make it. His volumes, *The Earthly Paradise and the Renaissance Epic* (1966), *Play of Double Senses: Spenser's Faerie Queene* (1975), and *Exile and Change in Renaissance Literature* (1984) are wide-ranging voyages arising not only from the passion of a man to

make enduring books but from a man seeking through literature connections to ages gone by in the interest of a contemporary purpose. He valued the Renaissance for its emphasis
upon humane life. He cared nothing for mere literary pick-
ings to make a scholar's reputation with. Giamatti was a Uto-
pian, a paradise-lover, a seeker of the garden, seeker of a
pastoral community, of a benign society to which, "perhaps,"
as Henry Adams hoped, one might "be allowed to return" to
find "for the first time since man began his education among
the carnivores, . . . a world that sensitive and timid souls
could regard without a shudder."

In some way, at a moment that was right for his idealism,
he conveyed himself or was conveyed by others to the decision-makers at Yale, who declared him president.

I was one evening in Giamatti's presence, at Davenport
College at Yale, April 8, 1978, for a dinner celebrating the
eightieth birthdays of Frederick and Marian Pottle, leaders of
the wondrous enterprise known as The Yale Edition of the
Private Papers of James Boswell. For this occasion the president-designate of Yale was called upon to speak. I groaned to
think what a president-designate might say. I feared his
turning my dear tortured sick drunken promiscuous venereal
James Boswell to respectability. But Giamatti was wise, precise, and humorous. He did not falsify or inflate either Boswell or the Pottles, did not pretend to know anything he had
not known in his bones—he had not sent a work/study presi-
dential assistant to the library day before yesterday to catch
hold of amusing anecdotes of Boswell. He refrained from re-
galing us Boswellians with Sam Johnson stories. No, he was
his own man, he was fluent and brilliant and honest. I did not
quite catch his name; would not have known how to spell it
the morning after.

At the time of his appointment as president, Giamatti presented himself as one who had never had this office in mind.
He had no strategy, he said, no policy. He made a little joke
bearing consequences: all he had ever wanted to be president
of, he said, was the American League. Yale needed, he said, "a
corporate strategy . . . a policy. I, of course, had no policies.

I had a mortgage and one suit, but no policies." He visualized himself issuing the following memorandum on his first day of office, July, 1978, "to an absent and indifferent University. It read, "To the members of the University Community. In order to repair what Milton called the ruins of our grandparents, I wish to announce that henceforth, as a matter of University policy, evil is abolished and paradise is restored. I trust all of us will do whatever possible to achieve this policy objective."

In his inaugural address he viewed Yale in one respect as he had viewed the Renaissance, as a place or a time whose best hope was to unite itself with transcendent ideals: the goal of Yale should be higher than Yale. "A civilized order is the precondition of freedom, and freedom—of belief, speech, and choice—the goal of responsible order. A university cannot expound those goals and expect a larger society to find them compelling, it cannot become a repository of national hope and a source of national leadership, unless it strives to practice what it teaches. If its goals are noble, so must be its acts."

It was President Giamatti's pleasure to imagine ideal circumstances even in the presence of reality in New Haven. Yale was to have become pastures of learning, a setting characterized by harmony among its constituencies. His objective was civility. He did not expect its arrival in his own term, but he saw himself as more than merely the manager of a vast corporation: it was his imperative to enunciate the ideal, lest it be forgotten.

He distinguished between management and leadership. Management was dull stuff, leadership divine. "Management," he wrote, summing up the experience of his eight-year presidency, "is the capacity to handle multiple problems, neutralize various constituencies, motivate personnel; in a college or university it means hitting as well the actual budget at break-even. Leadership, on the other hand, is an essentially moral act, not—as in most management—an essentially protective act. It is the assertion of a vision, not simply the exercise of a style: the moral courage to assert a vision of the institution in the future and the intellectual energy to persuade the community or the culture of the wisdom and validity of the vision. It is to make the vision practicable, and compelling."

He was prepared to return to teaching. The best job he had ever had, he said, was professor of English. "Being president of a university is no way for an adult to make a living." A few weeks before his resumption of his preferred life, however, he was asked to become president of the National League of Professional Baseball Clubs—the wrong league but president all the same. He could not resist. He held this position from 1986 until April, 1989, when he was chosen by the owners of the clubs to become commissioner of baseball, the highest position in baseball, created after the Chicago White Sox gambling scandal of 1919 to preserve the good name of the sport.

When Giamatti was president of the National League the Cincinnati field manager, Pete Rose, spoke of him as a good possibility for commissioner of baseball. "I like Bart," said Rose to the New York *Times*. "In fact, I get along damn good with him. . . . I think he'd make a great commissioner. He's an intellectual from Yale, but he's very intelligent."

I don't seem to be able to establish the identity of the master of numbers who first revealed in the media the possibility that Pete Rose as player, as baseball hitter, might some day exceed the record for safe hits, established by the so-called immortal and certainly ill-tempered player named Ty Cobb, who had hit safely 4,191 times during a career ending in 1928.

It could have been Rose himself who tipped off the press regarding the notable achievement he saw in his future. He knew the uses of the press, as he knew every aspect of his business. As hitter, he was a genius at studying the ball and how it was delivered from the pitcher to home plate. Once he addressed the writer Roger Angell in the following way: "Well, I don't think there's anybody going to get me out for long . . . Nobody's got a book on me. I switch hit and I hit the ball everywhere. I can hit the fastball and the breaking ball, and I might hit you down the right-field line one time and up the other way the next time. If some pitcher's getting me out I'll do one of six things. I might move up in the box or move back. I might move away from the plate or come closer. I might choke up more or choke up less. I can usually tell what I'm doing wrong by the flight of the ball. I've seen guys play major-league ball for ten, twelve years, and if they go oh-for-fifteen they want to change their stance, like it's the end of the world. That's ridiculous. The only thing that's rough about this game is that you can't turn it on and off like a faucet. If I'm swinging good, I'll come to the park even on an off day, just to keep it going. This game is mental. There's a lot of thinking in it. You watch the pitcher from the batter's box and see what's going good for him. You watch the ball and it's sending you messages—the knuckleball don't spin, screwball's got backspin, slider's got that dot. It's easy."

Every hit was a pleasure. It was his *pleasure* to hit. It was his pleasure to blister his hands practicing batting—he hardly let a day go by without practicing. He practiced in health or exhaustion. He practiced in solitude and played before multitudes. It was his pleasure to play baseball with unfailing enthusiasm.

On the blue morning last summer when Pete Rose was exiled from baseball he reiterated his *love* for the game: his love was natural enough, for those rewards which baseball gave him he could not have gained another way. He had once loaded railroad boxcars at the Cincinnati Union Terminal. "The major leagues is my home," he said. "It's all I've ever wanted to do in my life. I can't think of a single thing wrong with the game of baseball. It's clean and exciting, and it gives a guy like me a big chance to make a big man of himself."

In the big league he played first base, second base, third base, left field, and right field. This is virtually impossible to do. But he was a team player, not alone a careering specialist. He seldom missed a game. He cared for himself. He also cared for others. Some of his best friends were black. He set all sorts of exotic records—played more games than anybody else, played in more *winning* games than anybody, came to bat more often than anyone, hit 200 hits in a season more often than anyone, and so forth and so forth reckoned into the thousands. He amassed a fortune. He advertised Wheaties. Pleasure lay in things money could buy. He owned tons of cars and horses. He enjoyed gambling. He was a family man and yet not narrowly monogamous: his second wife said, "It was frightening to go into . . . marriage with someone like Pete, with everyone wanting him. I have to accept the fact that there are women out there who don't care that he's married."

In 1978, when Bart Giamatti became president of Yale, Pete Rose was in his sixteenth year as a player for Cincinnati. Rose was a household name and a household face. Giamatti, on the other hand, described himself as a household name only in his own household.

Seven years later—1985—Giamatti's penultimate year at Yale, Pete Rose had become playing manager of the Cincinnati Reds. Before the season began he required ninety-five hits to break Ty Cobb's record. The media gathered every day in greater force to follow him with stories and pictures to the end of his quest. On the day before Opening Day, "I told my players . . . Sure, going after the record would cause distractions, but I told them to have a lot of fun with it, too. The crowds will be large and there will be a lot of excitement. The electricity should help them. I also told them I'm just like every other player on the team—two arms, two legs and 4,000 hits!"

Every day his picture was in the newspaper, every day on the screen. How many did he hit today and how many more must he hit to break Ty Cobb's record? When will he do this great thing?

On May 5 he banged out three hits and was now only seventy-five hits behind Ty Cobb. "I'm swinging the bat real good right now." He'd been swinging the bat real good for years and years. The *Sporting News* had named him Player of the Decade for the 1970s, and here he was in 1985. He began the month of June with two hits. On the second day of June he got three hits.

On the last day of June he won the game for his Reds with

a hit in the ninth inning. He could hit blind: "This was a tricky game because it started at 4:05 in the afternoon. They did that because they had a concert after the game and the musicians said they couldn't play with the sun shining on their instruments. So they made us go through two-thirds of the game in twilight time. That's the truth. When I hit off Gossage, I couldn't see anything."

On July 18 he played in the annual all-Star game for the sixteenth time, throwing out the first ball for the game at the request of the then-commissioner, Peter Ueberroth. Ueberroth described Rose shortly thereafter as "a dedicated ambassador of good will for baseball [who] understood the significance of being a role model for children. . . . I was immediately won over by his spirit, the joy with which he played the game, and the wild abandon of youth that has never left him."

On the last day of July Rose got two hits and was twenty-five behind Ty Cobb. On August 17 and 18 he gathered five hits in two days and gave many interviews to agencies of the media. A reporter for the Cincinnati *Post* asked him to list and discuss his ten most memorable hits.

On September 8 in Chicago he tied Ty Cobb's record, and on September 11 in Cincinnati he surpassed it. A journalist wrote: "It was all over. Rose ran to first base with his usual vigor and rounded the bag as flashbulbs turned Riverfront Stadium into a light show. Rose's fifteen-year-old son Petey led the surge from the Cincinnati dugout. He had now hit more hits than any man: 4,192 . . . A bright red Corvette, with Ohio license 'PR 4192,' was driven onto the field and presented to Rose. Marge Schott, owner of the Reds, hugged him and planted a kiss or two on his cheek. Then, Rose became a lonely, confused figure as the ovation swelled. 'I didn't know what to do,' he said later, 'I've never been on a ball field and not known what to do.' "

Let's glance again at that bright red Corvette. Rose had been fleetingly distressed by the simultaneous public appearance of the automobile and the woman who owned the Cincinnati Reds. It was a *post hoc* illusion, the impression it gave was that it was she who presented Rose with the car, but it was not she, it was someone else. She was taking credit for something she had not done. He had never admired corporate managers nor ever concealed his distaste for them. He was strong for the players' union. In old-time baseball talk he was something of a bolshevik.

Now, ladies and gentlemen, let me ask you this: why is Pete Rose so much more celebrated than I? He became, like Giamatti, just what I wanted to be. I could have become a great baseball hitter if I had not been so hard-pressed by my family to prepare for livelihood. Doesn't anybody remember those solid sandlot singles of mine? Why doesn't the media follow me around keeping track of my achievement day by day, my statistics, the consecutiveness of my performance, my ten most memorable paragraphs, the ingenious ways in which I overcome difficult problems: this smooth essay you glide across required weeks and weeks of days and nights to write. I did not perfect my swing overnight. Pete Rose makes me feel that my own life is wasted, my wealth so meager: he owns tons of horses while I own but a single cat. He makes me ashamed of my anonymity. Nobody recognizes me on the street. A park is named for him, a street is named for him. When he is not driving his red Corvette he receives if he wants it *a free rental car from Hertz for life,* unless, I suppose, Hertz changed its mind when Rose went down. I would much rather be Pete Rose than Hertz the rented car man. I think of his pleasures, how much and how many he owns of everything, how far he travels, how free he goes, how many women long for him—women out there who don't care that he's married—how much money he has put away in safe places. No parks or streets are named for me. I thought we were a fair-minded nation—but is this what we Americans call *fair*?

Of course we all know or remember how the summer of 1989 was different from the summer of 1985. The case of Pete Rose had come to our notice in February, "when baseball received firm allegations," said Mr. Giamatti, "that Mr. Rose bet on baseball games and on the Reds' games. Such grave charges could not and must never be ignored." In March a special counsel for the commissioner began a formal investigation of the allegations. In early May counsel completed his preparation of a report of 225 pages "accompanied by seven volumes of exhibits" leading to the conclusion that Pete Rose had bet on baseball games. For his alleged offenses Rose could be banished from baseball.

A meeting on the evidence among Rose and Giamatti and their lawyers and advisors was scheduled for May, postponed, rescheduled for June, postponed again. It never occurred. Rose went to court to challenge Giamatti's authority, first to a friendly court in Cincinnati, later to a firmer court in Columbus. Simultaneously former friends or associates of Rose—*alleged* friends, *alleged* associates I suppose I should say—were on trial for one thing or another, weaving the famous name of Pete Rose through various proceedings.

It was a big show, it was the purest *pleasure* to follow, it was theater, after all, *tragedy*—we all recognized it as tragedy and gravely mentioned it in that respectful way—it was great stuff like other recent tragedies we all enjoyed so much, starring such prominent actors as Richard Nixon in Watergate, Spiro Agnew in Vice-presidential Bribery, Oliver North in Iran-Contra, God's TV evangelists in Thefts and Adulteries, Jim Wright of Texas in The Speaker's Expulsion, Evan Meacham of Arizona in The Plundering Governor, Leona Helmsley in The Hotel Queen on and on to the depths of larceny.

A friend has suggested to me the German word *schadenfreude,* in translation "the happiness . . . the delight . . . the *pleasure* with which we regard the misfortunes of others." And we can easily recall that memorable and amusing evening, not so long ago—19 October 1769—Boswell and his pal Sam Johnson "talking of our feeling for the distresses of others." "Why, Sir," said Johnson, ". . . it is greatly exaggerated." "But suppose now, Sir," Boswell replied, "that one of your intimate friends were apprehended for an offense for which he might be hanged." JOHNSON: "I should do what I could to bail him, and give him any other assistance; but if he were once fairly hanged, I should not suffer." BOSWELL: "Would you eat your dinner that day, Sir?" JOHNSON: "Yes, Sir, and eat it as if he were eating it with me. Why, there's Baretti, who is to be tried for his life tomorrow, friends have risen up for him on every side; yet if he should be hanged, none of them will eat a slice of plum-pudding the less. Sir, that sympathetic feeling goes a very little way in depressing the mind."

The drama of Pete Rose carried me to places I could not have gone unchaperoned, it introduced me to betting book-ies and immense thick wads of cash and men called street-enforcers who would break your bones—break even Pete Rose's precious baseball-playing bones—for debts dishonored, tuned me in *via* taped telephone conversations to men and women betraying one another, to the music of the trapped criminal singing to save his skin, conveyed me to hideaway saloons for illicit meetings in public lavatories smelling of brain-destroying drugs, to federal code names attached to Pete Rose like number 14 to his uniform, to tape recorders wired to informants, to steroids. All this crime and punish-ment was served to me for my entertainment with my morn-ing coffee, in my car radio; this is the literature of the com-muter train, the epic oral invocation of the office.

One of our chief pleasures is to see high-born mighty men and women brought down. Therefore a chief element of Amer-ican tragedy is the downfall of the mighty whom we have envied for their power, their wealth, their skills, their fame. On August 25, 1989, Pete Rose was exiled from baseball by Commissioner Giamatti—this "sad end of a sorry episode," the commissioner called it. Pete Rose gone! He who had tor-mented me for more than two decades with his superiority, his fame, his wealth—he who had lived that life of athletic excellence really meant for me—now at last was banished from the kingdom.

Perhaps we remember the standard schoolbook definition of Greek tragedy. The protagonist falls from happiness to misfortune as a result of his own tragic flaw. He falls from a high station of authority. He elicits from the audience pity and terror. He suffers retribution and the displeasure of the gods.

No teacher of literature in any school I attended had ever made tragedy clearer for me. Never had I so keenly felt its truth: tragedy is pleasure. The American chorus, the press, the bloke in the street were mercilessly impatient: public anger took the form of condemning Rose not so much for his crime as for his litigious delay. Justice should speed around the track like an Indianapolis racing car. Americans love capital cases, finding pleasure in executions. The public, our own Greek chorus, even in advance of the judges, feels itself in possession of sufficient evidence, and clamors for action. Due process is for the birds.

On the morning he exiled Rose, Giamatti described in remarkable phrases the terms of Rose's possible readmission to the kingdom: it was the "burden" of Pete Rose, he said, "to show a redirected, reconfigured, rehabilitated life." Yet, though Rose was gone the drama was undone. The gods were still displeased. Giamatti, too, was culpable—young president of Yale, young commissioner of baseball, he had served not only the idealism of the Renaissance but the corporate interests of America. It was to become *his* burden, in the eight days of life remaining to him, beneath the pressure and fatigue and tension and excitement of this crisis of his life, to confront in his secret heart the sources of his zeal.

Was Rose's betting really a crime? Rose had not violated public law. He had violated only a corporation rule whose object was corporate self-perpetuation. Rose, according to the commissioner, had threatened "the game's authenticity, honesty and coherence." "I believe," said Mr. Giamatti, that "baseball is a beautiful and exciting game, loved by millions —I among them—and I believe baseball is an important, enduring American institution. It must assert and aspire to the highest principles—of integrity, of professionalism, of performance, of fair play within its rules."

And who are these virtuous owners of baseball represented by the commissioner? Organized Baseball, as it is called, is a federation of leagues of corporations whose business is baseball. These men and women, from the accounts of many witnesses, love their money and despise their players. "The only owner I ever knew who gave a damn about his players was Bill Veeck," wrote the late Hank Greenberg, big-league slugging star of the 1930s and 1940s. "There was no integrity at all among the owners . . . It was pitiful the way they treated the Babe [Ruth] and guys like Jimmie Foxx and other great ballplayers. Baseball was a cold, cruel business. There was no sport in it when you could no longer produce. The public looked upon it as the great American sport, but the owners had a different feeling about the game." For example, less than a week after Rose's expulsion, after nearly four years of scrimmage in court, the owners of major-league baseball clubs were found guilty of colluding to deprive 139 baseball players of $10.5 million. This was not the first collusion case settled in favor of the players, and others now in litigation are likely to arrive at similar verdicts.

"Let no one think that it did not hurt baseball," Mr. Giamatti said of the Rose affair. Pete Rose's betting can ruin baseball corporations but cannot ruin baseball. The first and ultimate pleasure of baseball is the pleasure the boy or girl feels on the sandlot when he/she smacks the ball so solidly, or makes a leaping catch to the cheers of her/his mates. Those are the pleasures no betting scandal can kill, for boys can always get themselves together with bats and balls, and rocks for bases, and start this whole thing all over again. The living sport of baseball had not been threatened: only the corporation had been threatened.

"I don't abuse my body," the banished Rose once said, "I'm not a smoker or a drinker . . . I keep myself fresh. I sleep until twelve, one o'clock in the afternoon. I don't walk around much days—I save my legs. I go easy on the movies and television to save my eyes. In the summer you never see me sitting by the side of a pool much. Sitting in the sun all day takes the strength out of you. And none of that hamburger stuff for me. I eat good, thick steaks."

Giamatti smoked two packages of cigarettes a day. Smoking, he said, was his "primary vice." If Rose gambled at baseball Giamatti gambled at tobacco and lost, depriving his family of a father and a husband. What could he have done? Not so easy to redirect, reconfigure, rehabilitate one's life! Giamatti, like Rose, fell from high station, from authority to misfortune, delivering upon himself his own retribution. Richard Ellmann has written: "Tragic heroes in pursuing their destiny to the end, make death their accomplice rather than their adversary."

For me, happy playgoer, catharsis achieved, pity and terror satisfied, Rose brought down, Giamatti brought down, gods of power and fortune reduced to equality with me, no experience of theater could have rewarded me with greater pleasure. This is the pleasure tragedy brings us.

ROSE'S FATE UPROOTS FAN'S ILLUSION

◇ THE THING BASEBALL fans seemed to forget all along was that this was really harder on Pete Rose than it was on the fans themselves.

The case had lingered for months, hanging over the fans since spring training—ages ago. The whole matter so impeded the fan's proper appreciation of the season that he was often heard to say he no longer cared so much how it came out as he merely wished it were over.

Rose's fate was not only uncertain but it was of a different quality of uncertainty. This was no simple question of whether an injured player was likely to return to the lineup. Rose's disability was something else, it was moral, it was spiritual, so troubling, so confusing that the fan didn't know whether he wanted Rose at all. The drama was unclear.

The fan condemned Rose for dragging things along. The fan expected Rose to resolve the case, as in fact he could have by surrendering to the commissioner. But Rose declined to surrender as he had declined all his life to surrender to the circumstances and limitations of the game itself.

Rose had never been perceived as a schoolboy wonder at baseball. It had been said of him when he was a mere prospect that he wasn't likely to amount to much, that he did not appear to be a natural ballplayer. And when the veterans saw him play they named him for the quality of his presumably talentless ambition: Charlie Hustle.

For his refusal to surrender to life's limitations in happier

235

years, Rose had been cheered and rewarded. But for his refusal now, at the darkest turn of his career, to surrender to
the tidy bearded figure called commissioner, he was accused
by the fan of stubbornly delaying the outcome of things, of
prolonging uncertainty, of stretching suspense beyond endur-
able limits.

Rose had taught the fan to expect him to pursue every
twisting fly ball into whatever treachery of the fences, and to
run out every batted ball. The fan made the mistake of expecting of Rose that he have a character equal to his talent.

As a player Rose lived beyond even his own dream. He
proved to the fan that he was not only great but verifiably the
greatest, statistically, arithmetically (here was language the
fan understood), having banged out more base hits than any
man who ever lived.

The standard Rose set for himself as a player was built into
his character as well. At the end he fought the odds against
him as he had fought at the beginning, arousing the irritation
of the fan by struggling against surrender. This had been his
style of play forever.

The way he played the game was his problem. He was correct in his repeated claim that baseball was his life. The problem may have been that the right way to play baseball was
not the right way to live.

Rose had been playing baseball since he was seven years
old. When the playing was over for him, he was relegated to
the idleness of merely sitting, not as player but as manager,
an idle spectator growing fat and thick. He could no longer hit
the ball as hard or as often as he had been able to do once
upon a time. He had benched himself. He watched each game
from the dugout having restrained himself by his own order
from grabbing a bat and getting up there and winning the
game himself for his own team with his own hit.

He had never announced his retirement as a player. He
had never made an occasion of it, possibly as a means of offering himself the illusion that the day had not yet truly come.
In reality, he had retired. In spirit, he was restless.

He had hit more hits than anybody had ever hit. What was

left in life to do now that he had done such a stupendous thing? He possessed the memory of excitement to which he could never return. His body would not permit him to do so, and neither would his mind. He was a man made in a certain way. Other men are made differently and go away quietly. The variety of character among baseball players equals the variety of any other craft.

Rose, on the morning of his public sentencing, stood stocky and upright and his tie was pulled tight to his Adam's apple like a tie on a boy wearing a tie to please his mother. Did he appear stunned? Maybe he was only sleepless. (His new baby was only two days old.)

Another figure of baseball—Cynthia Garvey, once wife to the baseball player, Steve Garvey—has aptly spoken of the "faceless acclaim" to which Garvey responded. The crowds. The fans.

On the morning of his exile Rose said, "I love the fans not only of Cincinnati but in general."

Whom is Rose loving when he loves the fans of Cincinnati and everywhere? Loving everybody everywhere is loving nobody anywhere. He loved them because they loved him. He was adored. His signature was worth big money, and his baseball bats sold like pieces of the true cross.

It was faceless acclaim. He required wiser love even more, love with more mind and perspective to it, and that was difficult to come by, for Rose or for anyone. He required someone to help him discover what he was going to do with the rest of his life.

Toward this end the fan was no help. The fan had loved Rose as he was. The fan had not worried about Rose's future. Nobody had the answer for Rose, or if anyone did Rose could not hear it, for the faceless acclaim had seemed to be enough. He had confidently followed one course and no other, playing the game at which he had succeeded, which has brought him fame and money and everything fleshly and material.

When the best of all lives began to come to its end for him, when the excitement of play wound down, he apparently found in his craving for excitement the thrill of wagering on the running men and horses, and possibly even on baseball games. He had become, said the commissioner, in thrall to gambling and bookmaking.

But if the fan bets, why can't the hero bet? Baseball—Organized Baseball, baseball as a corporation—expects heroes and journeymen alike to respect almost the first rule of the sport. No gambling. So says the sign on every clubhouse wall. Official baseball expects the fan to expect that the hero be above reproach.

Yet surely the student of the Renaissance knows that life is more complex than that. The baseball Hall of Fame is the hall of *fame*. It is not the Hall of Goodness, and indeed at one level the hall enshrines many men never nearly so good-hearted as Rose.

Rose, whatever else he may have been, was never a race baiter, a fist-fighter—and certainly never a pious fake grooming an image. He was who he was, a unified man inside and out. He did not bring his hair under control or study grammar.

Fame and virtue are different things. I find it odd and unrealistic to hear the commissioner of baseball demand of Pete Rose that he be the unblemished hero history has not recorded since the legend of Caesar's wife.

MORALIZERS MAKE SPORT WHEN THE MIGHTY FALL

◇ DWIGHT GOODEN HAS turned himself in. He may yet go from the hospital to Cooperstown. The young pitcher does not need our lectures or our moralizing, but only our sympathy.

We're repeatedly absorbed by the decline, the fall, even the scandalous death, sometimes the happy recovery, of some great young athletic prospect who seemed to have fame within his grasp.

Then he blew it. He died of cocaine poisoning. He fought with the police. He went to jail. He drank. He was arrested for urinating in the public outdoors in Kansas City. He swapped wives, houses, children, cars, and dogs with a teammate, scandalizing his bosses.

The great home-run king Babe Ruth had been, in his decade, the most familiar, appealing face in America, but he was the victim of his own appetite. The story was that he felled himself with hot dogs, but as the years passed and censorship diminished, we began to hear that his immortal stomach ache might have been venereal disease.

Dwight Gooden is seeking help for himself. In the process, he stimulates a great deal of discussion. Some of us condemn him for squandering his gift. He had ahead of him a long, illustrious, rich career, comfort, fun, luxury, and fame, and he blew it. He was supposed to have reciprocated his extraordinary good fortune with proper behavior. He was not to fight with police officers or to ingest drugs. "Look what we gave you," we seem to say. "You had all the advantages."

But by the time we encountered him, he was not only equipped with the tools of his game but burdened by the history of his life. So are we all. If we now claim to care for him, we must care for him totally, flaws and all. We must platoon him, playing him for his virtues, commiserating with his weaknesses. We must care about the conditions under which young athletes live, not only when they stand upon the threshold of fame, but during the obscure years of their preparation.

The athlete leads a whole life. He is shaped by much that came into his existence in those schoolboy years before we ever heard of him. He has heritage, family, genesis, a psychic composition. He carries all these invisibly with him. His psychic weaknesses were not so scoutable as his questionable knee, his fragile shoulder. He is acclaimed as the greatest prospect since the man with the bellyache. We have decided in advance that he will shortly be a superstar.

Having made this decision, we demand that he live up to our expectation. We invite the young man (or woman) to be an athletic hero, but we complain because he is not also a moral hero. We insist upon a moral specimen verified by a urine specimen.

Some athletes lead orderly lives, take home their money and invest it in sound properties. Others seem to invest in cigarettes and whiskey and wild, wild women. That was Mickey Mantle's song. Mantle has told us in *The Mick* that he did not husband his body. He might have played longer. His family would have been happier. Life all around would have been more satisfying for him. But how could he have known at twenty or twenty-five or even thirty what he has since come to know in middle life?

It's a rare young man who can imagine life ahead. The practical long-term vision is incompatible with the energy and desire of ambitious youth. If the wondrous athlete had had that much vision at twenty, he might not have been the athlete he was. The skill for which we celebrated him was not his powerful insight into human behavior, least of all his own. Boys will be boys and girls will be girls. The fever of passion and foolishness accompany the body wherever it goes.

In all this, the only constant factor is youth. The media bring to us great young athletes doing the impossible things they do with baseballs and parallel bars and diving boards, but the media also eagerly bring to us their follies as soon as their follies can be exposed and announced. We who envy youth so much console ourselves with delight in their downfall, which seems to prove to us, sitting at home, that for all their fabulous skills these athletes lack our own moral virtues. No matter how well they do, they are only poor fallible weak vessels like us.

After all, we think, the life of the hero of sports is the life we dream of having as our own. If we had it, we could certainly protect it. We hear that a home-team athlete we admire earns $100,000 a month. We don't make quite that much ourselves. If we did, we would surely be so grateful to the gods who blessed us that we would behave ourselves. We would not become involved in drugs or sexual escapades. We would respect our bosses who pay our big wages.

But this is easier to say at forty, or sixty, than it is at twenty. The energy of his youth is the source of the athlete's power, and great physical health is not necessarily accompanied by visionary mental judgment.

Old folks condemning young folks are never attractive. Old folks who really try to be honest about their past recall that they did all those bad things the young folks do. They smoked and they drank and they blurted out intemperate opinions and they stayed out beyond curfew and they got the girl next door "in trouble"—with her cooperation.

It is terribly easy to say one would be much wiser if only one had the lucky opportunities of the great young million-dollar athletes now endangered by fearful addictions. But do we really know what we would do, given the confrontation with forbidden pleasures?

It is not enough to adopt a slogan, "Say No to Drugs." President Ronald Reagan, when he was governor of California, urged young people in the abortion controversy to remember that the best contraception was to shake one's head from side to side. No. Hard to do. Neither drugs nor sex is the constant. The constant is youth.

"HIT BY PITCHED BALL— BY MAYS (CHAPMAN)"*

◇ A SINGLE MOMENT of baseball has remained forever unlike any other. Memorable moments have winners and losers. This moment had no winners. Everybody lost.

At the center of this unique, landmark encounter stood two figures, sixty feet apart when their tragedy struck. One was the pitcher and the other was the batter. They had been born in the same year (1891) in the same state (Kentucky)—the pitcher in Liberty, the shortstop in Beaver Dam one hundred miles away.

The game in which they were playing occurred at the Polo Grounds in New York, then home of the landlord, the Giants, leasing their stadium to their upstart cousins, the Yankees. Yankee Stadium, some day to be known as the house that Babe Ruth built, was scarcely yet dreamed of. The Babe himself, still a frolicsome twenty-five-year-old in his first season with the Yankees, played on this day an errorless right field: he caught one fly ball. Batting third in the order, he hit safely once in four attempts. For the Babe, not a famous day.

The visiting team was the Cleveland Indians. It was Monday, August 16, 1920.

Ruth and the pitcher, whose name was Carl Mays, had been well acquainted since their minor-league playing days at Providence. They had left Providence together to join the

* from the box score, Monday, August 16, 1920

243

Boston Red Sox, and subsequently the Yankees. Someone along the way had thought to convert the Babe from a pitcher to an outfielder. Not a bad idea.

Though Mays and Ruth were to be teammates for a decade they never got along with each other. Come to think of it, Mays never really got along with anyone. He was disputatious and rigidly moral. He did not drink or smoke or chase about after women nor suffer in silence his teammates' vices. He had experienced bad luck and several encounters with the law—once for having hurled a baseball at a fan. He was aloof, apparently misanthropic. In a magazine interview quoted by Mike Sowell he said, "It was long ago made apparent to me that I was not one of those individuals who were fated to be popular. It used to bother me some . . . but I was naturally independent and if I found that a fellow held aloof from me I was not likely to run after him."

Mays's professional trademark was his "submarine" ball, a sidearm pitch he delivered with awesome speed. In Mike Sowell's remarkable, comprehensive book, *The Pitch that Killed,* indispensable to the preparation of this article, Sowell describes Mays's style as seen by a writer for *Baseball Magazine:*

> A pretty wise noodle, a crazy style of deliver, and not much else, have made Carl Mays one of the game's leading pitchers.
>
> Mays has less "stuff" than a whole raft of other boxmen, whom he outclasses in winning results, but his submarine delivery is mighty effective in torpedoing batters.
>
> Carl slings the pill from his toes, has a weird looking wind-up and in action looks like a cross between an octopus and a bowler. He shoots the ball at the batter at such unexpected angles that his delivery is hard to find, generally, until along about 5 o'clock, when the hitters get accustomed to it—and when the game is about over.

To this Sowell adds the vivid testimony of Muddy Ruel, who on this ill-fated afternoon was Mays's catcher: "His underhanded motion is not natural and at times some of the balls he throws take remarkable shoots, jumps, ducks, and twists. I have caught many balls thrown by Mays which I did not know I had. I have never known how I managed to catch some of them. I have never been able to understand how any batter gets a hit off him."

The shortstop for Cleveland who had come to the plate to lead off the fifth inning against Mays and the Yankees was a man who, by all accounts, possessed the sweetest disposition. Ray Chapman was five feet ten inches tall, weighed 170 pounds, and was variously described as handsome, dashing, high-spirited, good-humored. He was noted for his smile. He was seldom critical of his fellows.

Jack Graney, an outfielder for the Indians (afterward a popular baseball broadcaster in Cleveland), valued Chapman's "beautiful tenor voice." Graney, who had roomed with Chapman for eight years, spoke of him as "a great person. Ask any of our players who are still around Cleveland, George Uhle, Elmer Smith, Bill Wamby, they'll tell you the same thing. Chapman was one of the finest boys who ever lived."

A straight arrow, a clean liver. Sixty years after his death one Bob McDermott, son of a boardinghouse keeper in Cleveland, remembered him as "the nicest guy. He was the type who would stand up when a woman came into the room. A lot of the players would sit out on the porch and heckle the girls as they walked by, but Chapman wasn't like that. Everybody liked him, though. He was a good dresser and liked to tell jokes. He had a tattoo of a bird on his right shoulder and I got one, too, just out of admiration for him."

Chapman, in the modern phrase, was "upward mobile." He had begun his working life digging coal. Now his baseball salary was $6,000 a year. He had been married in high society the previous autumn—"above himself," so to speak—to Kathleen Daly, whose father was a millionaire Cleveland businessman. Chapman, twenty-nine, expected soon to retire from baseball to become his father-in-law's partner.

His best man at the wedding was Tris Speaker, player/manager for Cleveland, one of baseball's most notable figures in that year or any other. Speaker batted third in the order, following Chapman, who was said to be "an ideal" second-place hitter, "a difficult man to pitch to." "Ray Chapman crouched and crowded the plate. Chappie was an active, shifty right-hand batter. Usually he would pop back when the ball was thrown." He "was one of the swiftest men in baseball," according to one newspaper account. "He had a sharp eye. He led the American League in bases on balls in 1918 with thirty-four. He was the ideal second-place hitter, broke major league sacrifice hit records in 1917 with sixty-seven, led the American League in sacrifices the following two years." He could circle the bases in fourteen seconds. At a track meet in 1918, during his wartime period of Navy service, he had run the hundred-yard dash in ten seconds.

In 1962, forty-two years after the death of his roommate Ray Chapman, Graney recalled that "the night before the Indians left [Cleveland] for New York, Chappie and his wife, Kathleen, were never happier. They stopped by to pick me up on the way to the depot because they wanted to take me through the new house Kathleen's father was having built for them as a present . . . We were all in a gay mood as Chappie, Kathleen's brother, Dan [Daly], and I boarded the train. Kathleen saw us off then returned to her home. The next day on the elevated going to the Polo Grounds, Chappie was singing in that beautiful tenor voice of his. Between songs he turned to the Indians and announced, 'Mays is pitching for the Yankees today so I'll do the fielding and you fellows do the hitting.'"

The Indians on that day were clinging to first place in the American League. In forty years in baseball Cleveland had yet to win a pennant. After four innings, they led the Yankees 3–0. Chapman led off in the top of the fifth. Jack Graney remembered: "Mays threw a blazing fast ball and I saw Chappie bend his knees trying to duck under it. I thought the ball hit his bat above his shoulder because it bounced right back at Mays. But then I saw Chappie collapse."

When the ball bounced back to Mays he thought, as Graney and many other players and spectators also thought, that the ball had hit Chapman's bat. Mays threw the ball to first base for what he imagined to be an out. Chapman "sank to his knees," according to one newspaper account, "his eyes closed, mouth wide open. Muddy Ruel, catcher for the Yankees . . . and umpire Tommy Connelly called for a doctor." But Chapman regained his feet, the crowd applauded him, and for a moment it appeared as if his crisis had passed. In the next moment, however, "he collapsed and was carried into the clubhouse."

When Chapman collapsed, said Graney, "I helped carry him to the clubhouse in center field and I stayed with him until the ambulance came. He was conscious. He looked at me and tried to speak but the words wouldn't come out. I knew by the look in his eyes that he wanted desperately to tell me something so I got some paper and put a pencil in his hand. He made a motion to write but the pencil dropped to the floor."

Chapman also attempted to communicate with Percy Smallwood, the Indians trainer, to whom he had entrusted his diamond wedding ring before the game. The ring was a gift from his bride. Smallwood, interpreting Chapman's effort to speak as a request that the ring be returned to him, slipped the ring on Chapman's finger.

Chapman was conveyed to St. Lawrence Hospital, less than a mile from the Polo Grounds. John Henry, a close friend who had just retired as a player after nine years in the major leagues, saw Chapman at midnight and reported that he had sought to exonerate Mays. "Tell Mays I will be okay," he said. Chapman was taken to surgery. He lay on the operating table an hour. Then he was gone. "We waited up all night for the bad news," said Graney, "which came about three in the morning."

"The blow had caused a depressed fracture in Chapman's

head three and a half inches long," according to the report in the New York *Times* on Wednesday:

> Dr. Merrigan removed a piece of skull about an inch and a half square and found the brain had been so severely jarred that blood clots had formed. The shock of the blow had lacerated the brain not only on the left side of the head where the ball struck, but also on the right side where the shock of the blow had forced the brain against the skull, Dr. Merrigan said.

Graney remembered: "Tris Speaker, Dan Daly, several players, and I went down to the depot to meet Kathleen, who had been called after the accident. She didn't know Chappie was dead when she got off the train. Speaker had arranged for a doctor to be at her suite when she arrived at the hotel and then Speaker broke the news to her."

The flags of Cleveland flew at half-mast. The funeral was to have been held at St. Philomene's Church in East Cleveland, but because of the vast crowd expected to attend, the ceremony was held instead at St. John's Roman Catholic Cathedral. One newspaper reported that "thousands of persons stood with bared heads as the body of Chapman was carried to the altar, and the last rites performed."

The players of the Cleveland team arrived from New York on Friday morning. Some of the players at Chapman's funeral had been members of his wedding less than a year before. "The entire Cleveland team with the exception of Tris Speaker and Jack Graney, who were so grief-stricken that they were unable to be present, entered the cathedral in a body, taking seats near the front. As they filed down the aisle in pairs, a wave of subdued emotion stirred the congregation, which seemed to feel the loss of Chapman more keenly for its contrast with the youthful presence of his associates."

Chapman's funeral oration was delivered by Rev. William A. Scullen in style and language appropriate to the occasion. He extolled Chapman as the epitome of brave American manhood. The late player, said the clergyman, "played the game of life as he played the game that was his profession . . . He is the glorious example of our American manhood, because that spirit that is manifested in our national pastime is the same spirit that broke the shackles of British tyranny and laid the foundation for this republic . . . the same splendid spirit of American youth, trained on the baseball diamonds of this broad land."

Possibly the most striking aspect of Rev. Scullen's address was his advocacy of an attitude of generosity toward the pitcher Carl Mays who, in the moment of the tragedy, acquired a blackened reputation which was to follow him to the end of his days. "And, my dear brethren," Rev. Scullen appealed, "may there be no hostility of any sort toward the man who was the unfortunate occasion of this accident. He feels it more deeply than you do, and no one regrets it as much as he does. This great game that we play, that is our national pastime, could not produce anyone that would willingly do such a thing. Remember that these would be the words of the man who lies here, not to hold it against any man." This was the spirit of exoneration reported by Chapman's friend, John Henry—"Tell Mays I will be okay."

Nevertheless, Mays became in retrospect if not in reality a mean man, a bad fellow, remembered as a vicious creature who threw beanballs at opposing players. He never denied that he threw baseballs too close to batters for their comfort, but he claimed that it was all in a pitcher's day's work, that he "brushed back" batters no more than other pitchers. He insisted he had no hostile intention toward batters.

Mays, pitching to Chapman "crouched and crowded" at the plate, "expected," he said, "that he would drop as do others when pitchers swing them in close to drive batters away from the plate. Instead he ducked and the ball hit him. I found a rough place on the ball afterward and believe that made it sail far more than I intended."

Mays's problem in 1920 was identical to the problem of pitchers from his time to our own. "I know what the pitchers have to be thinking about," he told an interviewer. "You have to make up your mind whether you are going to miss the plate altogether to avoid hitting a batter, throwing the ball out where the batter can get the fat part of his stick on it—or pitch to the spots on the plate where you know you have to throw. You've got to throw the ball in the strike zone where you think you can get him out. The man I hit was a batter like that—crowding the plate with his hand and head over it. I didn't mean to hit him, of course. But I had to pitch in the strike zone. That's what I was paid to do. Get the ball over the plate."

In a mournful conversation with the *Sporting News* in 1963 he lamented, "Nobody ever remembers anything about me except one thing—that a pitch I threw caused a man to die. It was an accident, nothing else. But what happened to me in August of 1920 is the only thing anybody remembers."

Postscripts. One week after the death of Chapman, Mays resumed his pitching turn for the Yankees. He continued to play for New York through 1923, for Cincinnati thereafter, and finally, in 1929, for the New York Giants—once again the Polo Grounds.

Kathleen Chapman gave birth to Chapman's child, a girl, Rae-Marie. For nearly eight years after Chapman's death Kathleen fought a losing struggle against depression. She died a suicide in 1928. Rae-Marie died one year later of complications from measles. She was eight years old. Thus was the little family of Ray Chapman swept away.

The Cleveland Indians, who had begun the season of 1920 with Chapman at shortstop, won the pennant, and in the World Series defeated Brooklyn. Cleveland second baseman Bill Wambsganss who, with Chapman, had formed a sterling double-play combination, speared a line drive in the fifth inning of the fifth game, doubled a runner off second base, and tagged another approaching from first, to complete, for the only time in World Series history, an unassisted triple play.

THE
DESIGNATED
EXPERT

OF *CASEY AT THE BAT*

◇ THIS COULD HAVE happened to you. You came home with a briefcase filled with urgent work. But you walked into your TV room wondering what might possibly be on the tube, and you remembered that you forgot about the baseball game. You switched on the machine, and you quickly knew by the low growling quality of the crowd that you had entered at a moment suspending hope in a losing contest with despair.

Not all is lost. Something is up. It is the batter. You have seen his face before on this very tube, but you forget his name. You are alert for the imminent clue. The graphic line on the screen tells you his name at precisely the moment the announcer has told it to you. The batter's name is Cooney.

What is the score? Who are we and where? Things come clear. We are two runs behind, we are the home team, our half of the ninth inning has just begun. We feel we might yet win. Two runs are not impossible. But—"then when Cooney died at first, and Barrows did the same, A sickly silence fell upon the patrons of the game."

Don't go away, folks, says the voice on the tube. Aw, come on! Still, it's never over till it's over. Two men are out and the bases are empty, bottom of the ninth. The face on the screen is now Flynn's, with Blake on deck: Blake is the disappointing guy kneeling, awaiting his turn. Why he earns $800,000 a year you'll never know. This expensive Blake will bat if imposter Flynn ($650,000) can keep the game alive.

And "Flynn let drive a single, to the wonderment of all./ And Blake, the much despise-ed, tore the cover off the ball," which was to say that Flynn went to third and Blake to second—that much you saw—though whether Blake's hit will be

253

scored as a double you don't know. You wait for the announcer to tell you. Your perception of it is that Blake singled and went to second when the outfielder tried to cut down Flynn at third, but the announcer isn't helping you because he has been silenced by the engulfing excitement of the sudden shift in balance from despair to hope. "Then from 5,000 throats and more there rose a lusty yell;/It rumbled through the valley, it rattled in the dell."

Two out, two on, bottom of the ninth, and the batter is Casey. A single will tie the score.

Why didn't the nameless Mudville opponents walk Casey and take their chance with the next batter, whose name you do not know? You don't know the name of the enemy pitcher, either—all you know is that he has an "L" on his chest. The "L" must stand for "loony" because he is loony to pitch to Casey. Better to walk Casey, load the bases, have a play at every base. But go ahead, pitcher, be loony.

Yes, they pitch to Casey. It's a mystery. A lot of things are a mystery. Where is Mudville? You know the names of only five players on the Mudville team: Cooney, Barrows, Flynn, Blake, Casey. You'll never know another. For 100 years this half-inning has defied the record book. You don't know a soul on the "L" club. You hadn't even remembered there was a ballgame on the air, but when you tuned in you easily guessed what had happened during the eight and a half innings before your splendid arrival. You were seized by the heart in the bottom of the ninth.

You're stuck, man, woman, now, you couldn't leave this scene, you couldn't depart, conscientious worker that you are, briefcase in the other room overflowing with critical documents.

Yet somebody stuck to business at David R. Godine, the publisher, in Boston, for here we have the fruit of an excellent plan to reprint the poem *Casey at the Bat*. The poem's little-known subtitle, "A Ballad of the Republic," suggests a sound and stimulating historical direction for Donald Hall's afterword to stanzas composed by a young fellow named Ernest Lawrence Thayer. Thayer's poem was first published by his

school chum William Randolph Hearst, in the San Francisco
Examiner, in June, 1888. The present book is charmingly illustrated by Barry Moser. But nothing could have come to
anything without the gem at the center, fifty-two lines of
mock-heroic narrative somehow imperishably attuned to the
American ear.

INTRODUCTION TO
THE BASEBALL CHRONICLES

edited by David Gallen

◇ Hey, Jackie Brandt, how are you? Where are you? Fancy meeting you here. Where have you been? Haven't seen you in ages.

Haven't seen him in fact for more than thirty years. It was 1959. He was playing baseball for the San Francisco Giants and I was covering the Giants for an article. Jackie was a blond fellow—boy, man, twenty-five years old, handsome chap, neither friendly nor unfriendly, ready to speak, I suppose, if he were spoken to, and so was I. I was a stranger in the clubhouse. We nodded. We never spoke.

I remember him on that day as one whose demeanor belied the logic of the moment. He appeared glum when he should have been happy. He had just won a game for his team with a home run. He hit twelve home runs that year. Not bad, right? Hadn't he every reason to be a happy man? He was a big-league baseball player. Nobody could ask for more than that.

Now here he is again, just today, on a page of this book. He is no longer in the uniform of the Giants but of the Baltimore Orioles. For Baltimore he is playing center field.

The game is at Boston in the bottom of the first inning. Ted Williams, who has walked on four pitches, has arrived at third base, whereupon another Bostonian—at any rate one Lu Clinton, a player for Boston—sends a fly ball to Jackie

Brandt in center field. "Williams tagged up and ran home," says the author. "As he slid across the plate, the ball, thrown with unusual heft by Jackie Brandt, the Oriole center fielder, hit him on the back." It didn't hurt. Williams scored the run.

That day's game, written up by John Updike, was the occasion of Ted Williams's last appearance as a player. Williams had played more than 2,000 games. Lu Clinton, who hit the fly ball, had played less than a hundred. I hadn't thought about Jackie Brandt in thirty years. Every thirty years we meet. He was up, he played, he was gone. I don't know where he is now. Maybe someone will write me a letter and tell me.

Today I see him once again for a moment through Updike's eye, hurling that ball with "unusual heft" into Ted Williams's back. Does Jackie Brandt remember that moment? Does Ted Williams remember that moment? There were an awful lot of ballgames to remember. "Bangin' around the way I was," says Satchel Paige, "playing for guarantees on one team after another that I never heard of, in towns I never seen before, with players I didn't know and never saw again, I got lonesome."

In my lifetime at college I met two students whose late fathers had been big-league baseball players. Both students were women. Both fathers (this is a marvelous coincidence, don't you agree?) had been catchers for the same team, though in different years. Both catchers were obscure. They did not catch much. You will not have heard of their names even if I tell you.

These two fathers possessed in common the memory of their unique craft, and the pale taint of their obscurity offset by their fame in the minds of their daughters. It is their daughters' idea that their fathers played much longer in the big leagues than they did, that they were more illustrious than they were. Perhaps these young women heard these things from their mothers. Mothers do not always tell their daughters the truth of the past.

Of course, with the *The Baseball Encyclopedia* at my elbow, I could have corrected the memories of those daughters.

"Dear girl, your father was an obscure player—you could look it up."

No, I would never say such a thing. We are obscure. The planet is crowded and fierce. However famous we may be to ourselves, to our heirs, to our family, to our descendants, we endure only for a limited term in the minds of the living, as Jackie Brandt in mine, as two dead catchers in the minds of their daughters.

Almost everyone inflates his career, doesn't he? Some people have told me they played baseball in the big leagues, but I cannot find them in the *Encyclopedia.* Everyone contends that he really did it all a little better than perhaps he did. Nobody feels that he quite got a fair shake—the memorable error he once made, which cost his team the game, the pennant, the world, should never truly have been scored as an error: consider the extenuating circumstances, the bad hop the ball took, the wind, the sun, the bad condition of the turf.

But what we have here in this book exceeds customary reality. These few men of baseball could hardly have been exceeded even in their own imaginations. They are who they are and they did what they did beyond question or cavil or dispute. Their achievements are clear and unclouded. They are not doubtful figures, furtive or shrouded, but players on a scene whose every act was open and observed. Everyone may see every pitch and catch or hit or out. Baseball players "cannot hide from clear responsibility," the late Commissioner Giamatti writes in these pages, "as in football or Congress."

These men were physically so tough they could play this aching game of baseball even when they were broken into pieces. Mickey Mantle required his friends to hoist him out of taxicabs. He played with steel pins drilled through his collarbone, and a wide assortment of injuries to his knees, thighs, shoulders, and groin—according to Arnold Hano, "a lifetime of pain." Mantle said to Hano, "I think I've been real lucky, but I can't help wondering how far I'd have gone with two legs." John McGraw, struck by a taxicab, walked around unknowingly for days with a broken leg. Lou Gehrig, "The Iron Man," played 2,130 consecutive games and died all in a day at thirty-eight. Dizzy Dean, struck in his big toe by a batted ball, ruined his arm compensating for his toe. The scientist Satchel Paige analyzes his own arm. "I just explained to the gentlemen that the bones running up from my wrist, the fibius, which is the upper bone, and the tiberon, which is the lower bone, was bent out, making more room for my throwing muscles to move around in there. I attributed most of my long life, and so on and so forth, to them two bones. The gentlemen was amazed to hear about that."

Some of these men were unspeakably fierce, like Ty Cobb, McGraw, Durocher, or they were essentially gentle like Honus Wagner and Walter Johnson.

Hear how the savage Cobb exploited Johnson's gentleness:

> I had to figure Johnson out. I realized quickly that he wasn't a vicious pitcher, despite all that speed. I saw him wince when he fired one close to somebody's head, and he used to tell me that he was afraid someday that he would kill a man with that fireball. So I used to cheat. I'd crowd that plate so far that I was actually sticking my toes on it when I was facing Johnson. I knew he was timid about hitting a batter, and when he saw me crowding the plate he'd steer his pitches a little bit wide. Then with two balls and no strikes, he'd ease up a bit to get it over. That's the Johnson pitch I hit. I was depending on him to be scared of hitting me.

Where have all the young men gone? Ted Williams has gone to the Hall of Fame. Jackie Brandt has joined the less exclusive company of the *Encyclopedia:* he shares his little space with the 13,000 men who have played at least one official moment in the major leagues of baseball.

Ty Cobb played twenty-four years, mainly for the Detroit Tigers, immediately preceded in the *Encyclopedia* by Joe

Cobb, who played one game for the same team, in 1918, batted once, drew a walk, and that was all. Ty Cobb is immediately *followed* in the *Encyclopedia* by Dave Coble, who came to bat twenty-five times in fifteen games for the Philadelphia Phillies in 1939, stroked seven safe hits (one a double), and scored two runs. Fate deals unevenly. Babe Ruth hit 714 home runs. Jim Rutherford, who follows Babe Ruth in the *Encyclopedia* lineup, played one game, hit no home runs.

The thought occurs to me that the indelible moments of baseball are associated in general with players often unremembered except in the context of their isolated moments of triumph or chagrin: Merkle's omitting to run to second base, Mickey Owen's dropping the third strike, Ralph Branca's fateful pitch, Bobby Thomson's home run, Bruckner's error, Lavagetto's hit, Sandy Amoros's miraculous catch, Wambsganss's unassisted triple play, John Vander Meer's back-to-back no-hit games, Don Larsen's perfect game. These were good players—nobody plays in the big leagues who is not a good player—but the superstars, Ruth, Cobb, Gehrig, Speaker, Paige, DiMaggio, appear to be remembered for their lives as a whole, for lifetime performance, rather than for isolated moments of their play.

In Stephen Jay Gould's learned essay, "The Streak of Streaks," Gould examines the other side of the "capricious character" of those events I have just mentioned. "Single moments of unexpected supremacy . . . can occur at any time to almost anybody," he writes. "But a streak must be absolutely exceptionless; you are not allowed a single day of subpar play, or even bad luck . . . Thus Joe DiMaggio's fifty-six game streak is both the greatest factual achievement in the history of baseball and a principal icon of American mythology . . . one sequence so many standard deviations above the expected distribution that it should not have occurred at all . . . DiMaggio's streak is the most extraordinary thing that ever happened in American sports."

* * *

Hey, Leo, what's up?

Leo don't answer. He's too tough and gruff. I had the feeling he didn't like me.

Somebody on the bus mentioned Babe Ruth. Leo had once
been a teammate of Babe Ruth. Mention Babe Ruth and Leo
tells of the time he picked a clubhouse fight with Ruth, who
was twice his size.

Hey, Leo, remember when we rode a bus together? He don't
remember. Who am I that Leo should remember me? Nevertheless it happened. One day late in cold January of 1966 I
rode in a bus somewhere south of Chicago with Leo and Ripper Collins and several Chicago Cubs baseball players. It was
a ticket-selling promotional tour arranged by the Cubs in
their own behalf. The front office was represented by Charlie
Grimm.

Leo sat up front beside the driver, huddled in his overcoat,
staring at the treacherous road ahead. In the back of the bus
Ripper Collins smoked his cigar. Durocher hated Collins's cigar and made him sit in back. I had thought a man called
Ripper would be fierce, but Ripper no longer ripped. He sat in
back. The years had tamed him. In the center of the empty,
hollow bus the baseball players played cards.

On the following morning we boarded the bus for another
day's tour. One of our players was missing. He had been out
bowling late last night and was therefore a little slow getting
started today. We would fall behind schedule. Late to leave
meant late for the luncheon. Late for the luncheon meant late
for the dinner. People were waiting for us. Wasn't anyone
worried? The players in the bus were not worried. They broke
out the cards. Leo assumed his seat up front, Ripper Collins
fired up his cigar in the back, and Charlie Grimm's impassive
face told me all I needed to know. He could not worry. Give
Charlie several baseball players and one of them is bound to
have been up too late last night. This had always been so, and
it was not less likely to be so this winter morning. Charlie
Grimm had been playing this game, boy and man, player,

coach, manager, and front office since 1916—exactly half a century—and he knew that the baseball player was immortal, that his species endured, that he repeated established patterns. There was always going to be one baseball player up too late last night, and nothing in the world Charlie Grimm could do about it.

Hey, Old Pete, there you are. Do you remember me? I punched you in the stomach once—how can you not remember?

Grover Cleveland Alexander had been wounded in World War I. He drank thereafter and suffered a variety of afflictions of body and mind. He had earned money at baseball but saved none of it.

When his career ended he lived marginally on small sums earned for humble work or taken as gifts. He appeared for a while, half celebrity half freak, for a so-called museum or flea circus on Times Square in Manhattan. Manhattan had been a scene of triumph for him. He had pitched two complete games for victories for the St. Louis Cardinals against the Yankees in 1926. In the seventh game he came to the mound as a relief pitcher in the seventh inning with the bases loaded and two men out. He struck out Tony Lazzeri to end the inning, pitched two scoreless innings beyond, and saved the World Series for the Cardinals.

The Times Square flea circus attracted boys like me, drawn to the scene by promises of marvels. I paid my way in. Grover Cleveland Alexander's name meant nothing to me. He had been gone from baseball for almost a decade, too long for my memory, and he was featured instead by a shrewd management not as the exceptional baseball player he had been but as a man with an iron stomach whom any boy could punch for a price.

I was not yet sensitive to other people's dignity. I punched him in the stomach. He had won 373 big-league baseball games. Only two men in the history of baseball had won more games than he.

* * *

In his chapter on John McGraw, Jack Sher writes, "It annoyed McGraw that baseball was not always considered the most important thing in American life, on a par with the scientific discoveries that were changing our nation and the policies that were being formed in the White House." In search of the most important thing the people of the United States of America have ranged among options.

Baseball has competed among the options for our affection. We have sentimentalized it and we have commercialized it, and it persists.

How fitting that baseball's late, brief commissioner should have been a man so erudite and so humane as Mr. Giamatti of Yale! He treasured the game in spite of impurities not likely to have been observed by Mr. McGraw. Giamatti said:

> We are a nation of immigrants always migrating in search of home . . . The hunger for home makes the green geometry of the baseball field more than simply a metaphor for the American experience and character; the baseball field and the game that sanctifies boundaries, rules, and law and appreciates cunning, theft, and guile; that exalts energy, opportunism, and execution while paying lip service to management, strategy, and long-range planning, is closer to an embodiment of American life than to the mere sporting image of it.

My own hope is that baseball, with all its impurities, will prevail among the options. Conquerors, warrior-presidents, tyrants, mad leaders of nations and tribes, arrogant liberators, and self-appointed saviors, take heed. Stop. The humblest man in *The Baseball Encyclopedia* will have done more for humankind than you. In all the history of the big-league

game only one man was ever killed at play. One in 13,000
men in *The Baseball Encyclopedia*! I can almost say with
Pete Rose, "I can't think of a single thing wrong with the
game of baseball."

GALLEN

LOVE AFFAIR
IN SAN FRANCISCO

AIRPORT

The road trip could have been worse (ten wins, eleven losses), but the night itself could not have been more nightmarish: the Dodgers' pitcher had struck them out eighteen times. It was 2:30 in the morning, and their lead was one game. They had gone away three weeks before with a game and a half, but somewhere back east they had lost their half.

Maybe if they had come home with a larger lead they would have been greeted by a larger crowd. Baseball fans are like that. The little boy's father said there was supposed to be a brass band to meet them, and the little boy's mother replied that anybody with brains enough to blow through a horn would be home in bed. Even so, there were 300 people, some with signs like THIS TOWN LOVES YOU, and the morning was chilling, as mornings in San Francisco always are.

Manager Bill Rigney, his warm breath visible, addressed the faithful briefly, saying, "We're in first place, and I'm confident we're going to stay there," and a shivering young lady said, "I like hearing him say it, though I suppose it's what he *would* say," and the players filed down. Shortstop Ed Bressoud, a widower at twenty-seven, carried two sleepy children. Hank Sauer, after two decades as a player (he hit his last home run eight weeks ago in San Francisco), was now a coach. Trainer, clubhouse man, a few wives. Newsmen. Many of the faces were familiar but only two of the voices: down out

267

of the sky came Russ Hodges and Lon Simmons, broadcasters.

There was nothing anybody could do about anything at half past two in the morning, but the little boy clung to a sign reading NOW! ON TO THE PENNANT. He fully forgave the Giants for striking out eighteen times, and for losing their half game. "I'm not worried," he said, but his mother was terribly tired.

EMBARCADERO

From Coit Tower on Telegraph Hill a tourist can see Alcatraz prison through a telescope for a dime. Among the tourists were the Chicago Cubs, to whom the Giants had been too cordial all season. On the Embarcadero a teamster said, "Don't mention my name, but if they can get past Chicago then St. Louis comes in, always a patsy for us. We can be four, five games ahead by the time L.A. wakes up. I been on strike for three weeks. Who's pitching?"

He was told that Mike McCormick was pitching.

"I mean for them," the teamster said.

"Ceccarelli."

"I'm half Irish and half Italian myself," the teamster said. "That's common here. The first time I heard the name of McCovey I said to the wife, 'The Giants got another Irishman.' But he sure can hit the ball, I'll tell the cockeyed world."

The recorded national anthem at Seals Stadium was played, but midway through it failed, and the teamster was uncertain whether to be embarrassed or amused. The Cubs' lead-off batter flied to left, the teamster held his breath, but Cepeda made the catch.

"It's a hell of a time to start learning left field," he said. The next two Cub batters struck out, and the teamster lit a cigar. "I smoke when the Giants bat. It brings them good luck. They're in first place, ain't they? I love that team."

Danny O'Connell struck out.

"I think it's going to win," the teamster said.

Willie McCovey, who had hit safely in fourteen straight games, struck out.

"It's a big-league town," he said. "We deserve a big-league team."

Willie Mays struck out.

"I don't know why they ever left the Seals go," the teamster said. "The Seals were only a bush team but these are only a bush team either, eighteen strike out down there in L.A. and three strike out now and it ain't even two o'clock. Why don't they send them back to New York? Send McCovey back to Phoenix, nothing would suit me nicer. I could do better myself. I could at least stuck my bat out in front of the ball. Strike out, strike out, strike out, that's all they do."

A mixed chorus sang of Dual Filter Tareyton Cigarettes, but the breast of the teamster was not soothed. "Rigney's no manager," he said. "I could manage them better, the bums."

FISHERMAN'S WHARF

Brother Joe has gone away, brother Dominic has gone away, brother Vince lives across the Bay, but brother Tom comes every day to the restaurant. Fish run in season, the fishermen mend their nets, and the wind is brisk on Fisherman's Wharf.

Willie Mays catches two fly balls in a row, and a gentleman with spectacles says, "I feel secure when I hear that Mays is waiting."

Schult singles, Chicago has a runner, and the fisherman in the boat pauses at his work. "There was only one DiMaggio," he says. Dark grounds to Bressoud, who tosses to O'Connell for the force play at second base, and the fisherman returns to his labor. Daryl Spencer is still ailing, Jimmy Davenport still hurting, but Mike McCormick has pitched two fine innings.

"I think," says the gentleman with spectacles, "that if the Giants can get off to a good start on this home stand they'll go all the way."

The fisherman offers no opinion, but when Cepeda singles, and Brandt, on the hit-run play, pokes another through shortstop, the fisherman's hope rises. "Maybe," he says.

The batter is Felipe Alou, a Spanish-speaking outfielder with an innocent bronze countenance, whom manager Rigney intuitively inserted today in right field in place of Willie Kirkland, who is lounging in the bullpen in a long, warm coat. The Giants have three players named Willie, each of whom was born in Alabama; three who speak Spanish; two named Jones. Alou flies out to center field, Cepeda scoring after the catch.

"In baseball," says the gentleman with spectacles, "the past participle of 'to fly' is 'flied'."

"It's a funny game," says the fisherman.

"At any rate," says the gentleman with spectacles, "we've got a run. We have drawn—as the sportswriters say—first blood."

Bressoud and Hegan pop out.

"I was hoping for a big inning," says the fisherman, lowering his radio for the passage of the commercial. "If they'd have a big inning I could stop listening and start working." His boat rocks upon the water.

At Seals Stadium, where brother Joe and brother Dominic and brother Vince once played, the inning turns. At the Wharf, salt mist forms on the gentleman's spectacles, he removes them, wipes them, replaces them. "A run is a run," he says.

"Maybe," says the fisherman.

CANDLESTICK

The bare-chested mason at Candlestick Park thought he'd sit out the third inning. His companions were a transistor radio, a thermos bottle of coffee, and a critical observer who asked, "How are you going to build a ballpark sitting down?"

"Listen," the mason said, "I've been working like a slave since before the Giants got out of bed this morning."

Some of the light towers were up. Some were still lying on the ground. Some of the roof was on. Some was off. Some of the seats were in. Some weren't. The wind stirred the dust, and a man on a mowing machine rode back and forth across the outfield where a World Series would be played if the Giants won and the park were done.

Chicago was retired one-two-three. "That's the way to do it," the mason said. "Some day I'll tell my grandchildren, 'See this ballpark. I built it.'"

There had been many delays. There had been a teamster strike. There had been harsh exchanges between the architect and the contractor. Mayor Christopher—running for re-election as the man who "gets things done"—had been drawn into the dispute. "I am apprehensive lest the absence of Mr. Bolles [the architect who designed the stadium] delay some of this important construction," the mayor said, but some things can't move any faster than they can move, not even for the mayor of San Francisco.

McCormick fanned, but O'Connell walked.

"She'll be a beauty," the mason said. "She'll be done."

McCovey lined out.

Mays popped up.

The mason said: "If nobody hits any better than that what are you hurrying me to build this ball park for?" He capped his thermos bottle.

At Candlestick Park the dugouts are built flush with the turf. "A dugout isn't a dugout any more," the observer said.

The mason slipped his transistor into his pocket, replied, "So what?" and strolled back to work. From his pocket came a song of praise by a mixed chorus: "Falstaff Beer, right beer anywhere . . . brewed with special care . . . sing out now, the time is here. . . ."

CHINATOWN

The Chinatown pharmacist reports, "Sure, there's a lot of interest in baseball in Chinatown, and a lot of betting, especially among doctors." In the Temple of Heaven saloon the bartender and his patrons gossip in Chinese but talk baseball in English. The patron orders a Sneaky Dragon and asks who's up.

It is Thomson. There are three players in today's game who were in the Giants' lineup on yet another Wednesday afternoon—October 3, 1951. Willie Mays had been on deck and Alvin Dark had hit safely earlier in that inning when Bobby Thomson hit his "miracle home run" eight years ago. Now Bobby Thomson, this time for Chicago, hits another home run.

A patron orders an Oriental Passion.

Schult pops up. Dark, like Thomson, plays for Chicago today. He fouls out to catcher Hegan.

"How come Hegan is catching?" the first patron asks.

"Some rookie," the second patron replies. "They're giving him a try."

The rookie, Jim Hegan, who has been a big league baseball player for nineteen years, flies out to open the Giants' half of the inning. McCormick strikes out, O'Connell grounds to Dark, the patrons toss off their Sneaky Dragon and their Oriental Passion, Bobby Thomson and Alvin Dark jog into the Chicago dugout, and Willie Mays assumes a defensive posture in center field. It is not the spacious garden Mays knew at the Polo Grounds—but then, it is not the same Willie Mays, either. He feels that he has five good years of baseball left. Eight years ago, in the on-deck circle when Bobby Thomson hit his miracle, Willie Mays was not counting years. No doubt the bent old Chinaman, his face creased with wisdom, knows some ancient proverb with which to console humankind caught up in the awful fleetness of time. He enters the Temple of Heaven, he speaks, he says, "What's the score?"

UNION SQUARE

The caps were all the rage. They kept the wind out of a man's hair, the sun out of his eyes, and they announced his loyalties. A great many people wore them who labored in neither wind nor sun.

The men in caps at Union Square worked without distraction during the Chicago fourth. It was a quick three outs. O'Connell caught a pop fly, Cepeda a fly ball, and Brandt threw out Ernie Banks. Plastic figurines of Banks were on sale in shops at Union Square, but not of Brandt, who was to be a hero of the Giants' afternoon.

A moment later Felipe Alou hit a home run. At Union Square, in front of the St. Francis Hotel, a lady snapped off her transistor, snapped open her purse, dropped the transistor in, and snapped the purse shut. Then she walked downhill past the workmen in caps.

NORTH BEACH

One cannot hear, in the Coexistence Bagel Shop, the song of Falstaff Beer. Here in North Beach they do not sing of Dual Filter Cigarettes. The jukebox plays advanced jazz, far out.

The patron orders garlic sauce and potato salad (fifty-five cents). Coffee is fifteen cents (with food, ten cents). The patron says, "I don't dig baseball. I don't approve of competitive sports."

The baklava—a delicious pastry made of chopped nuts and honey—is thirty-five cents, and the tourist eats and asks, "What's the score?"

"For my part," says the patron, "you can stuff baseball in a gray flannel sack of commercialism."

But a second patron mercifully agrees to go out somewhere and ask a square. He disappears into Grant Avenue.

"He's a phony beatnik," the patron asserts. "He's just on an unemployment kick. He's got clothes at home. Me, I'm a real beatnik. I'm unemployed forever. I exist in a state of true indifference."

He rolls a cigarette.

The second patron returns. "Three to one," he says.

"Favor who?" the tourist asks. "Who's got the three?"

"I don't know," the second patron says. "To hell with everything."

"It makes a difference," the tourist insists.

"Not to me."

NOB HILL

The Pacific Union Club on Nob Hill also coexists, Almost anyone can apply for membership as soon as he becomes enormously wealthy. Here the news is received that Mr. Raymond Lee Walls Jr., an associate of a Chicago firm, flies out to Mr. O. Manuel Cepeda, whose winter address is Puerto Rico.

As often happens, even in the best of baseball games, a lull has developed. The Giants appear to be firmly in control of the transaction. The Cubs appear to be ineffectual in achieving their terms. There have been very few base hits (only six, in slow trading). There has been no tension, no dispute, no conference at the pitcher's hill. Truly, it has been a dull game. Dull, dull. One relaxes.

By direct wire, further information is received: Mr. Ernest Banks, of Dallas and Chicago, pops out to Mr. Edward Francis Bressoud, who is preparing for a pedagogical career at the University of California at Los Angeles. During the summer months he represents a San Francisco house, calling at Los Angeles, St. Louis, Chicago, Milwaukee, Pittsburgh, Cincinnati, and Philadelphia.

Dull, dull, dull, the mind relaxes, drifts. Stocks in the Giants was at $100 a share in New York, at $175 after their removal to San Francisco, and would sell today for $800–$900, if anybody cared to sell.

Mr. R. Brown Thomson of Chicago, who hit a home run eight years ago, and in his last time at bat, is struck out by Mr. Michael Francis McCormick. In an earlier negotiation, Mr. McCormick received a bonus payment reported at $65,000.

At Seals Stadium rich and poor rise for the seventh-inning stretch.

POWELL STREET

The score is posted at the corner of Powell and O'Farrell, across from Omar Khayyam's Restaurant. The bells of the cable cars clang, the cable itself hums underfoot, and the man says, pointing, "Formerly I put the speaker inside so it didn't radiate outside, where if you cared to hear the progress you stepped inside, but I now put it up outside and let it radiate for somebody else."

He gives a good shine—twenty-five cents—and he says, "Come back, hear?"

Felipe Alou walks, steals second base, and a small crowd forms to listen. Bressoud strikes out.

A passerby asserts that he has been a lifelong Yankee fan, that he would not know whom to root for in the event of a World Series between the Yankees and the Giants.

Hegan grounds out.

The shoeshine shop is sheltered from the wind by Macy's. The proprietor of the shop is a Missourian, but he has also lived in Indianapolis and Minneapolis. He has shined shoes in San Francisco since 1943. He was an admirer of the San Francisco Seals, but he now wholly accepts the Giants, and he sighs with disappointment when McCormick grounds out to end the inning.

Radiating outside, as he chalks the new zero, is a message from the Golden West Radio Network on behalf of Folger's Coffee, carefully selected, famous, fresh-brewed *real* coffee that makes you want to wake up and live. The crowd, which had begun to form around the loudspeaker in the hope of a rally, disperses.

"Come back, hear?" says the shoeshine man.

TWIN PEAKS

"Confidentially speaking," said the man in the house near Twin Peaks, "this confounded baseball season has cost me a lot of time. You see, I work at home. I must concentrate on what I'm doing. I tell myself. 'Don't touch that dial,' but it's like a drug, I'm hooked."

He continued: "Analytically speaking, I can save a certain amount of time by scientific listening. For example, in a game like today's, I began by listening only to the Giants at bat. Then Alou's home run put the Giants ahead by a couple of runs, so I shifted from offensive listening to defensive listening. Right now I'm listening defensively."

The Cubs were retired in the eighth, and he turned his radio off.

The Giants were also retired in the eighth, and when he turned his radio on again Averill was batting for Ceccarelli, the Cubs' pitcher, in the top of the ninth. Averill grounded out to Davenport, who had replaced Brandt at third base: manager Rigney was also listening defensively.

"This one's in the bag," the man said. "Hopefully speaking, I think McCormick is back on the track again, and we're in. The Cubs have been the spoilers, but we're knocking them off."

"Cautiously speaking," his guest said, "while you were hopefully speaking Taylor singled."

Then Altman singled, too. The tying run was on first base, only one man was out, and the Giants' infield was joined by manager Rigney in conference with McCormick. In the bullpen, Sam Jones was warming.

"Frankly speaking, it's been a dull game." The man fed his fireplace. At Seals Stadium, fans who had been shuffling toward the exits resat themselves, and Sam Jones, who had been watching the game first from the dugout and then from the bullpen, walked slowly toward the pitcher's mound. He was chewing a toothpick.

When Davenport replaced Brandt at third base, Brandt moved to left field, where he belongs, and Cepeda to first base, where *he* belongs. McCovey was in the Giants' dugout. Lee Walls was now replaced at bat by Dale Long, and the man in the house near Twin Peaks began to pace between his fireplace and his picture window. In short, there was a good deal of agitated shuffling of souls.

Sam Jones struck out Dale Long. Two men now were out, the tying run was still at first base, and Ernie Banks was the batter.

"Statistically speaking," said the guest of the man with the view of Twin Peaks, who was pacing more rapidly than before, "Banks is leading the league in homers and RBIs."

"My whole summer has been squandered," his host replied.

"You could always turn the radio off," his guest said cheerfully.

"Don't touch that dial," the man commanded.

LEFTY O'DOUL'S

A tense moment at Lefty O'Doul's. The consensus was, after Jones fanned Long, that manger Rigney had been wise to relieve McCormick, but when Banks singled, and a run scored, the feeling was that McCormick had been removed too soon. The tying run moved up to second base, and when Walt Moryn singled, it scored.

"They can't get past Chicago," somebody said. "They sit up nights figuring ways to lose it."

Noren pinch-hit for Schult, and Sam Jones struck him out.

At Seals Stadium the fans who had resettled themselves during their interrupted journey to the exits unfolded their blankets and spread them once again across their knees. At O'Doul's it looked like an extra-inning game, maybe twelve or thirteen innings.

Cepeda flied out.

"Cepeda don't hit in the clutch any more," somebody said.

Don Elston was pitching for Chicago. He was fresh and fast. His first pitch to Brandt was a ball. His second pitch was also a ball, and a man in O'Doul's said, "He'll walk."

"Then who'll drive him in?"

"Maybe he'll hit a home run."

"Not him."

Jackie Brandt said in the clubhouse afterward that he had no idea, when he hit the ball, where it was going. He just ran, as he had run out an uninteresting pop foul in the fourth inning. When he rounded first base he heard the crowd, and he knew. At home plate, Felipe Alou shook his hand. At Lefty O'Doul's the consensus was that manager Rigney was doing a damn fine job, that Jones and Cepeda were great, that Brandt was always a threat at the plate, that the Giants would get past Chicago, beat St. Louis, and go all the way. The tourist had not met so many brilliantly clairvoyant people anywhere in the city. However, he could find nobody at O'Doul's who would tell him with absolute certainty what would happen *tomorrow*.

MAYBE WHAT
BASEBALL NEEDS
IS A HENRY DAVID THOREAU

◇ A TRILLION YEARS ago, about 1937, a fellow named Sam Leslie sometimes played first base for a baseball team strangely named the New York Giants, which played 154 games a season, all in the afternoon. When Sam Leslie was asked his opinion of a proposed rule permitting a pinch hitter to bat more than once in a game, he replied, "They'd never have a rule like that." Such a thing could never come to pass; it was all pure academic speculation (though that might not have been the phrase Sam Leslie used), all one big What If— like What if they could shoot a man to the moon? and What if they ever allowed *colored* players into organized baseball? and What if you were shipwrecked on a desert island with Jean Harlow? I was a boy in Mount Vernon, New York, and I read all these things in the New York *Sun* (defunct).

More recent than Sam Leslie is a funny comedian named Bob Newhart, who has enacted on a phonograph record (must I say *album*?) the invention of baseball. Someone calling himself Abner Doubleday telephones a manufacturer of patented commercial games. Mr. Doubleday's idea goes something like this: A fellow pitches a ball to a second fellow, who tries to hit it with a stick. There are nine men on each team. "Why *nine* men?" the manufacturer asks. "Why *three* strikes but *four* balls? Why *three* bases and yet a fourth under a different

279

name—*home plate*?" Such an arbitrary numerology inside an insane nomenclature vexes him until, in a twinkling, all things become clear: It's all a hoax. "Abner *Double*day indeed!" "Hey," he laughs in sudden enlightenment, "is this one of the guys in the office?"

Yet we and Bob Newhart and Sam Leslie, home again in Moss Point, Mississippi, see during the current season all whimsy rationalized: pinch hitters hitting more than once in a game, and pinch runners, too, coming and going more than once. To our astonishment, the player pinch-hit for or pinch-run for does not even leave the game. Those of us with the sharpest eyes see that the pitcher's mound has been lowered from fifteen inches to ten.

For every new thing we see, much more has been suggested: seven-inning games instead of nine, games abandoned by consent of a submerged team, the pitcher's mound moved farther from the plate (it's sixty feet six inches now, the hoaxster's round number), and the distance shortened from home plate to first base. Encourage bunting, some say; no, say others, nobody cares for bunting. Some suggest that the ball and turf be increased in "resiliency" by ten percent, while inhibitions be placed upon the use of relief pitchers. Let the automatic walk be truly automatic—no balls thrown ritualistically to the plate. Let the distances to the fences be uniformly shortened. (They already have been in Philadelphia, and the scoreboard lowered in Cincinnati.)

The purpose of all this is to increase scoring, generally upon the theory that most people who watch baseball games prefer big scores to small ones, as do mesmerized people who linger at pinball machines; that people in the age of rocketry love to see things flying out of sight—"out of sight" in contemporary slang means "terrific"—and that they wish to see whatever happens happen very fast, without delay or waste of time, thus making upon baseball the paradoxical demand that scores be eleven to nine, not three to two, with these twenty runs scoring in less time than five.

Some of the proprietors of baseball have taken up the challenge of the paradox. The customer is always right, they say.

Give him more quicker. In public, baseball people drown in sentimentality. When they aren't in season they are weeping at the sound of fading names—weeping mainly, one supposes, at the prospect of their own mortality. In private, however, they think themselves very practical people with dry hand-kerchiefs. Baseball, they say, is really Show Business, and they cite tabulations showing the size of their Audience, their Box, their Vote, and, above all, their ratings—for they are not only Show Business, but that particular branch of Show Business that is Television Business. Can baseball exist without the customer?

The proprietor says no. The philosopher says yes and asks, "Did you ever see a bunch of boys playing baseball to no audience but themselves? Indeed you did. Perhaps the customer is expendable, and the proprietor, too. Who owns baseball?"

Like any manufacturer of patented commercial games, of shoes, or a thousand instantly obsolete items, the proprietors of baseball have made various "scientific" studies of their product. In time-motion studies conducted last season in Baltimore, they saw that half a game of baseball is "dead time" between pitches, that one-fifth is "dead time" between innings, that one-quarter is "dead time" passed in miscellaneous ways (catcher rubs up the ball, players confer, replacements enter the game, batter goes for new bat, etc.), and that only the remaining five percent is devoted to actual play.

To anyone with a passion for continuous, ceaseless action these are very bad numbers, like those that show us that we sleep away one-third of our lives and spend most of the remainder eating, shaving, dressing, undressing, and parking our cars, except, perhaps, for an infinitesimal minimum spent in love. To the baseball proprietor the numbers suggest why the game is competing poorly, especially on television, against professional sports having less "dead time," as well as high scores and the attraction of speed and violence.

True, games other than baseball possess qualities responsive to that invisible spirit called by Mr. Mike Burke, president of the New York Yankees, "the changing velocity of American life." But velocity is, by definition, a quality of motion, and the motion may be in a circle for all we know. Proprietors tinkering and tampering with the game ought really to meditate instead upon American velocity.

Gentlemen of baseball, friends of baseball, lovers of the small infinitesimal moment, Mr. Burke, and you with the stop watch in Baltimore: You must accept history, understanding its meaning and riding it through. Velocity, too—so much of it made in America—rockets to obsolescence. Gentlemen, don't panic. "If you try to make up points in a few minutes," says basketball coach John Wooden of UCLA, "you usually get farther behind. That is where poise comes in." Try for poise. Don't envy the upstart games their crowds or their television fees. Are you really and truly practical men? Then you must live in history apart from any one moment's velocity. Velocity passes, history remains.

Don't hurry the pitcher. He cannot just fire away because it's good for business. It's not good for *his* business, and every effort to hasten the duel between pitcher and batter only hastens the decay of the game itself. Anyone who has ever played baseball knows the intensity of the split second when the pitch is on its way. The spectator shares with batter and pitcher the suspense preceding the pitch, and he understands, too, the anxiety of the player tugging for comfort at cap, ear, shirt, or belt.

Shall we read upon the credits: "Baseball, adapted for television from an idea suggested by Abner Doubleday"? Every boy heard very early from someone wiser than he, "Don't play to the grandstand. Play to the ball, and the grandstand will come to you." Of all lessons, it is the most difficult to learn.

Gentlemen of baseball—practical men, as you think yourselves: Not in the name of sentiment, but in the name of absolute, hard-nosed, hard-headed pragmatism, the man you need may be Henry David Thoreau, and what you need may be not expansion but contraction, not speed but the nourishment of old roots, not closer fences or lowered scoreboards but a renewed connection between the game and its essential followers, not the eye of the camera but the vision of Time Past and Time to Come. Don't speak of "dead time" to living children.

"Simplify, simplify," Henry David would tell you. Don't expand your income, but reduce your desires. The bigger you get, the harder you'll fall. Enterprises that burst from their own greed never engage our commiseration.

If the year is wrong for baseball, let the game dwindle, shrink, sulk if it must, and revive again as time once again seeks it. Born in the last century, it grew with this one. It was a thing of Nature. When it discovered—in the era of Babe Ruth—that Audience loved the home run hit out of sight, the hitting game was encouraged, and Audience remained. But the moment was real, not fake, consonant and harmonious with Colonel Lindbergh and Jack Dempsey in an age of solo power.

In other years, even the biggest cities were, more or less, Moss Point. From the ramps of the Polo Grounds one saw the children of Harlem playing baseball in the shadow of the stadium. Neighborhoods, towns, and villages played to watch themselves play by daylight and dusk, not by the light of the tube.

Nobody ever denied "dead time." Nobody needed time-motion studies to tell him that the pitcher prima donna was squandering the time of thousands of people hitching up his pants, kicking at the dirt, spitting out his juice. That much all men could see, and they respected and admired the pitcher for it, for he was king of the hill (now lowered from fifteen inches to ten). One day, many thousands of people halted their lives to watch Lefty Gomez gaze at an airplane crossing the sky. Kings and princes and goofy lefthanders were entitled to our time because we knew how hard their job was. In the "dead time" between innings we waited; suspended, for Hughie Critz, at second base, to stoop to the grass for his opponent's glove, and toss it a few feet to a better place.

And, after "dead time" came some moment of excruciation. It was no long moment, either—measured in inches and fractions of seconds—but the culmination of all dead time. You had waited for it all afternoon or all year, and, when it came, you remembered it forever, for it was all your boyhood and all your nostalgia, and you could not have had it otherwise.

Where is the brilliant proprietor of baseball—someone at least as brilliant as the inventor of the bunt or the curve ball, some Wee Willie Keeler hitting them where they ain't—who will lead baseball to its source, who will cut back and get little? "I much prefer," Henri de Montherlant wrote in *Les Olympiques,* "to the official grounds of famous clubs where the fine ladies along the touch-line burst out laughing if you sprawl on the turf with the ball, those patchy suburban sports fields, where you play on a litter of old tins, to an audience of thirty shivering citizens."

For an American baseball executive, the Frenchman's truth may be hard to digest. Yet, it may be necessary for baseball to shrink in popular appeal—to cease entirely to compete with the violent, brutal sports in a violent and brutal time—and so breathe its own life on quiet sidelines until its own time shall come again, preserving its ancient rules and customs, even as artists have done, awaiting the time of rediscovery.

The velocity will abate. We'll not want the moon when we have it, as we deplore uninhabitable cities now that we have them, or highways paralyzed, or airplanes stacked in the polluted sky. It is not that we were a better country or a better people in those old days when baseball ruled. It is only that we were different, living at another pace, and baseball was opposite to that pace, like the two-lane highway and the railroad train, the genuine slow book, the long wait for news, radio voices whose faces we never saw, and surface mail—when the moon was a metaphor of the unachievable.

Baseball can be transfused by speed and expansion, but only a wise obedience to Nature can save it. Attendance this year may rise a little, but the margin might not measure more than curiosity to see new rules applied. Thousands of people will buy at least one ticket for a glimpse of Ted Williams.

If the age of baseball has passed, let it pass for this hour, not into extinction like last year's TV show, but back into its origins and local affections, town clubs and small devoted ownership. Let the big, ambitious owner surrender; let the brute sports thrive and flourish. Let Time have its way with baseball as with all natural, enduring things until one day, as I suspect, America, like Ted Williams, having fished all the waters of the known world, will return to the game that bespeaks its myth at a pace to match the reconciliation.

EPILOGUE

◇ PEOPLE ASK ME, "Are you a fan? How many games do you go to every year? Of course you have season tickets." I understand how disappointing I become when I say I see only a game or two a year. I wouldn't know what to do with a season ticket if I had one. I admire the game of baseball but I am not necessarily a fan of any of the people who play it or of the cities they pretend to represent. I go to a game to be with the companions I go with. If possible I sit in the shade, because the sunshine is hard on my head. I do not drink ballpark beer because along about the fifth inning I'd need the men's room.

Some people over time have been eager to go to ballgames with me because they think I know the hidden secrets of baseball. As the game progresses they see that I have failed them. I do not seem to know anything special. I do not speak in an enlightening way. I am not a sterling speaker. If I have something illuminating to say I go home and write it, stepping into baseball long enough to write an article, an essay, becoming intensely involved from the moment a good idea comes to mind and my research begins, until the moment I round off the last ambushed passage and drop the work into the mail. Then I withdraw from baseball and go away for a while.

Beyond a certain age I ceased to "follow" baseball in the usual sense, and I do not follow it now. I do not subscribe to magazines of sport. Once or twice a week I read the daily paper, but never on Sunday, and never the sports statistics in microscopic type. I cannot tell you the names of twenty players playing this moment in the big leagues, and those I can name are mostly those I saw on television during the most recent World Series. I do not know who is leading the pennant races in the various divisions of the leagues, and indeed I'm not certain which divisions which teams are in.

Sometimes I dwell pessimistically on the futility of sport, how much effort we give to it, spend on it, watching strong young people play games while the rest of us lie about wasting away. American cities are strangling themselves with professional franchises at incalculable costs in humane planning, repair, and beautification.

And yet, I remember against the background of Philistine ruin an encouraging moment I like to mention from time to time. One Saturday afternoon at a vast university in the Corn-and-Bible Belt of the United States of America I was walking to the library, hearing above the silence of the golden afternoon the cheering of the football crowd at the stadium. It was exactly the sound of the Romans calling for the death of the gladiator. I thought, how terrible to think that everyone at this university is at that bloody game, that this whole enterprise is given over to sport, that thousands and thousands of mindless students and their mindless faculty have nothing better to do with their minds than watch football players. Then came my own moment to cheer, for when I entered the library I was astounded to see how many people were working there at one thing or another, as if no football game were occurring. I felt, after all, a surge of hope for America.

Friends of mine devour statistics. They tell me things in numbers about which I could not care less, trivia, records, odd or ironic baseball coincidences. Games come right into my house. The play-by-play broadcasters rattle on, speaking of new records set almost every minute, a barrage of statistics.

In my house I prefer to watch the game with the sound down, but even then I do not quite watch it, either. I'm like the fellow—indeed, I *was* the fellow—earlier in these pages who listened to the radio scientifically. "You see," he said, "I work at home. I must concentrate on what I'm doing . . . Analytically speaking, I can save a certain amount of time by scientific listening. For example, in a game like today's, I began by listening only to the Giants at bat. Then Alou's home run put the Giants ahead by a couple of runs, so I shifted from offensive listening to defensive listening." Thirty-five years later my home is still my workplace. I spend hours in my workroom, free of TV and radio. My wife is a fan. Sometimes she strolls past my door to advise me that So-And-Sos have got a rally going, something might be building. The dull game has developed tension. I wander from my workroom to the TV to see the tension through, for whereas it may be true that most moments of most games are dull, it is also true that some moments of some games are excruciatingly tight, tense, heart-stopping, marvelous beyond words, memorable beyond manufactured drama.

Many of the essays and articles in this book were written against topical deadlines, when, for a short time, everything seemed to matter a great deal to the editors for whom I worked, and to me, too, of course. Did those things matter for the players, too, whom I "covered" in these articles? If so, they never spoke of it to me. I have a friend who as a full-time veteran journalist has written hundreds of articles for a major American magazine of sport. He tells me he has never received a word of response from any of his subjects. Not a line. Not a phone call.

I think of all the fierce exciting games seen or heard of, and I wonder how we can so often renew our enthusiastic partisanship, our shouting, our rejoicing, our memories of impossible plays turned to reality, our hard and bitter feelings of loss and regret. It is all so soon over, and the players' names not even remembered. During thirty-nine years as major-league player and manager Casey Stengel saw so many players come and go he gave up trying to remember their names. He gave them nicknames matching their conspicuous physical or mental characteristics.

I have heard of the retired player who was asked by a fan at an old-timers' game, "Who did you used to be?"

I think of the boys with whom I played baseball in neighborhood games in Mount Vernon, New York, cousins and uncles, my brother. I spy my father shyly watching me from the sidelines. And now, quick as a flash, suddenly I'm not my father's son but my son's father. My son is a highly skillful baseball player, a leader, organizer, manager. I too was always on the telephone, rounding up my players, and indeed I am still active at a slower pace, as I tell in this book, in "The Bonding."

I am not the fan of the day but the periodic fan. My pleasure in the game has come not from immersing myself in it as daily fan, but by visiting it, as in writing, distant and aloof, understanding it by solving the writing problem it presents, as I could not have understood it by passively watching from the grandstand. I see that the thing that matters, the thing that lasts and endures, has never been so much the names of the players or their statistics, but the game itself, which is the real thing, surviving everyone.

Forty years ago I read a novel called *The Year the Yankees Lost the Pennant* (afterward the musical play *Damn Yankees*), by Douglas Wallop, in which a mournful fan named Joe Boyd suffers year after year for the Washington Senators, who never win a pennant. One night out of the shadows there appears to Boyd a man named Applegate, the devil himself, who offers Joe Boyd the chance to play for the Senators. Applegate promises to endow Joe Boyd with such remarkable skill that he will lift the Senators from the lower depths to victory over the Yankees. Joe will become the greatest player who ever lived. For his matchless future Joe Boyd need pay the devil only the devil's usual fee.

I'd have made the deal once, at a time when I thought life was longer than it is, in the old days, when I was a boy and did not know how richly life extended beyond baseball; did not know how soon money, fame, and body were spent.

Tell me, would you spend eternity in hell in exchange for the grandest baseball career any man ever enjoyed?

You say you would?

Then *you're* a fan.